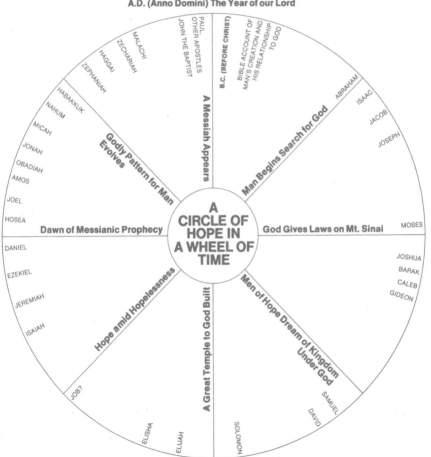

Jesus Christ—The Hope of the World
A.D. (Anno Domini) The Year of our Lord

A CIRCLE OF HOPE IN A WHEEL OF TIME

- PAUL, OTHER APOSTLES
- JOHN THE BAPTIST
- B.C. (BEFORE CHRIST)
- BIBLE ACCOUNT OF MAN'S CREATION AND HIS RELATIONSHIP TO GOD
- MALACHI
- ZECHARIAH
- HAGGAI
- ZEPHANIAH
- HABAKKUK
- NAHUM
- MICAH
- JONAH
- OBADIAH
- AMOS
- JOEL
- HOSEA
- DANIEL
- EZEKIEL
- JEREMIAH
- ISAIAH
- JOB?
- ELISHA
- ELIJAH
- SOLOMON
- DAVID
- SAMUEL
- GIDEON
- CALEB
- BARAK
- JOSHUA
- MOSES
- JOSEPH
- JACOB
- ISAAC
- ABRAHAM

A Messiah Appears
Man Begins Search for God
Godly Pattern for Man Evolves
Dawn of Messianic Prophecy
God Gives Laws on Mt. Sinai
Hope amid Hopelessness
Men of Hope Dream of Kingdom Under God
A Great Temple to God Built

ALL THE BIBLE'S
MEN OF HOPE

ALL THE BIBLE'S
MEN OF HOPE

Edith Deen

DOUBLEDAY & COMPANY, INC.
GARDEN CITY, NEW YORK
1974

Library of Congress Cataloging in Publication Data
Deen, Edith.
All the Bible's men of hope.
Bibliography.
1. Bible—Biography.   2. Hope—Biblical teaching.
I. Title.
BS571.D4   220.9′2   [B]
ISBN 0-385-05100-X
LIBRARY OF CONGRESS CATALOG CARD NUMBER 73-22786

May the God of Hope fill you with joy and peace in your faith, that by the power of the Holy Spirit, your whole life and outlook may be radiant with hope.

Romans 15:13, Phillips translation

Acknowledgments

When my editor at Doubleday suggested I write on men of the Bible, I felt unequal to the task because my whole writing career, more than twenty-five years as a woman's editor and daily woman's columnist, on through four religious books, had been about women.

After I finished my first book, *All of the Women of the Bible* in 1955, readers then asked that I write on *All of the Men of the Bible*. But I soon discovered I could not do justice to so comprehensive a subject in one volume, because in the Bible are many more men than women.

One afternoon soon after my editor made the suggestion, I was standing in my garden with Maurice C. Clemmons, then manager of a local book department, when the idea of a book about men in the Bible came up. His immediate response was, "Why don't you key your theme to the Bible's men of hope? Theologians and philosophers are placing new emphasis on hope. And a search for this force by present-day humanity is awakening with increasing emphasis."

The next day I wrote my editor suggesting a book on the Bible's men of hope. The return mail brought a letter from him saying, "This idea is excellent. It will really give the book focus, and as far as I can see, it will be the exact right focus."

With that I went to work. For more than three years I have

climbed my way to a mountain top, expanding the theme to *all* the Bible's men of hope. I have been thrilled every step of the ascent, for it all has been a highly illuminating experience.

One of my most enthusiastic helpers has been Dr. William L. Reed, noted archaeologist and an eminent Bible scholar, who read the manuscripts of three other books of mine. I have great confidence in his judgment, for he is knowledgeable on every phase of Bible study and internationally known as director of the American School of Oriental Research in Jerusalem and co-director of the excavations at the Qumran cave, near the west shore of the Dead Sea. Recently he investigated buried cities in Yemen, where ancient inscriptions and artifacts provide new information about an impressive ancient civilization in southwest Arabia. Dr. Reed holds a top post in the religion department of Texas Christian University in my home city of Fort Worth, Texas.

As he has read my chapters these last three years, some several times, he has made valuable suggestions and corrections. If any biblical errors occur, I accept them as my own, because I continued with revisions after his readings. But even in my first chapters, crude though they were, he inspired me with enthusiasm for my task.

I must acknowledge, too, the help of many scholars who for centuries have labored on Bible translations, so as to make this greatest book of the ages more understandable. We are now living in the Golden Age of Bible translations, and this gives our work its most difficult, and yet its most challenging, perspective. We who write about the Bible have our choice of more important new versions than at any other time in the world's history. My basic text for this study has been the Revised Standard Version; however, I have quoted from others listed in the bibliography.

Another faithful helper, Ella Higginbotham, a neighbor and friend, who has worked with me more than twenty years, often labored nights and weekends in typing the manuscript. Out of my badly typed and scribbled lines, she produced excellent copy, and she gave me a lift each time she presented it to me.

My excellent housekeeper, Versie Roberts, who has also been with me more than twenty years, set me free to work in my study.

She also kept my home in beautiful order and fed me well as I labored.

Now as this book goes forth, I am more keenly aware that we never do anything alone. Often when I thought my task was beyond me, I felt a guiding presence in my paneled yellow study, where the sun pours through gold glass windows.

Prologue

This is the first biblical study centered on the theme of hope as it unfolds through all the Bible's men of hope, from the patriarchs on through Christ and the Apostles, a period covering more than two thousand years.

Hope, these biographies reveal, has many synonymous connotations: faith, trust, promise, a sense of wonder, prophecy, expectancy, confidence, belief, optimism, aspiration. It also has many anchors: spiritual renewal, physical restoration, and, most of all, righteous living.

Like many other periods in civilization, today's world has been passing through a fascination with despair, but the lives of the Bible's men of hope present an unbroken call to look to the future with hope. The way they confront their challenges and trials makes known that the universe and all of us in it are controlled by a God of hope, who, like a radiant arc, surrounds us in all his glory.

We come to see that hope in all of these men is not based on a fantasy but on a spiritual experience that implies an adventure, a confident search, a going forward in an expectation of the good, a power that pierces the ever-mysterious radiance of beauty, truth, and goodness. While other ancient civilizations died, Israel survived because its leaders fixed their minds on noble goals they knew only God could bring about.

A new school of scholars see biblical hope as the rainbow sign of tomorrow, "a new form of consciousness," as it were, guiding us toward a new future with God, one which signifies wonder and beauty. And the many new books on hope in the last decade present us with inspiring, optimistic, and stimulating challenges.

In a path-breaking study on this subject, the German scholar Jurgen Moltmann, in *Theology of Hope*, speaks of the sin of despair. He says that "if faith thus depends on hope for its life, then the sin of unbelief is manifestly grounded in hopelessness" (p. 22). He further discloses that "the world is full of all kinds of possibilities, namely all the possibilities of the God of Hope. It (Christian eschatology) sees reality and mankind in the hand of him whose voice calls into history from its end, saying, 'Behold, I make all things new,' and from hearing this word of promise it acquires the freedom to renew life here and to change the face of the world" (p. 26).

Carl E. Braaten, in *The Future of God*, a book based on the revolutionary dynamics of hope, says "the whole Old Testament is a book of hope . . . The religion of Israel, in its innermost essence, is hope toward the future of God . . . The Book of Psalms is the prayer and hymn book of the people who place their hopeful trust in God . . . The Psalmist is hoping in God for our salvation . . . His hopes are projections from the promises of God which have already been declared . . . He waits for God . . . with still unfulfilled promises" (p. 49).

Again and again this is apparent in the lives of these great men of hope. They reveal a hope that is not as an abstraction but a reality.

"The Golden Age is not behind us, but ahead of us" (p. 131), declares Johannes B. Metz in *New Theology No. 5*, a book edited by Martin E. Marty and Dean G. Peerman. This quote is from an essay, "The Creative Hope," in which Metz also says, "the Old Testament is not primarily a word of information or even a word of address, nor is it a word of expressing the personal self-communication of God, but is rather a word of promise . . . The principal word of promise points to the future . . . . the world for the first time has a history ordained to the future—in contrast to the Greeks for whom the world appears as a consistent and closed cosmos" (pp. 133–34).

Writing on "Hope in a Posthuman Era," also in the book *New Theology No. 5*, Sam Keen places hope in an attitude of wonder, in which we experience life as a gift, and learn to bring "order out of chaos, meaning out of contingency, triumph out of tragedy." Keen further points out that "the question of God is not the question of the existence of some remote infinite being. It is the question of the possibility of hope. The affirmation of faith in God is the acknowledgment that there is a deathless source of power and meaning that can be trusted to nurture and preserve all created good. To deny that there is a God is functionally equivalent to denying that there is any ground for hope" (pp. 86–87).

One book can not contain one ethereal concept in all its fullness. But if this book can now shed a tiny light on a new pathway and not forget the cross, it may be a small means of releasing us from some of our fears and frustrations.

Contents

TWO
A NEW HOPE
A NATION UNDER GOD

THREE
IN TIME OF DESPAIR
HOPE

FOUR
JESUS CHRIST
THE HOPE OF THE WORLD

FIVE
OTHER MEN OF HOPE
IN THE BIBLE

Contents

ALL THE BIBLE'S
MEN OF HOPE

SECTION ONE

The Patriarchal Period
A Time of Promise

Although a new discovery on the origin of man of our own species had its genesis more than 100,000 years ago, according to recent findings in Border Cave in southern Africa, man's relationship to God had its genesis in the patriarchal period, beginning with Abraham's birth in Mesopotamia in the Middle Bronze Age, somewhere between the twentieth and nineteenth century B.C.

This patriarchal period continued on through the birth of Abraham's son Isaac and Isaac's son Jacob, afterward to be called Israel, the father of the twelve tribes of Israel. More than two centuries are thought to have elapsed from the time of Abraham's life in Canaan to the patriarchal family's descent, led by the one hundred and thirty-year-old Jacob, into Egypt.

Joseph, the youngest of Jacob's twelve sons and the most promising, is included in this section because he made it possible for his family to journey from famine-stricken Israel to Egypt and provided for them there. One of his last requests was that his body be returned from Egypt to Israel for burial. His tomb is traditionally located one half a mile north of Jacob's Well at Shechem in Samaria.

The patriarchal era is one of confidence in God's promises (the very essence of hope), first made to Abraham when he left his native land. The entire patriarchal saga centers around the promise, first, for land and posterity. Nomads as they were, there was nothing the patriarchs desired so much as land and continuity in family life.

These promises, demanding of the believer trust in God, were later sealed by the patriarchal covenant based on the divine promise. Israel's heritage came to signify a solidarity between its people and the chosen ones of God, so-called because they chose to worship God, the Eternal Spirit, who seeks to make all men his sons.

CHAPTER 1

Abraham: The Father of Faith and Hope

Man's hopeful search for God, primitive but inescapable, dawns. Abraham's three promises from God are fulfilled, with faith as the framework for their realization.

Beginning with Israel's first great patriarch Abraham, the God of history begins to reveal himself as a God of hope. "When hope seemed hopeless, his [Abraham's] faith was such that he became 'father of many nations'" (Rom. 4:18, NEB), according to God's promise. "This promise, then, was valid before God, the God in whom he put his faith, the God who makes the dead live and summons things that are not yet in existence as if they already were" (v. 17).

"And what is faith?" The answer is "Faith gives substance to our hopes, and makes us certain of realities we do not see" (Heb. 11:1, NEB).

Abraham was subjected to three precarious and uncertain adventures in hope: first, a journey to a new land, not knowing where it was; next, a long and perplexing deferment of the birth of his son of promise, Isaac, and finally Isaac's release after Abraham took him to be sacrificed as a burnt offering. Never once doubting God, Abraham responded through every trial with an incredible power to believe. He was never afraid or doubtful, because "he looked forward to the city which has foundations, whose builder and maker is God" (Heb. 11:10).

He willingly accepted apprehension and suffering for a redemption that he never doubted. For his hope was in God, the governing power in his future. When he accepted this fact, hope became the very heart of his existence, kept alive his pioneering spirit, and left no place for the indecision so common to those who move toward a new and uncertain future.

Abraham had to suffer the incongruity of circumstances. He hoped for the Promised Land but first had to wander as a nomad and live in a tent. Famine awaited him when he arrived at his destination. His hope for a son of promise and heirs as numerous as the stars was seemingly lost in a delay encompassing many years. Finally, in their old age, Isaac was born to Abraham and his wife, Sarah.

All this time Abraham's hope was so fixed on God that he never tried to superimpose his own will. His serene attitude makes us know that hope that is seen is not hope in its truest sense. For who hopes for what he can already see?

Abraham had that which is central to hope, the wisdom to wait and the ability to handle apparent hopelessness. Through him we better understand what William F. Lynch says in his *Images of Hope*, "When a moment comes which is impossible we can at least wait for the emergence of a larger moment and a larger time" (p. 29). We also see we must learn to liberate hope and at the same time acknowledge and assert it. Lynch also tells us, "Hope is truly on the inside of us, but hope is an interior sense that there is help on the outside of us" (p. 31). Abraham kept hope aglow amid many years of heartaches and uncertainty.

His Call to Leave Mesopotamia

"The God of glory appeared to our father Abraham, when he was in Mesopotamia, before he lived in Haran, and said to him, 'Depart from your land and from your kindred and go into the land which I will show you.' Then he departed from the land of the Chaldeans, and lived in Haran. And after his father died, God removed him from there" (Acts 7:2–4) into Canaan. Abraham had no land of his own there, "not even a foot's length" (7:5).

Land, however, was promised to him and his posterity, though he had no child at the time. God further told Abraham that "his posterity would be aliens in a land belonging to others, who would enslave them and ill-treat them four hundred years" (7:6), but also that his posterity some day would once again worship in Canaan.

Abraham's hope was active and this gave his life, based on change and mobility, a forward direction. He must have come to realize there is nothing so certain as change and that mobility is a part of change. So the obedient Abraham took life as it came, guided by an unflinching faith that he was moving toward, not away from, God.

When Abraham and his wife, Sarah, and his mother and his father, Terah, migrated to Haran in northern Mesopotamia from Ur of the Chaldees, it is quite possible that "one reason for the choice of Haran might be that both Ur of the Chaldees, their original dwelling place, and Haran had famous sanctuaries of the moon god" (Avi-Yonah and Kraeling, *Our Living Bible*, p. 26).

W. F. Albright, foremost authority on the archaeology of Palestine and the Middle East, suggested that Abraham's father, Terah, was a legendary hero, who had been honored by the Canaanites and Hebrews as a moon god. Terah was also the name of a town near Haran, and Abraham's father Terah had a brother named Haran (Lot's father). It is easy to conjecture that the families not only were prominently connected with the area but doubtless were moon worshipers themselves.

When God commanded Abraham to move on to Canaan, he carried with him a deeply implanted impression of the moon god, thought to be the parent of the revolving hosts of heaven, guardians of the world at night. Moon worship later developed into a worship of the moon god himself.

In any case, Abraham came from an ancient Sumerian civilization that saw wonder in the sun, the moon, and the stars, not too unlike that expressed in Genesis, "And God made the two great lights, the greater light to rule the day, and the lesser light to rule the night; he made the stars also . . . And God saw that it was good" (Gen. 1:16, 18).

In Abraham's Sumerian civilization the stars were said to be like an army maneuvering with mysterious strategy. Then astrology was born and out of it, astronomy. So advanced were ancient Chaldeans in the latter that they are said to have estimated a year to be three hundred and sixty-five days, six hours, fifteen minutes, forty-one seconds, within a few minutes of what modern instruments record.

The eminent Protestant minister Harry Emerson Fosdick wrote in his book *The Hope of the World* that "the steady stars themselves give meaning to constant change that is all about us." He recalled Walt Whitman's listening to a lecture by an astronomer. Later Whitman wrote:

. . . I became tired and sick,
Till rising and gliding out I wandered off by myself,
    In the mystical moist night-air, and from time to time,
Looked up in perfect silence at the stars

(p. 114).

Abraham migrated from a part of the world that found intangible beauty in the universe. And he took with him into Canaan a sublime faith in a creator of wonders unexplainable.

The Early World of Abraham

The age of Abraham formed an era of transition from the last king of Sumer to the first dynasty of Babylon, whose greatest king was Hammurabi, the Babylonian codifier of laws resembling Hebrew laws.

Even while in Mesopotamia, Abraham's maturer years were highlighted by a new hope, not in a separate ideal of an ancient Sumerian culture, but in a supreme power of the universe, centralized by neither time nor place nor belief in a false image, but trust in the controller of the creative process, the object of man's highest reverence and aspiration.

In order to experience fellowship with his creator, Abraham had to possess hope and faith or he could not have gone forward. He showed, too, that he was ready to give up the old moon-god sanctuaries for a simple altar, first beneath an oak tree at Shechem.

Though the city he looked for so long was like an illusive mirage, his hope did not crumble as he waited.

In Paul's doctrine of justification, he asks the Galatians: "Did you receive the Spirit by works of the law, or by hearing with faith? . . . Does he who supplies the Spirit to you and works miracles among you do so by works of the law, or by hearing with faith?" (Gal. 3:2, 5) Then Paul speaks to the Galatians of the witness of Abraham, in which he declares that Abraham " 'believed God, and it was reckoned to him as righteousness.' . . . So you see that it is men of faith who are the sons of Abraham. . . . So then, those who are men of faith are blessed with Abraham who had faith" (3:6-7, 9).

To Abraham faith and hope seemed to be interlocked gifts only God could bestow. Consequently, God was Abraham's anchor and defense. Because he had the faith to see from afar into the future but died before God's promises were realized in all their fullness, all men of faith, inheriting from Abraham this same hope, can live in great anticipation too.

Before Abraham left Mesopotamia for Canaan, he had an awareness of the universality of God. This prepared him for an uncorrupted worship of God in Canaan amid a more modest way of life. In Mesopotamia he had enjoyed life at its primitive best. Not only did he have access to elaborate moon-god sanctuaries there but also to homes that were among the finest in the ancient world. Archaeological studies reveal that these ancients had two-story houses with a central court and stairs leading to the upper stories with rooms opening upon a balcony looking down on the court below.

When he and his wife, Sarah, and his nephew Lot left on their arduous journey, Abraham took sheep, asses, servants, camels, silver, and gold. His picturesque caravan left the green valleys of his own Fertile Crescent and crossed the desert to Shechem. Later his slow-crawling caravan moved to the mountain on the east of Bethel. There he pitched his tent, with Bethel on the west and Ai on the east, and here he built a second altar. When famine later swept the whole area, Abraham took his caravan down to Egypt.

Although he experienced abundance in Egypt, he ran into new and unexpected situations. Before he arrived he told his wife, "I know that you are a woman beautiful to behold; and when the Egyptians see you, they will say, 'This is his wife'; then they will kill me, but they will let you live. Say you are my sister, that it may go well with me because of you and that my life may be spared on your account" (Gen. 12:11–13).

In these ancient times, when travel was hazardous, it seems that a husband's life meant more than his wife's honor. Later Abraham and his descendants were to learn that God was leading them to a clear perception of moral law, which found its fulfillment in the time of Moses.

When Pharaoh took Sarah into his own harem, he gave to Abraham sheep, oxen, men servants, maid servants (one of whom was Hagar), she-asses, and camels, and then when he learned that Sarah was Abraham's wife and not his sister, he said, "Take her, and be gone" (Gen. 12:19).

Sarah and Abraham and his nephew Lot went back into the Negeb. Rich in cattle, silver, and in gold, but with strife between their herdsmen, each now needed more land. The magnanimous and believing Abraham gave Lot his choice. He took the well-watered Jordan Valley. Abraham could have been disheartened, but he was not, for God said to him, "Lift up your eyes, and look from the place where you are, northward and southward and eastward and westward; for all the land which you see I will give to you and to your descendants for ever" (Gen. 13:14–15).

And so Abraham finally came to Hebron, his permanent home, the scene of his third altar, and later the family's burial place.

The Heir of Promise

Abraham now had the land that God had promised him but he did not have the "heir of promise." Still barren, Sarah decided to give, according to the custom of the time, her Egyptian maid, Hagar, to her husband as a concubine. To Hagar was born Abraham's first son, Ishmael, but not the heir of promise. Finally, after much disappointment and frustration, the promise of a son to Sarah and Abraham was miraculously fulfilled.

Problems over child rights between the first-born of the Egyptian slave woman and the son of the beautiful and favored Sarah soon arose in the household. The law was on Sarah's side. Her son, Isaac, received the birthright, and when he did, Hagar was expelled with Ishmael from the household and sent into the desert near the Egyptian border. Ishmael became the progenitor of twelve princes (Gen. 25:12–16). The Moslems still hail him as their ancestor.

Abraham faced the severest trial of his life when God said to him, "Take your son, your only son Isaac, whom you love, and go to the land of Moriah, and offer him as a burnt offering upon one of the mountains of which I shall tell you" (Gen. 22:2).

In Abraham's godly obedience, the primary function of faith, he set forth with Isaac to the mountain. One can scarcely imagine what complete faith it took for Abraham, on arrival there, to build an altar, lay the wood, bind his only son, place him on the altar upon the wood, stretch forth his hand, and take the knife to slay him.

God did not demand such a sacrifice from Abraham however. He provided a ram instead. When Abraham saw this ram miraculously appear in a bush, he took it and offered it in place of his son. Again Abraham learned "the Lord will provide; as it is said to this day, 'On the mount of the Lord it shall be provided'" (Gen. 22:14).

From this moment the seed of hope for Isaac's future was planted, and Abraham knew that it would flourish.

THE CULMINATION OF HIS FAITH AND HOPE

When Isaac reached maturity, after the death of Sarah, Abraham set about to select a bride for him. Since Abraham still had ties with his family in Haran, he sent his trusted steward Eliezer there to find a bride for Isaac. The steward was miraculously led to the beautiful Rebekah (Rebecca), the daughter of Bethuel, Abraham's nephew by his brother Nahor. The steward perceived that here was a maiden who possessed the same qualities inherent in her uncle Abraham, courage, determination, and the stamina to move into a strange land.

Hastily, arrangements were made through her father, Nahor, to take Rebekah and her maids back to Canaan. There Rebekah became Isaac's bride, and "he loved her." For twenty years Rebekah was barren. When she did conceive, she discovered she was to have twins, for she felt them struggling within her. Finally, when the time had come for their delivery, sons—first Esau and then Jacob—were born.

Through Jacob's marriage to the sisters Rachel and Leah came the twelve tribes of Israel, and through them, Abraham became the "father of many nations," as it had been foretold.

Abraham did not live to see these grandchildren and their children, but he died with the assurance that God would multiply his descendants as the stars of heaven, just as he had miraculously fulfilled his two other promises, all now about to become a solid certainty.

Much must remain obscure about this story of Abraham, the first patriarch, such as the exact years he lived and died, how many people (a clan or only his own family and servants) crossed with him from Mesopotamia into Canaan. Although Abraham's story has emerged out of mystical obscurity and some scholars refute some of it, the important truth is there, that Genesis is a story of man's first faithful search for God.

For that reason Abraham, the first patriarch, towers in primeval history as a credible witness of God, the first to receive "the promise of the Spirit through faith" (Gal. 3:14).

In Abraham, the pioneer of faith, dawns a hope in man that develops by stages as he gropes his way toward a more profound relationship with God, the Creator of the Universe.

CHAPTER 2

Isaac: A Humble Man of Simple Faith

Although not as illustrious as his father, Abraham, or his son Jacob, Isaac is an important link in the family saga based on God's promises.

As befitting Abraham's son of promise, Isaac's life is a continuation of the theme that God is not some remote human being but a source of infinite power and wonder and that he can be trusted to nurture and preserve all created good. Isaac quietly manifested this kind of faith, and it was sustained in a mood of hope, because he, like his father, was "fully convinced that God was able to do what he had promised" (Rom. 4:21). As the heir of promise for his generation and with his father's supporting faith, Isaac perceived that God's covenant would be fulfilled in him and his children. His father's experiences confirmed his faith, which continued through his long life.

"Faith, like hope, is not a prediction of the future; it is the vision of the present in a state of pregnancy," says Erich Fromm in his book *The Revolution of Hope*. "The statement that faith is certainty needs qualification. It is certainty about the reality of the possibility . . . it is the certainty of the uncertain. It is certainty in terms of man's vision and comprehension; it is not certainty in terms of the final outcome of reality," continues Fromm (p. 14).

Both faith and hope acknowledge that which is not yet revealed. They can bring triumph out of tragedy, order out of tumult, and meaning out of unforeseen occurrences, as can be seen in Isaac's story, both during his long life and after his death.

Isaac's explicit confidence in God's promises was the essence of his hope. He acted as one certain that his family's destiny would be determined, not by external situations but by the wonder of God's creative power.

Although the least conspicuous of the three patriarchs, Isaac takes his place among Bible immortals, for it is written again and again, first in Exodus 2:24, "God remembered his covenant with Abraham, with Isaac, and with Jacob." And this covenant became the basis of Israel's greatness and the center of its hope.

His Younger Years

Born to believing parents, Abraham and Sarah, in their old age, as related in Chapter 1, Isaac was the second link in the genealogical line destined to develop into a mighty nation. Through a long, weary pilgrimage, he could have forgotten that God is absolutely faithful to his word, but he did not. Despite the circumstances, Isaac held to his faith, the kind that Dr. Elton Trueblood, the wise Quaker philosopher and author, refers to "not as a blind leap into nothing but a thoughtful walk in the light."

Modest and retiring from his youth, Isaac developed into a passive young man of so few words that his faith in and obedience to God were less apparent than in his activist father. When he went with his father to Mount Moriah to be sacrificed, according to God's command, the faithful Abraham's heart was broken, but Isaac's life was in question. But he unequivocally yielded to his father's demands, only to learn that he and his father were to remain under God's love and protection, for God was only testing their faith.

Without a murmur, Isaac calmly watched his father stack the wood on the altar and then come forward with the fire and the knife. Isaac was then twenty-five years old, according to Josephus, the Jewish historian. He was filled with all the dreams of youth, but he knew how to suffer and be still. So he surrendered himself to his father and his God, and his father's faith was strengthened by God's providence when the ram miraculously appeared and was offered for sacrifice instead of Abraham's only beloved son.

His Family Life

The next important episode in Isaac's life was his marriage to Rebekah. Because Abraham wished to retain the purity of religion, according to the sacred family tradition, he sent his old servant back to his homeland to select a bride for Isaac. As Isaac was the inheritor of God's specific promise, it was not thought to be the time for him to leave Canaan; and again his activist father usually made the family's major decisions, even the selection of a bride for his son.

Whatever the reason might have been, the Isaac–Rebekah romance would have lost much of its idyllic charm had Isaac made the long journey by camel caravan himself.

Before the beautiful and graceful Rebekah appeared in a caravan from her native Haran, Isaac, a prayerful man, "went out to meditate in the field in the evening; and he lifted up his eyes and looked, and behold there were camels coming. And Rebekah lifted up her eyes, and when she saw Isaac, she alighted from the camel, and said to the servant, 'Who is the man yonder, walking in the field to meet us?' The servant said, 'It is my master.' So she took her veil and covered herself. And the servant told Isaac all the things that he had done. Then Isaac brought her into the tent, and took Rebekah, and she became his wife; and he loved her" (Gen. 24:63–67).

Isaac gave Rebekah the honored place in his affection when he took her into his deceased mother's tent on his wedding night. Because he so loved and trusted Rebekah, he left to her some of the major decisions of the family, just as his father had done with his mother, Sarah.

Though blessed in many ways, Isaac and Rebekah remained childless for twenty years. Rebekah was barren like his own mother for so long that Isaac could have doubted God's promise for children by her. Instead of resorting to complete despair, the prayerful Isaac asked God for children. One can hear an echo of this prayer in Psalm 119:

> Let thy steadfast love come to me, O Lord,
>> thy salvation according to thy promise . . .
> Remember thy word to thy servant,
>> in which thou has made me hope . . .
> Uphold me according to thy promise, that I may live,
>> and let me not be put to shame in my hope!
>> (119:41, 49, 116)

It is written, "The Lord granted his [Isaac's] prayer, and Rebekah his wife conceived" (Gen. 25:21). There was conflict between the twins, Esau and Jacob, soon after their conception. This conflict deepened after their birth. Esau was born first and then Jacob came from his mother's womb. This discord came about largely because of the divided loyalty of the parents. Isaac had a selfish fondness for the roving Esau, a skillful hunter who lived in the open; Rebekah favored the quiet Jacob who kept to his tents. The first dissension between Esau and Jacob is dramatically expressed.

"Once, when Jacob was cooking a stew, Esau came in from the open, famished. He said to Jacob 'Let me gulp down some of that red stuff; I'm starving.' . . . But Jacob replied, 'First give me your birthright in exchange for it.' 'Look,' said Esau, 'I'm on the point of dying. What good will any birthright do me?' But Jacob insisted, 'Swear to me first!' So he sold Jacob his birthright under oath. Jacob then gave him some bread and the lentil stew; and Esau ate, drank, got up, and went his way. Esau cared little for his birthright" (Gen. 25:29–34, NAB). The latter signified the rights or inheritance of the first-born. These now belonged to Jacob. The pleasure-loving Esau had thoughtlessly given them away, all because he wanted pottage ("red stuff") more than priesthood.

The Later Years of His Life

Isaac spent his first years in the Negeb, in or near Beer-sheba, where his father had settled, but when famine came, he, like his father, took his family to Gerar, an ancient inland Philistine city-state, on the border between Palestine and Egypt. He dwelt in the south country near the well Beer-lahai-roi, and after he sowed crops there for several seasons, he became wealthy in cattle and land, thus adding to the cattle and land left him in Canaan.

After Isaac reopened some of his father's water wells covered up earlier and acquired larger flocks, herds, and work animals on his own, the local inhabitants became envious of him. They ordered him, saying, "Go away from us, for you are much mightier than we" (Gen. 26:16). When Isaac's servants dug in the valley, the herdsmen of Gerar told them, "The water is ours" (v. 20). Isaac dug other wells and then went to Beer-sheba again and built an altar. Here he was visited by Abimelech and his army commander, Phicol. When Isaac asked them why they had come, they answered, "We see plainly that the Lord is with you; so we say, let there be an oath between you and us, and let us make a covenant with you, that you will do us no harm, just as we have not touched you and have done nothing to you but good and sent you away in peace" (vs. 28–29).

Seeing they wanted to be friends, Isaac gave a feast for them, and they worked out a covenant of peace together. In doing so, Isaac won a victory of nonresistance against a former enemy. During this, the most successful period of his long life, he was no longer subordinate to his father or son, but clever and capable in his own right.

New family sorrows awaited Isaac. His blindness, which occurred probably forty or fifty years before his death, is mentioned the first time in the poignant scene with his most promising son, Jacob. Esau had married women from idolatrous races of Canaan, and "they made life bitter for Isaac and Rebekah" (Gen. 26:35). Isaac remained passive, but Rebekah complained about these Hittite women and began to scheme with her more promising son, Jacob. While Esau was in the field hunting one day, Jacob, with the help of his mother, impersonated Esau in dress, manner, and voice and went in to his father and asked that he bestow the family blessing upon him. The power inherent in the spoken word of the blessing, plus the birthright received earlier, now gave Jacob all of the rights of the first-born son over Esau.

The trickery, to be delineated more fully in the next chapter, was achieved because of Isaac's trusting nature. Before he realized it, the blessing was now Jacob's and not Esau's, and this gave Jacob full precedence over Esau in the family line.

Loving father and husband that he was, Isaac could have despaired because of the deception practiced upon him by his wife and son (it was too late to retract what he had done), but he had to suffer and be still. Esau was the one who showed great emotion and anger when he returned from the field and realized what had been done.

Also preparing savory food for his father, he went to him and begged, "Bless me, even me also, O my father!" (Gen. 27:34). But Isaac told him, "Your brother came with guile, and he has taken away your blessing" (v. 35). When Esau realized he now had to take second place, he said to his father, " 'Have you but one blessing my father? Bless me, even me also, O my father.' And Esau lifted up his voice and wept" (v. 38).

Esau so hated his brother that Isaac could no longer remain silent. He faced Jacob with the report that Esau was planning to kill him. Then Isaac charged Jacob to arise and go to Haran and find there a wife from one of the daughters of his mother's brother Laban, a wife born with a higher sense of values than the pagan women. Isaac's last words to Jacob were, "God almighty bless you and make you fruitful and multiply you" (Gen. 28:3).

Little more is written about Isaac until Jacob's return from Mesopotamia, where he spent about twenty years. Rebekah is dead. Isaac is living at Hebron, the home of his father. Jacob made his last visit to his father shortly before his death. He went with Esau, with whom he was now reconciled. Together they buried their father at Machpelah beside their mother and grandparents.

His Qualities of Character

Acted as it is upon a small stage, it is difficult to bring Isaac's life into words. Everywhere Isaac appears, he emerges as a sec-

ondary character, second to his eminent father, Abraham, second
to his beautiful and clever wife, Rebekah, second to his aggressive
son Jacob. Wherever he confronts any of these, he is standing on
the side lines, an easygoing, yielding, self-effacing character, con-
tent to submit to the will of these stronger ones.

And yet Isaac glorifies the commonplace. He is unforgettable,
because he is the only one of the three great patriarchs who represents the level of ordinary humanity, with whom the average
person can best identify. The plain, unassuming Isaac therefore
gives a very human aspect to the patriarchal saga.

When Abraham dominates him, as is so often the case of a
great father who produces a less conspicuous son, when Rebekah
overshadows him, when Jacob takes advantage of him, Isaac remains the affectionate, believing, co-operative, faithful character
in a drama acted out by these three decisive ones.

Amid all the demands, the counterplots, the strife, and the strat-
agems in which he found himself, Isaac continued to look to God
as the source of every blessing in his own life. Not as outwardly
religious as his father, who was described as "the friend of God,"
he was nevertheless a prayerful man filled with faith.

One of Isaac's other great qualities was that he never stooped
to littleness when others took advantage of him. Needless to say,
he remained the channel for God's continuing goodness to his
family.

Even toward his half-brother Ishmael by Abraham's concubine,
Hagar, Isaac showed no enmity, though they were separated in
their formative years because his mother, Sarah, objected to Isaac
being raised beside the child of her husband's concubine. But
when Abraham died, again Isaac showed brotherly co-operation
with Ishmael.

Forgetting the differences of their youth, the two went together
to bury their father Abraham beside Isaac's mother, Sarah. Isaac
was now the second patriarch of his people, while Ishmael was
the first patriarch of the desert tribes of Arab, an area known as
Arabia. The Moslems still honor as their ancestor Ishmael, who
lies buried with his mother at Mecca, while Isaac lies in a grave at

Machpelah with his parents, his son Jacob, and other members of his family. The Jews to this day honor Isaac as one of their great ones.

His Place in Bible History

There is no formal eulogy to Isaac but as the son of promise, Israelite tradition pays tribute to him in a variety of ways. The Apocryphal Ecclesiasticus (44:22) honors him with the other ancestors of Israel, beginning with Enoch "who walked with the Lord" and continuing on through the three patriarchs. In Christian liturgy Isaac is glorified again and again with the two other patriarchs. He is honored among the heroes of faith as one who "invoked future blessings on Jacob and Esau" (Heb. 11:20).

The New Testament also applies God's promise to Isaac, when it declares, "Now we, brethren, like Isaac, are children of promise" (Gal. 4:28). Isaac's story, like that of the other two patriarchs, is treated as a theme pregnant with a future of promise, a theme that found its rebirth, its liberation, and its validation in Christ. Isaac "died in faith, not having received what was promised" (Heb. 11:13), but he saw it and greeted it from afar.

The Bible is a record of the way these promises were woven into the fabric of Israel. Genesis highlights the struggle, Psalms assure the victory, and the New Testament stresses the fulfillment. One begins to realize that hopes are projections from the promises of God already declared.

As one of the three builders of the Land of Promise, Isaac is a part of the history that has an unbroken continuity from Genesis to the present. As the son of promise, he is a living symbol of God's gracious dealings with Israel. Finally, like his father and son, Isaac chose God. He became to each of them a personal God, with whom they walked and talked. In such a close contact with God, Isaac, Abraham, and Jacob transcended the experiences of other men of their time and help us to understand better that the God of Promise also will fulfill hopes through our own family, generations to come, for God is dependable, even when his children are weak and vacillating, and as J. B. Phillips says in his book

God Our Contemporary, "If there is a God at all he must be 'big enough' to fit into the modern scene (and that naturally means a conception of the Creator a million times greater than that held even a century ago)" (p. 3).

CHAPTER 3

Jacob: His Hope for His Descendants

After his name is changed to Israel, Jacob fathers the twelve tribes of Israel. Through the tribe of Judah, he is an ancestor of Jesus Christ. Joseph is his most eminent son and Rachel his most beloved wife.

Jacob, the direct ancestor of the Israelites, never lost hope for his family because he took seriously what God promised to his grandfather Abraham, to his father, Isaac, and finally to him.

The somewhat materialistic hope that his descendants will multiply "as the stars of heaven and as the sand which is on the seashore" (Gen. 22:17) takes on greater spiritual significance when it is promised that if Israel obeys God's voice and keeps his covenant, it shall be "a kingdom of priests and a holy nation" (Ex. 19:6).

During a long, arduous process of change, Jacob arose as the faithful servant of God under the promise that if he obeyed God, if he strived with God and men, and if he prevailed through tragedy and suffering, his name would no longer be Jacob but Israel. Unlike hopeless men who do not believe in God's promises, Jacob emerged as one led by God; and as he did, his hope moved toward better things. He was transformed into a new man who thought of God, not as far off but near, not as the God only of his father and grandfather, but as his God too.

Like his father and grandfather, Jacob learned to walk and talk with God, and in doing so he transcended the limits of the ancient people's common ideas about God.

His Emergence as a Patriarch

When Jacob was born in Canaan to Isaac and Rebekah, "he took hold of Esau's heel" (Gen. 25:26). All through their youth Jacob, the second-born, held Esau by the heel, as it were, whenever they came to grips with each other. These brotherly differences were not resolved until their later years.

As a youth, Esau was so "irreligious and immoral" (Heb. 12:16) that he was unable to share the expectant faith of either his father or his grandfather or to have serious regard for his rights and privileges as the first-born. Careless and motivated by animal appetites and material pleasures, Esau sold his birthright for a single meal. In this foolish withdrawal from family responsibilities, Esau scorned his natal claim.

Later, when he desired the family blessing (the culmination of the birthright), he was rejected, though "he sought it with tears" (Heb. 12:17). On the other hand, Jacob so coveted the ancestral birthright and blessing that he schemed to get them. These entitled him to what was probably a double portion of the inheritance from his wealthy father, also the precedence and authority over the family at his father's death, and the priestly prerogative in the home.

With his clever mother's support, Jacob obtained the blessing from his father. Together mother and son planned that Jacob wear the garments of Esau and cover his hands and neck with the hairy skins of goats, so that his own smooth skin would feel like Esau's hairy skin. Imitating the voice of Esau, Jacob went before his blind and aging father and asked that he bestow the family blessing upon him. The deception fooled the believing Isaac, as related in the preceding chapter. All too late Esau learned of the subterfuge played upon him by his mother and his brother.

His Wives and Children

Jacob had to pay for his fraudulent act in a twenty-year exile in Haran, several hundred miles from his homeland. While there his mother's brother Laban also practiced chicanery on him, in both his property and marriage rights.

For Laban's daughter, the beautiful Rachel, whom Jacob loved at first sight, he had to give fourteen years of labor, when he had promised only seven, because Leah, her more unsought and plainer sister, was sent to him first by her scheming father. She arrived heavily veiled and unrecognizable in the dark of the bed-chamber. Jacob learned all too late that he now had as his wife Leah instead of his lovely and lovable Rachel.

Tradition has it that although Jacob had to serve fourteen years as a shepherd for Laban, in dowry payment for his two daughters, Rachel was finally brought to him a week after the marriage festivities of Leah. But Jacob faced new problems with his polygamous household, which also included Bilhah, Rachel's maid, and Zilpah, Leah's maid. Jacob took both maids as secondary wives.

About fourteen years after her marriage Rachel gave birth to the beloved Joseph, Jacob's last son to be born in Haran. Rachel's second son, Benjamin, was born later in Canaan. Rachel's maid Bilhah bore Jacob two sons, Dan and Naphtali. Leah's maid Zilpah bore Jacob two sons, Gad and Asher. Leah was the most prolific of all. She bore Jacob six sons, Reuben, Simeon, Levi, Judah, Issachar, and Zebulun, as well as a daughter Dinah.

In Haran Jacob endured much, including other clashes with his father-in-law and idolatry inside his own family. When Joseph was only six or seven years old, Jacob was divinely guided to return to the land of his fathers. One of his lurking fears was that his children might become imbued with the idolatry so common in Haran. Jacob realized that if he were to receive the ancestral promises for his family, he must conduct himself as God's own; and as time passed, he came to know that the changes in his life were ordained for his ultimate good.

And so it was that Jacob developed into a person led by God, one who never doubted his promises regarding his descendants.

THE RELUCTANT WANDERER

Jacob's life falls into four periods: his residence with his parents in Canaan; his twenty-year sojourn with his mother's brother Laban in Haran, where eleven of his twelve sons were born; his return to Canaan; and finally his migration to Egypt.

In his more productive years, Jacob continually moved about the western area of the Fertile Crescent, where his grandfather had grazed his way into the Promised Land. That semicircle of fertility constituted a cultivable fringe between the mountains on one side and the desert on the other.

Jacob's story reflects the nomadic life and customs of the Hebrew people as they wandered, first seeking water wells and afterward erecting altars. When famished spiritually, they learned to appease their spiritual hunger at altars at Shechem, Bethel, Hebron, Moriah, and Beer-sheba, just as they had quenched their material thirst at flowing springs and water wells in the dry stretches of land. The most famous of these wells is at Shechem, still known as "Jacob's Well." (It was here that Jesus, wearied from his journey, paused to ask the woman of Samaria for water to drink.)

Jacob changed into a worthy patriarch through a long process of adversity, family bereavements, disappointments, doubts, fears, loneliness, and moments of shocking weakness in his own character. These changes evolved gradually for the better as he faced many heartbreaking and sometimes horrifying experiences. They make us better understand Paul's words, "We rejoice in our sufferings, knowing that suffering produces endurance, and endurance produces character, and character produces hope, and hope does not disappoint us, because God's love has been poured into our hearts through the Holy Spirit which has been given to us" (Rom. 5:3–5).

So victorious was Jacob that he, along with his father and grandfather, is honorably mentioned by Peter in his second sermon to the men of Judea in Jerusalem. He declares that God, who glorified the three patriarchs, "glorified his servant Jesus, whom you delivered up and denied in the presence of Pilate" (Acts 3:13) and killed, but whom God raised from the dead. A second time, Jacob, along with his father and grandfather, is pictured as sitting at Christ's table in the kingdom of heaven (Matt. 8:11), also as one loved by God (Mal. 1:2; Rom. 9:13), and as an heir of the divine promise.

His Spiritual Transformation

Jacob's spiritual awakening took place immediately before and after his return from Haran. On his way there, weary and guilt-laden after having falsely obtained the family birthright and blessing, Jacob lay down to rest at a place he afterward called Bethel.

There he dreamed of the angels of God ascending and descending a ladder set upon the earth. Amid all of his entanglements, the wrath of Esau, his mother's sorrow at giving him up, and the disappointment of his father at his deception, Jacob now realized it was God with whom he must come face to face.

In Jacob's dream at Bethel, God confirmed his covenant, first promised to Abraham, then to Isaac, and now to him to whom God spoke clearly, "Behold, I am with you and will keep you wherever you go, and will bring you back to this land; for I will not leave you until I have done that of which I have spoken to you" (Gen. 28:15). When Jacob awoke, he suddenly realized, "Surely the Lord is in this place; and I did not know it . . . This is none other than the house of God, and this is the gate of heaven" (vs. 16–17).

In appreciation for his undeserved promise from God, Jacob made this vow, "If God will be with me, and will keep me in this way that I go, and will give me bread to eat and clothing to wear, so that I come again to my father's house in peace, then the Lord shall be my God, and this stone, which I have set up for a pillar, shall be God's house; and of all that thou givest me, I will give the tenth to thee" (Gen. 28:20–22).

When Jacob erected his first altar at Bethel, where he had his first dream, he was alone, with neither friends, property, nor a hopeful future. But in these moments of dire despair, Jacob found God and then confidently went forward into Mesopotamia, where he found Rachel and her family.

Twenty years later when he came back to Bethel, he had family, friends, and wealth, but he needed divine protection more than ever so that he might fearlessly face his brother Esau, whom he had wronged.

Sending his two wives, his two concubines, his children, and his flocks and herds across the river Jabbok, Jacob did not cross with them, but remained alone for the night on the far side of the river. The ancient writer's way of telling this is that "a man wrestled with him until the breaking of the day" (Gen. 32:24). This man was God, who blessed him and gave him the new name of Israel. After this his twelve sons were to be called the "children of Israel" and Canaan was known as the "land of Israel."

As Jacob wrestled all night and came face to face not only with God but with his old self, he stepped up to a new level of experience, now illuminated by the typical virtues of the patriarchal ideal. His character had mellowed. Though once covetous, tricky, selfish, deceitful, and ambitious for material things, he was now humble, stable, purposeful, diplomatic, and spiritually sensitive.

Prayerfully, Jacob finally crossed the Jabbok alone, joined his family, and took up a new life in his own homeland. On his arrival there, instead of showing malice toward him, Esau embraced Jacob, and there was peace between them at last.

In Canaan Once More

Jacob now moved to Succoth, east of the Jordan, and later to the green valley of Shechem, the land of gushing springs and verdant pastures where his grandfather had set up his first altar and where he now erected an altar with the significant inscription EL-ELOHE-ISRAEL, meaning "the God of Israel." Another time Jacob went up to Bethel, more than ten miles north of Jerusalem on the road to Shechem, again to renew his covenant promises. He was grateful to God, who remembered even the unfaithful.

Daily he was strengthened for the crushing sorrow that awaited him, the death of his beloved Rachel when she gave birth to Benjamin near Ephrath (Bethlehem). Jacob set a pillar upon Rachel's grave and grieved for her until the end of his long life.

Family problems of another kind awaited him. When his caravan reached the edge of Shechem, his daughter Dinah by Leah was defiled by Shechem, prince of the area, who professed his love for Dinah and wanted to marry her. But Jacob's two sons Simeon and Levi, acting like angry fools, seized their sister, plundered the town, and slew Shechem and other men in the city, as well as their wives and children. Jacob's eldest son, Reuben, committed incest with Jacob's concubine Bilhah. Not even on his deathbed did Jacob forgive his sons for their treachery and godlessness.

After the death of his father, Isaac, Jacob took up his residence in the ancient city of Hebron, situated in a valley surrounded by sloping hills and vineyards, springs and water wells. Here Jacob dwelt securely for a time, tenderly rearing Joseph, his most promising child.

Jacob's older sons, jealous of Joseph, conspired to kill him. First they stripped him of the princely coat his father had made for him. Then they cast him into a pit to die but when they saw a caravan of Ishmaelite traders coming from Gilead en route to Egypt with their camels, they sold Joseph to these traders, who took him on into Egypt with them. On their arrival there, they sold him to Potiphar, an officer of Pharaoh.

When Jacob thought Joseph had been killed, he could not be comforted in his grief. Finally, during a famine in Canaan, Jacob sent his ten eldest sons down to Egypt to buy grain.

When the ten brothers returned with the grain, they told Jacob about meeting the "lord of the land," who thought them to be spies but finally released them, only under the condition that they bring back their youngest brother Benjamin. (This "lord of the land," it later was learned, was the long-lost son, Joseph, now the distinguished prime minister of Egypt.)

Unwillingly, Jacob sent his last son Benjamin down to Egypt with his other ten sons. There Joseph invited the eleven brothers to dine with him, but he did not disclose his own identity until he had tested the older brothers.

The lonely Jacob, longingly waiting in Canaan for the return of his eleven sons and still grieving for Joseph, thought he had lost Benjamin also. But joy filled his heart when the ten elder sons returned with Benjamin from Egypt, also with an abundance of grain and an invitation from Joseph that their father return with all twelve of them on their next journey to Egypt.

His Migration to Egypt

With the famine still serious in Canaan and now certain that Joseph was in Egypt, Jacob decided to go there. Jacob, his wife, Leah—he had buried Rachel at Bethlehem—his children and grandchildren, maids, goods, and cattle set forth for Egypt in wagons sent by Pharaoh.

As Israel's large entourage reached the border of Egypt, there to greet them was Joseph, riding in a regal chariot. He settled them in the "best of the land, in the land of Rameses, as Pharaoh had commanded" (Gen. 47:11).

Centuries later the people of Israel would sing Psalm 105, a call to thanksgiving in the temple at Jerusalem. It records glory to God for the Abrahamic covenant, for sending Joseph to Egypt, for bringing Jacob and his family safely there during the famine, for the Exodus of the Israelites decades later, for the desert wanderings and finally their return to Canaan.

Jacob lived in Egypt for seventeen years, but as death approached, he asked Joseph not to bury him in Egypt but in Canaan, the Land of Promise. Jacob's last official act in Egypt as the family patriarch was to bestow the family blessing on Joseph's sons Ephraim, the younger, because he sensed special strength in him, and then Manasseh, the elder (both half Egyptian through their mother, Asenath). Finally, Jacob blessed Joseph and his brothers.

History fulfilled the wisdom shown by Jacob. Ephraim's tribe grew to a multitude. The land allotted to him was the best in Palestine. This half tribe of Ephraim and the other half assigned to Manasseh were assimilated into Israel's family and became one of the twelve tribes of Israel. The sons of Levi, who committed the horrible violence against Shechem, were later denied territory

in the Promised Land. However, they later fathered the line of
Moses, Aaron, and Miriam. Because of his earlier incest, Reuben,
a son of Leah, was denied pre-eminence in the family but re-
tained a place in the family tribal line, along with Simeon, Levi,
Judah, Issachar, and Zebulun, Leah's other five sons. The seventh
and eighth tribes were the combined tribes of Ephraim-Manasseh
and Benjamin, the heirs of Rachel. The ninth and tenth were
Gad and Asher, the sons of Jacob's concubine Zilpah, and the eleventh and twelfth were Dan and Naphtali, the sons of the other
concubine Bilhah.

During the Exodus, centuries later, the twelve tribal divisions
had been preserved, and out of them emerged a distinct people,
the Israelites, according to God's promise to Abraham:

> I will make of you a great nation,
>   and I will bless you; . . .
> All the communities of the earth
>   shall find blessing in you.
>   (Gen. 12:2–3, NAB)

Before his death Jacob spoke again of his sorrow over the loss
of his beloved Rachel, whom he had entombed years earlier at
Bethlehem. He knew he could place his greatest hope in her son
Joseph and his heirs, because Joseph had remained "separate from
his brothers."

Jacob died in Egypt and was taken back to Canaan for burial
in the field of Machpelah beside his grandparents, his parents,
and his wife Leah.

With all the family problems that Jacob had had to suffer—defilement of his only daughter Dinah, his son Reuben's incest, and
the jealousy, lies, and tortures of Joseph by his brothers—one wonders if any father ever had more to endure.

There must have been moments when Jacob's faith wavered
and when the seeds of hope vanished. And yet they came to life
in all their fullness in Joseph; so in the end, Jacob learned that his
hope became a movement toward good rather than away from it,
as had been promised.

Joseph was "the fruitful bough" (Gen. 49:22), as his father had predicted, and his blessings were "mighty beyond the blessings of the eternal mountains" (v. 26).

The life and work of the noble Joseph made the difference between hope and hopelessness in the family of Israel, as becomes so evident in the next chapter.

CHAPTER 4

Joseph: A Hope That Never Wavered

A shepherd in his boyhood, a slave and prisoner in his youth. During famine in Canaan, he brings his people into Egypt when he is prime minister there.

When Joseph was cast into a dark pit by his brothers to die, he never lost hope. When he was afterward sold into slavery by them, he did not despair. When Potiphar, at the insistence of his wife, cast him into prison for a crime he did not commit, he was not discouraged. When seven years of famine struck Egypt, during his administration as prime minister, he was not dismayed. When he learned of the famine in Canaan and that his father and brothers were without grain, he brought them new hope by arranging a rich land grant for them in Egypt.

Joseph was never hopeless in any situation, no matter how gloomy, for he was a man of God, and godly men do not lose hope. So loving was he in his attitude toward all those who caused his hardships, so confident was his faith in the future, and so filled was he with that divine fire of hope that he saw every event in his life, the good and the bad, as God at work.

Even Pharaoh, on first meeting Joseph, sensed that he was a prince among men. And so he asked his servant, "Can we find such a man as this, in whom is the Spirit of God?" (Gen. 31:38). Although Pharaoh and his people were not believers in the God of Israel, Pharaoh recognized something very special in Joseph.

His Early Boyhood

Born in Haran, his mother Rachel's birthplace, Joseph showed promise at a young age. He was the favorite child of his father, Jacob, and seemed destined to greatness by the divine promise to his father's house.

Joseph takes his place in the family line as one of the chief figures of the patriarchal period. He brings distinction to his father's line because of his ability, his discretion, his integrity, and his humility, wisdom and faith.

Joseph was born, too, with the spiritual fortitude to endure much—the jealousy of his brothers, slavery in Egypt, temptation from Potiphar's wife, famine in Egypt, and finally tremendous responsibilities as prime minister of Egypt. Through each experience he grew stronger in character, and no matter how heavy his burdens, he maintained a faithful, tranquil spirit that set him apart from his brothers.

It was he who accepted humiliation as the way to exaltation, he who willingly endured servanthood as the way to humility of spirit, and he, too, who lovingly forgave those who committed wrongs against him, even the ten brothers who sought to kill him.

Because Jacob's favorite wife, Rachel, died at the birth of Benjamin on the way to Bethlehem when Joseph was probably only seven or eight years old, it was only natural that Jacob should place his greatest hope in Joseph, her eldest son.

"Separate from His Brothers"

Probably without realizing it, Joseph's father made him a prince over his brothers when he fashioned for him a long robe of many colors, probably of fine Egyptian linen, with sleeves that came to the wrists, while his brothers wore common shepherds' coats. Such a princely coat as Joseph wore seemed to foreshadow his being made the heir over his brothers, especially Reuben, the eldest, and other older sons who had lost their father's favor by their misconduct. The very sight of Joseph in his fine clothes intensified the brothers' angry feeling against him.

They belittled him, calling him "the dreamer" because he had a dream showing his sheaf of grain rising higher than their own sheaves. Another time he dreamed of the sun, the moon, and the eleven stars bowing down to him. His brothers grew more jealous of him, but his father, upon reflection, remembered Joseph's dreams.

The brothers' hatred probably first flamed as the family was returning from Haran to Shechem, when Joseph, along with his mother, was given the place of greatest safety in the caravan. The jealousy of the ten brothers finally reached such proportions that they conspired to murder Joseph, but without shedding blood. First they stripped him of his princely robe and threw him into a pit, as related in Chapter 3.

As they sat eating, Arabian desert merchants, on their way to Egypt, passed by and offered twenty shekels of silver for Joseph. It seemed more advantageous to the brothers to sell Joseph than to leave him in the pit to die, so they bargained with the traders, who took him to Egypt, where they in turn sold him in the slave market there.

After seeing the caravan disappear in the distance, Joseph's brothers took his robe, killed a goat, and dipped the robe in the blood. Then they brought it to their father, who, recognizing the robe, said, "It is my son's robe; a wild beast has devoured him; Joseph is without doubt torn to pieces" (Gen. 37:33). The indifferent brothers remained silent when their grief-stricken father refused to be comforted.

His Early Days in Egypt

In none of these experiences was Joseph bitter toward his brothers or distrustful of God. On the other hand, he knew in his heart that God was testing him and preparing him for his divine destiny.

Even Potiphar, Joseph's master, saw that "the Lord was with

him, and that the Lord caused all that he did to prosper in his hands" (Gen. 39:3). As overseer over all that Potiphar had, Joseph looked after Potiphar's slaves, his grain, cattle, and other varied activities of the field and of the estate.

He saw in the young Joseph such noble qualities of character that he entrusted him with his most valuable possessions as well as the custody of his wife. It turned out, however, she was not trustworthy.

Like other rich matrons of Egypt, she probably indulged herself in every luxury—a couch of ebony inlaid with ivory, boxes of perfume, bronze mirrors, richly embroidered tunics, and jewelry for her arms, ankles, and hands. Her material possessions and her sensual pleasures so occupied her thoughts that one day when the young, handsome Joseph entered her private boudoir she tried to seduce him. But he was a man of such high moral standards that he refused her entreaties, saying, "My master has no concern about anything in the house, and he has put everything that he has in my hand; he is not greater in this house than I am; nor has he kept back anything from me, except yourself, because you are his wife; how then can I do this great wickedness, and sin against God?" (Gen. 39:8–9).

Day after day, Potiphar's wife clamored for the honorable Joseph's attention, but he resisted her entreaties. Angered because he always retreated from her advances, "she caught him by his garment, saying 'Lie with me'" (v. 12). But he left the garment in her hand and fled from the house. She then called the other men of her household and said, "See, he has brought among us a Hebrew to insult us; he came in to lie with me, and I cried out with a loud voice; and when he heard that I lifted up my voice and I cried, he left his garment with me, and fled and got out of the house" (vs. 14–15).

When her husband returned she told him that the Hebrew servant had insulted her, and she showed him Joseph's garment as her proof. Potiphar had Joseph put in the prison, where the king's prisoners were confined. The keeper of the prison, soon recognizing Joseph's superb qualities, made him keeper of the prison.

Imprisoned with Joseph were Pharaoh's butler and baker, who

came to Joseph to relate some of their disturbing dreams which they hoped he could interpret. Joseph interpreted the dreams of these two so satisfactorily that Pharaoh, hearing of Joseph's power, had him brought from the prison to the palace to interpret his own dream. Joseph said that Pharaoh's dream meant that Egypt would have seven years of abundance followed by seven years of famine. He advised Pharaoh to prepare for the famine by storing reserves of grain during the years of plenty while the Nile was filled to its banks.

A Prime Minister

Seeing that Joseph had great wisdom and discretion, Pharaoh appointed Joseph, at age thirty, over all he had. His position equated that of prime minister. Pharaoh took his signet ring from his hand and placed it on Joseph's hand. This was his credential as prime minister. The sacred cartouche on the ring, when rubbed with ink and then pressed on a state paper, verified any document brought to him. Pharaoh also arrayed Joseph in fine linen, the apparel of a priest; and he placed upon his neck a golden chain that was the official sign of his authority. He also set at Joseph's disposal the second royal chariot, which took him through the streets of Memphis to make known his exalted position.

Furthermore, he arranged that Joseph marry Asenath, the daughter of the priest of On, a city of lower Egypt, and a seat of learning. During the period of seven years of plenty, Asenath bore Joseph two sons, first Manasseh and then Ephraim.

These were good years for Joseph and all Egypt, for there was such an abundance of grain raised that when stored, it seemed as plentiful as the sands of the seas.

Joseph's management of the surplus before the years of famine showed that he understood the principles of economy and management. As administrator, he had to initiate countless details. Storage silos had to be built. Contacts had to be made, transportation provided, and the farmers had to be persuaded to cultivate all available land. In all these Joseph exhibited great patience and

wisdom. The land not only prospered then, but Joseph was hopeful for Egypt's future, even in the succeeding years of famine.

Scholars have established that Joseph's rule as Prime Minister
of Egypt is now set in the period of the Hyksos, influential contemporaries of the Hebrews between 1720 and 1550 B.C., who are
thought to have come originally from Asia. Their powerful kingdom included Palestine, Syria, and for a time Egypt.

The Hyksos era was one of material prosperity. Some of their
innovations were the introduction of horses and war chariots in
Egypt, huge earthen enclosures for their horses, as well as other
new ideas that made Egypt flourish. It is understandable that
Joseph, who came into Egypt during the early part of the Hyksos
era, was a man of hope.

THE REDEEMER OF HIS PEOPLE

Among the visitors who poured into Egypt from adjoining coun-
tries to buy grain were Joseph's ten older brothers. They made
several trips. He knew them at the start, but they, not recognizing
Joseph as their long-lost younger brother, now bowed in obeisance
to him as one of the great men of Egypt. They came without Benjamin on the first trip, but Joseph requested that they bring him
with them on their next trip, and they did.

Joseph gave a banquet for his eleven brothers. Later as they
started homeward with grain again, he tested their integrity as well
as their loyalty to Benjamin. When he saw that they had matured
at last as worthy sons of his father Jacob, he told them, "I am your
brother, Joseph, whom you sold into Egypt. And now do not be
distressed, or angry with yourselves, because you sold me here; for
God sent me before you to preserve life. For the famine has been
in the land these two years; and there are yet five years in which
there will be neither plowing nor harvest. And God sent me before
you to preserve for you a remnant on earth, and to keep alive for
you many survivors. So it was not you who sent me here, but God;
and he has made me a father to Pharaoh, and lord of all his house
and ruler over all the land of Egypt" (Gen. 45:4–8).

Then the magnanimous Joseph shared with his brothers Egypt's rich store of grain, and he extended an invitation to them to bring his father and other members of his family to Egypt to live.

To his brothers Joseph sent asses, wagons, and more grain and bread for the journey.

When the brothers told their father that Joseph was still alive and ruler over all Egypt, "his heart fainted, for he did not believe them" (Gen. 45:26). But when he saw the wagons and other provisions sent by Joseph for the journey to Egypt, he said, "Joseph my son is still alive; I will go and see him before I die" (v. 28).

On Jacob's arrival in Egypt, Joseph was filled with such joy that when he came to his father, he fell on his neck and wept. Israel said to Joseph, "Now let me die, since I have seen your face and know that you are still alive" (Gen. 46:30). Joseph then took his father to Pharaoh, who blessed him, and directed that Jacob be given the best of the land in Goshen.

Later, so severe was the famine that the people had no money left to purchase grain, either in Egypt or in Canaan. First, Joseph permitted them to pay for their grain with their cattle. When all of their herds were gone, the people begged of Joseph, "Buy us and our land for food, and we with our land will be slaves to Pharaoh; and give us seed, that we may live, and not die, and that the land may not be desolate. So Joseph bought all the land of Egypt for Pharaoh" (Gen. 47:19–20).

Afterward he gave all of the people seed for the land, and in time of the new harvest, he told them that a fifth would belong to Pharaoh, and four fifths to them. And so the people, both his own family and the Egyptians, became slaves to Pharaoh. So long as there had been a just Pharaoh in power, Joseph's people prospered and multiplied in number.

The famine was so prolonged that Joseph finally was forced to take land as Pharaoh's payment for the grain. From this time onward, when there was a harvest, all of the people had to give a fifth of their entire crop to Pharaoh. But in spite of this new tax on crops, Joseph's own people prospered and multiplied in number.

In later times, when Moses blessed the people of Israel, he spoke of the great bounty provided by and to Joseph and of the strength that had come to Israel through his family line, the "ten thousands of Ephraim . . . and the thousands of Manasseh" (Deut. 33:17). The Psalmist, in his later prayer for deliverance from calamities, cried out,

> Give ear, O Shepherd of Israel,
>   thou who leadest Joseph like a flock!
> Thou who art enthroned upon the cherubim, shine forth
>   before Ephraim and Benjamin and Manasseh!
> Stir up thy might,
>   and come to save us!
>
>   (80:1–2)

Thus it was that Joseph's example of nobility and good management signified hope for the Israelites in the centuries that followed.

After Jacob's death and burial in Canaan, Joseph's brothers feared that Joseph would now hate them and pay them back for all the evil they had done to him. But when the weeping brothers came before Joseph penitently, he spoke to them, "Fear not, for am I in the place of God? As for you, you meant evil against me; but God meant it for good, to bring it about that many people should be kept alive, as they are today. So do not fear; I will provide for you and your little ones" (Gen. 50:19–21). Thus he reassured and comforted them. And Joseph lived to see the third generation of the children of his sons, Ephraim and Manasseh.

When Joseph was one hundred and ten years old and knew that death was near, he directed that his bones be returned to the land which God had given to Abraham, Isaac, and Jacob. During the Exodus, when the people of Israel went back to Canaan, "Moses took the bones of Joseph with him" (Ex. 13:19), as Joseph had directed. These were buried at Shechem in the portion of ground that belonged to the three patriarchs, Abraham, Isaac, and Jacob.

Joseph, in a sense, was the fourth patriarch, for his son Ephraim received from Jacob the best land in Canaan. At the time of the conquest of Canaan by Joshua, the Ephraimites, "a numerous people of great power" (Josh. 17:17), again were favored in the allotment of the land of the twelve tribes.

Joseph is honored in Acts 7:9–16 as one favored by God. He is honored again as one saved through faith, who "made mention of the exodus of the Israelites and gave directions concerning his burial" (Heb. 11:22).

Joseph's kind of faith is best defined in Eph. 2:8–10, which says, "For by grace you have been saved through faith; and this is not your own doing, it is the gift of God—not because of works, lest any man should boast. For we are his workmanship, created in Christ Jesus for good works, which God prepared beforehand, that we should walk in them."

No character in the Old Testament better represents such faith, which, when combined with hope and love, completes that great biblical triad. These qualities, like shafts of light, led Joseph to God, who brought through him many good works to many people.

A New Hope
A Nation Under God

Between the last scene of Joseph's provision for his family in Egypt and his own death and the Exodus is a great silence, finally broken only by the sighing and groaning of the subjugated Israelites. The sojourn in Egypt was once thought to have lasted more than four hundred years, but today's scholars say "a far more likely figure would be between 140 and 210 years, allowing forty or fifty years for each generation" (*The Interpreter's Dictionary of the Bible*, Vol. 1, p. 582).

Under Joseph and the Hyksos pharaoh of his time, there was a generous sharing with the Israelites in Egypt, but during this time lapse, a new dynasty of pharaohs ruled.

Although the children of Israel endured much misery during their long bondage in Egypt, there is no doubt that the experience there had much to do with the making of a valiant people. Had these later Egyptians been more compassionate, the Hebrews might have been absorbed into the complex world of the Nile Valley population. But the bitterness of their bondage was the occasion for their departure to continue their destiny in Canaan.

This sense of divine decree is strong in Hebrew history. Crushed and hopeless in Egypt at the last, they learned that in the vicissitudes of life they usually drew nearer to God.

Out of their suffering arose one of their own, Moses, a towering figure, regarded as next to Christ in the history of religion.

His delivery of his people in the Exodus became a primary element in the nation's consciousness. God spoke to Moses on Mount Sinai, "I have seen the affliction of my people who are in Egypt, and have heard their cry because of their taskmasters; I know their sufferings and I have come down to deliver them out of the hand of the Egyptians" (Ex. 3:7–8).

Here was another divine promise, says Walther Zimmerli, in his book *Man and Hope in the Old Testament:* "We hear again of people on the move, making for a goal. In place of the patriarchal families with their eyes on the fulfillment of the promise of offspring and settlement in the land, there is now the pilgrim people of God, preparing, under the promise of a land flowing with milk and honey, for an exodus (a going out) . . . In the difficulties of the wilderness wanderings they are continually in danger of looking back, longing for the fleshpots of Egypt. Again and again they are called by Moses to trust in the divine promise of a new future in the land" (pp. 52–53).

A new kind of hope filled their hearts, the hope of liberation and the hope that God would redeem them "with an outstretched arm."

This section traces the leadership of Moses and Joshua and these other men of hope, from the deliverance through the rulership of David and Solomon.

CHAPTER 5

Moses: Back to Canaan Through a Door of Hope

Born into a priestly family but adopted and educated in Pharaoh's court, Moses remains a Hebrew at heart. After much suffering, through God's power he gains the strength to lead his people out of bondage in Egypt.

Even when his oppressed people in Egypt were filled with hopelessness and despair, Moses never lost hope. The remarkable thing about Moses was that he had to create hope in the suffering Israelites, whose faith had been dormant so long. His refusal to accept difficulty and darkness was a connotation of his denial of them.

Foremost in his religious heritage were God's promises to Israel. Revived at Mount Sinai (Horeb) by his newly awakened faith in God's presence and power, first Moses brought his people into a cohesive whole at Goshen, where they had first settled, and then led them southeastward toward Succoth. The wilderness trek to Canaan, a mission seemingly impossible in these ancient times, began with the miraculous Exodus across the parted waters of the Red Sea.

The faith of Moses to accomplish such a task was first kindled when God appeared to him in the burning bush on Mount Sinai, after which he achieved pre-eminence: leadership in the Exodus; the uniting of the community of Israel under their first civil and religious laws; the direction of the building and furnishing of the first mobile tabernacle; delivery from the Amalekites, chronic enemies of Israel; and finally entrance to the immediate passageway into Israel.

Moses bore many crosses for his people during their forty years of wilderness wandering. Despite their groaning and complaining amid extreme difficulties, he confidently pushed forward in his inspiring leadership until the community of Israel learned what it was to be borne on eagles' wings across the divided waters of the Red Sea, what it was to be fed manna and quail when they were starving, what it was to see water pour from flinty rocks, what it was to be delivered from the merciless Egyptians.

Amid all of these trials and wonders, Moses was able to stir his people out of their apathy and despair and to assure them that they bore a unique relationship to God, their real deliverer.

God said to Moses on Mount Sinai, "I will certainly be with you." For Moses, God was no longer a voice to be heard but a presence to sustain.

Finally, at the end of his long life, Moses looked into the Promised Land "from the plains of Moab to Mount Nebo to the top of Pisgah, which is opposite Jericho." From this high point Moses gazed upon a glorious spectacle—his own ancestral land. He could rejoice that he had reached the borders of Israel, a land that would serve as a fortress for true religion. Moses would never set foot there himself, but his mission was accomplished and his hope for the community of Israel was fulfilled. And that was enough.

His Birth, Adoption, and Preparation

Miracles surround Moses from the time of his birth until his death. Scholars compare some of his experiences to Christ's. Like him, Moses seemed destined from birth for greatness. He was tempted but mastered evil. He fasted for forty days while communicating with God in the solitude of Mount Sinai. He had power to control the sea and to feed a multitude. He endured grumblings from these he helped the most. Because of all this, he is mentioned more often than any other person in the Old Testament.

His story unfolds in all its fullness in Exodus, Leviticus, Numbers, and Deuteronomy. These four books with Genesis form the Pentateuch, the first five books of the Old Testament, sometimes called the "Five Books of Moses." At least his name and his work dominate the first four of them.

Moses was prepared by birth and adoption for his inspiring leadership of the community of Israel. His father, Amram, and his mother, Jochebed, were members of a priestly Hebrew family. His mother seemed to realize from the moment of her son's birth that he was favored by God, so she took special means to hide him from the midwives who had been ordered by the ruling pharaoh to kill all male offspring of Hebrew mothers. (The Egyptians feared the growing power of the Hebrews in their fast birth rate.)

Moses' birth is introduced in all of the imagery common to the ancient Near East. His mother contrived the idea of hiding him in an ark of bulrushes, beside the Nile, where Pharaoh's daughter found him when she came to bathe. The child's sister Miriam, watching nearby, stepped forward to inquire of Pharaoh's daughter if she wanted to employ a nurse. And when told that she did, Miriam rushed to bring back the child's own mother, who then went into the palace and nurtured him for several years without having it known that Moses was her own son.

As this author says of Moses' mother, Jochebed, in her book, *All of the Women of the Bible*, "the whole character of Moses displays his mother's holy guidance. She it was who instilled in her son a belief in God, creator of heaven and earth, of man and beast. She it was who imparted to him the sacred traditions of Israel and who told him of the divine promises to Abraham and his descendants that they would become a great nation" (p. 53).

In the court of Pharaoh, Moses was educated in the wisdom of the Egyptians, probably at the school at On, the finest in the ancient world. He no doubt received instruction in Egyptian architecture, a knowledge he later used in the design of the first tabernacle and its fittings. He also was trained in the occult. This planted the seed for some of his later experiences with the supernatural. Other studies probably included philosophy, literature, and writing. These all prepared him for his duties as a high officer in Egypt before he took up the cause of his own people.

And now the faith of Moses began to give substance to his hopes. "By faith Moses, when he grew up, refused to be called the son of Pharaoh's daughter . . . By faith he left Egypt, for he was resolute, as one who saw the invisible God" (Heb. 11:24, 27, NEB).

A Shepherd on a Mountain Top

The New Testament records that "when Moses was forty years old, it came into his heart to visit his brethren, the Sons of Israel. And seeing one of them being wronged, he defended the oppressed man and avenged him by striking the Egyptian. He supposed that his brethren understood that God was giving them deliverance by his hand, but they did not understand" (Acts 7:23–25).

Certain that Pharaoh would have him killed for slaying the Egyptian, Moses fled to the Midian desert, where he paused to help seven sisters, daughters of the priest of Midian, as they watered their father's sheep. One, Zipporah, later became his wife and the mother of his sons, Gershom and Eliezer.

A stranger in a strange land, Moses now kept the flock of his father-in-law. Although reared in the palace of Pharaoh, he was to learn what it was to live in a coarse black tent, to wear coarse haircloth, and to wander over blistering sands and up grim wadis, amid only the sound of bleating sheep. But this silence was a blessing. Moses had time to commune with God.

Here he came to know God as being infinitely superior to everything human, as a fundamental principle elevating the soul beyond the limits of this little world, as a spirit lifted by high thoughts and noble deeds, all as indefinable as the mightiness of God himself.

God's Voice from a Burning Bush

Finally, Moses the shepherd "led his flock to the west side of the wilderness, and came to Horeb, the mountain of God. And the angel of the Lord appeared to him in a flame of fire out of the midst of a bush; and he looked, and lo, the bush was burning, yet it was not consumed" (Ex. 3:1–2).

Here, unsuspectingly, Moses stumbled upon his commission from God, who said to him, "I have seen the affliction of my people who are in Egypt, and have heard their cry because of their taskmasters; I know their sufferings, and I have come down to deliver them out of the hand of the Egyptians, and to bring them out of that land to a good and broad land, a land flowing with milk and honey" (Ex. 3:7–8).

Moses' new historical task came through three magnificent symbols he perceived on the mountain top: the burning bush, the holy ground, and God's voice. These miraculous encounters with God set Moses apart for a particular task in a moment of time, and prepared him to establish later, not a democracy with the supreme power vested in the people, but a theocracy with the supreme power vested in God.

For God had given Moses three distinct affirmations of his presence when he said, "I am come down to deliver them . . . Come, I will send you to Pharaoh that you may bring forth my people, the sons of Israel, out of Egypt . . . I will be with you" (Ex. 3:8, 10, 12). The diffident Moses asked, "Who am I that I should go to Pharaoh?" (v. 11).

But in God's power he went forward to this Pharaoh, one of the eleven pharaohs of the nineteenth and twentieth dynasties in Egypt. Most probably it was Rameses II (1301–1234 B.C.), who built the great hypostyle hall in the temple at Karnak, the Rameseum at Thebes as his mortuary temple, the great cliff temple at Abu Simbel in Nubia. He also erected an amphitheater at Memphis, as well as other monuments in Egypt, Nubia, and Asia, so that, according to J. A. Wilson (in *The Interpreter's Dictionary of the Bible,* Vol. 4, pp. 10–11), "it is entirely possible that

the Children of Israel were employed as slave labor in the huge
building enterprises of Rameses II, in the cities of Pithom and
Rameses."

The Last Days in Egypt

After Moses had the encounter with God on Mount Sinai, he
feared no one, not even Pharaoh. And so he went forth with vision uncorrupted by the manners of a tyrannical court, a mind
unperverted by personal ambition, a life untouched by materialism, a new love for God, and compassion for his suffering people.

Confidently he called upon Pharaoh to plead for certain privileges for the community of Israel. These were quickly denied. A
second time he appeared before Pharaoh, this time accompanied
by his more eloquent brother, Aaron. Again the demands were
curtly denied. Had Pharaoh granted these rights to another people within his own borders, it would have been tantamount to
acknowledging them as a free nation within the borders of Egypt.

Instead of gaining freedom, the Israelites found their trials
multiplying. Pharaoh ordered his foremen to refuse Israelite
workmen straw to make bricks. They were forced to gather their
own straw and flogged unmercifully as they labored. A very old
painting found in a rock tomb west of the royal city of Thebes
impressively illustrates Ex. 1:13–14, "They made the people
serve with rigor, and made their lives bitter with hard service, in
mortar and brick, and in all kinds of work in the field."

The time had now come for Moses to lead his people out of
Egypt. Before they would believe that God would deliver them,
they saw the Egyptians tormented by plagues. Their drinking water from the river turned to a deep blood-red color. Frogs invaded
their houses and fields. Gnats, flies, and locusts swarmed everywhere. Other plagues included three days of darkness, fire, hailstones, and lightning, all signs to reveal that self-will and pride,
such as that of the Egyptians, destroy human well-being.

About to be born was the unified nation of Israel, with a religious heritage separate from that of all other ancient nations.

Amazing forces were unleashed in preparation for this stupendous event, the Exodus from Egypt.

Moses took all the preparatory steps. First he held the Feast of the Passover. Though a similar feast had been celebrated earlier by Israel, this one was transformed into something more meaningful. A census was also taken of the number of Israelites in Egypt. Some "six hundred thousand men on foot, besides women and children" (Ex. 12:37) prepared to journey from Rameses in Goshen to Succoth, with their cattle, their flocks and herds, and their unleavened dough. The time that their people had dwelt in Egypt was "four hundred and thirty years" (12:40). Some scholars now say it was not so long, according to our method of recording time, probably a little more than two hundred years.

THE EXODUS AT THE RED SEA

The Israelites journeyed from Succoth and encamped at Etham, on the edge of the wilderness, "And the Lord went before them by day in a pillar of cloud to lead them along the way, and by night in a pillar of fire to give them light, that they might travel by day and by night" (Ex. 13:21).

Finally, on reaching the Red Sea they were overtaken by the Egyptians. As the Israelites saw the iron chariots, drawn by fast-stepping horses, pressing close upon them, they complained to Moses asking, "What have you done to us, in bringing us out of Egypt . . . it would have been better for us to serve the Egyptians than to die in the wilderness" (Ex. 14:11–12). But God spoke to Moses, "Tell the people of Israel to go forward" (v. 15). And his faith gave substance to his hopes again. "By faith the people crossed the waters of the Red Sea" (Heb. 11:29). The waters divided, and the Israelites marched forward on dry ground. The pursuing Egyptians in their chariots, drawn by fine horses, came after them. All sank into the wet sand and they were drowned as the winds blew the waves against them.

The skeptical may discount the miracle of the parted waters of the Red Sea. But Immanuel Velikovsky has written two books, *Worlds in Collision* and *Ages in Chaos*, which are said to support

the Exodus scientifically. In researching old records of this phenomenon from other parts of the world (from Iran to China, from
Babylon to Mexico and South America, from Egypt to Finland),
Velikovsky found events of a similar nature occurred at the same
time in these other parts of the world. He discovered there also
was a lifting of the sea into giant tides, a pillar of smoke, fire, and
earthquakes. His explanation of the violent change is that a planet-
like body was in near contact with the earth at this time and that
the earth almost collided with what he thinks was the planet
Venus. He records that this took place about 1500 B.C., but most
Bible scholars say the Exodus was about 1250 B.C. While the God-
loving take many of the miracles of the Bible on faith, scientists
may confirm their authenticity centuries later.

The Exodus, more awe-inspiring to the beholders than today's
miracles, such as moon flights, brought triumph into the hearts of
the Israelites. In the beginning their fathers chose God, and now
drawing close to him, they went forth singing their ancient national ode, "The Song of Moses" (Ex. 15:1–8), which begins,

> I will sing to the Lord, for he has triumphed gloriously:
>   the horse and his rider he has thrown into the sea.
> The Lord is my strength and my song,
>   and he has become my salvation;
> This is my God, and I will praise him,
>   my father's God and I will exalt him . . .

Joining her brothers Moses and Aaron, Miriam, their prophetess
sister, led the women and children, singing and playing her tim-
brel as the Israelites advanced through the Red Sea.

FORWARD INTO THE WILDERNESS TO SINAI

After walking through the parted waters, the Israelites headed
for what was their immediate goal, a plateau in the high mountains at the apex of the Sinai Peninsula. Here in a wide valley facing the mountains, they set up a new community, based upon
God-given laws. Their progress toward God was slow. Oftentimes
they were like children, vexed and impatient in their slow march

across the wilderness, first to Marah, then to Elim, and then to Rephidim.

At Marah they found neither food nor water, and they "murmured against Moses and Aaron . . . saying to them, 'Would that we had died by the hand of the Lord in the land of Egypt, when we sat by the fleshpots and ate bread to the full; for you have brought us out into this wilderness to kill this whole assembly with hunger'" (Ex. 16:2–4). They were all disheartened and discouraged, and there is nothing so hard to bear as a disappointed hope.

As time went on they came to understand the wonders of God's provision for them, such as the quails that covered the camp and a fine flakelike substance called "manna" (probably a secretion exuded by tamarisk trees) on the ground. This they found at Marah. At Elim they came upon seventy palm trees and twelve springs of water. When they reached Rephidim, there was still no water to drink, but God directed Moses to strike a rock, and water came gushing forth.

From Rephidim they set out for the wilderness of Sinai, where they encamped. Here they faced Mount Sinai, where Moses had had his first mystical experience with God. In the grandeur of this setting, where a tall cliff rose in front of them like a huge altar, they too sensed God's presence.

The Ten Commandments and Other Laws

Unlike other historical commanders, Moses did not lead his people against Pharaoh because of his tyranny, but away from him in order to re-establish Israel under new religious and civil laws. He did not know how these laws would come forth, but he had the hope to believe that Israel would become "a kingdom of priests and a holy nation," as God had promised.

Here on Mount Sinai the miracle of the Ten Commandments and other laws took form. When God called Moses again to the top of the mountain, he gave to him orally the Ten Commandments. He and Aaron afterward brought them back to the people.

Standing there in the solitude of the mountain, awaiting the return of Moses and Aaron, the congregation of Israel comprehended better what Moses said when he came down, "If you seek him [God] with all your heart and soul, you shall find him." They were to find that the Ten Commandments now repeated to them were to form the foundation for their society, and because the Commandments are an expression of the moral nature of God, they are a starting point of all true religion. Forming as they do an epoch in the history of the human race, these ten ancient precepts are as relevant to today's conflict, confusion, and immorality as they were to the conflict, confusion, and immorality experienced by nearly all levels of society some three thousand years ago.

Exalting as they do the sanctity of the home, human life, the sex relationship in marriage, the sacredness of property, the pledged word, and so on, the Ten Commandments still remain the high point in the law of civilization.

Afterward were added other religious and civil laws, which form the Covenant Code. The latter gave the people an awareness of national security guaranteed under God's protection. This they had never experienced before.

First conceived in a patriarchal society and later evolving to fit the growing needs of the community of Israel in its wilderness wanderings, this Covenant Code set down by Moses is considered by many scholars to be the oldest extant body of the Hebrew law. Repeated in Deuteronomy as the Decalogue, it is also called the Code of Mount Sinai, the place of its birth.

For his leadership in forging these God-centered guidelines some three thousand years ago, Moses made more tangible a new hope in an entire legislative code.

THE FIRST WILDERNESS TABERNACLE

Moses also directed the construction of the first tabernacle, a portable sanctuary that became a celestial light to succeeding generations. He planned the design and the furnishings, appointed the craftsmen, both men and women, and set up the first priestly organization under the direction of Aaron.

When the people first assembled for its dedication, "the cloud of the Lord was upon the tabernacle by day, and fire was in it by night, in the sight of all the house of Israel" (Ex. 40:38).

The Ark of the Covenant, also called the Ark of God, was housed in the tabernacle, a movable tentlike sanctuary. The contents of the Ark were believed to contain the two tablets of stone on which were recorded the Law given by God to Moses on Mount Sinai. ("Some authorities believe that the first ark, like the synagogue Torah arks, looked not like a chest but like a miniature building," according to *Harper's Bible Dictionary*, p. 43.)

But even before the tabernacle was built, the future of Israel had been threatened when the people sinned greatly.

> They made a calf in Horeb,
>   and worshiped a molten image,
> They exchanged the glory of God
>   for the image of an ox that eats grass.
>   (Ps. 106:19–20)

Even the frightened Aaron yielded to their idolatry. Moses could have given up, for he was so long burdened with troubles that were not of his making. When again he climbed Mount Sinai, he spoke to God, "Alas, this people have sinned a great sin; they have made for themselves gods of gold. But now, if thou will forgive their sin—and if not, blot me . . . out of thy book which thou has written" (Ex. 32:31–32). When God faced Moses, this indomitable leader of the Jewish commonwealth, he was filled with compassion for these ignorant, idolatrous people, and now commanded Moses to lead them forward on their journey.

They went from Sinai to Kadesh, with the portable sanctuary ahead of them, and with Moses, Aaron, and Aaron's priestly sons guiding them. With God's promises firmly imprinted upon their hearts, the Israelites arrived at Kadesh, the starting point for their final march into Canaan.

FULFILLMENT AT LAST

Before taking action to enter Canaan, Moses chose a representative of each of the twelve tribes and sent them as spies into Canaan, in order to view the land, to see whether the people there

were weak or strong, few or many, and whether the land was fat
or lean. This and the appointment of Joshua as his successor to
guide Israel into the Promised Land were the last official acts of
Moses.

He now realized that his hope for his people was no longer an
invisible dream but a visible reality. And he was comforted at the
end of his long life. "His eye was not dim nor his natural force
abated" (Deut. 34:7). Buried at Beth-peor, no man knows the
place of his burial to this day. Like Elijah it is thought Moses took
on a glorified body. At Christ's transfiguration, the first three
Gospels tell that Elijah appeared with Moses before Peter, James,
and John and that Peter said to Jesus, "Master it is well that we
are here; let us make three booths, one for you and one for Moses
and one for Elijah . . . and a cloud overshadowed them" (Mark
9:5–7; also Matt. 17:1–8 and Luke 9:28–36).

In transforming the lives of his people, Moses himself had been
transformed. While in the presence of God in the solitude of
Mount Sinai, he had in a sense been transfigured, until his face
shone with a new radiance.

It is no wonder God could speak of him as "my servant Moses,"
one who brought hope out of hopelessness, because he had such
zeal for the glory of God. With all this, Moses was humble and
unwearied in every undertaking, vigilant in governing his heavyhearted people, resolute in loving them, patient in bearing with
them, and hopeful in his goals for them.

Although Moses died in loneliness, within sight of the Promised Land, he was never alone.

Sensing a call from God for renewal, Joshua now moved forward
to take his people into the Promised Land.

CHAPTER 6

Joshua: Through the Divided Waters of the Jordan

*A religious enthusiast, a victorious soldier and a resolute reformer,
Joshua stands tall in the early history of Israel. After he leads the
Israelites into Canaan, he wins battles over hostile groups there
and then assigns the land to the twelve tribes who had returned
from Egypt.*

As the central figure in the Bible book which bears his name,
Joshua takes his place among the eminent leaders of early Israel,
one who was divinely prepared for his task of unifying the returning refugees in their homeland. The Apocrypha calls him "the
great liberator of the Lord's chosen people" (Ecclesiasticus 46:1,
NEB). In both war and peace he showed them possibilities that
could become sound expectations. This provided a candle of hope
that burned in Israel all during his leadership.

First as the Israelite general, Joshua won a victory over the
Amalekites in the Sinai Peninsula. As a firm believer in the God
of his fathers, he assisted Moses in the tent meeting during the
desert wanderings. (Moses sent Joshua into Canaan to report
conditions in the Promised Land before the Israelites entered
there, as explained in the preceding chapter.) And before his
death, Moses designated Joshua as his successor. After he was commissioned, ordained, and charged with Moses' office, Joshua was so

filled with "the spirit of wisdom" that he was given the courage to lead his people across the flooded Jordan River.

When peace came, he formed an alliance with the conquered people and those who had crossed with him in the Exodus from Egypt. Wherever Joshua led, he was divinely guided. "Have not I commanded thee?" God asked him. "Be strong and of good courage; be not afraid neither be thou dismayed: for the Lord thy God is with thee whithersoever thou goest" (Josh. 1:9, KJV). Ever since the King James Version was translated more than three hundred years ago, these exact words have strengthened the dejected and depressed. It is remarkable how often Joshua was told to be strong and of good courage, first in Deut. 31:23, and finally, in his address in his last years, he said, "Therefore be very steadfast to keep and do all is written in the book of the law of Moses" (Josh. 23:6).

Wherever Joshua came upon seemingly difficult obstacles, such as war with the Gibeonites at Gilgal, he heard God's voice again say, "Do not fear them, for I have given them into your hands" (Josh. 10:8). After that, great hailstones blinded the enemy, and Joshua's army was victorious.

His successful exploits hammer out the theme that God is active in history. Although Joshua's first years in Canaan are intermingled with war and conquest and God is conveyed as a God of war, a connotation we can never associate with God today, the Bible unfolds as living history. This theme is grimly relevant to every society in which man suddenly thinks he is sufficient unto himself and acts accordingly. All of these historical circumstances constitute an integral part of the final revelation of God's own Son, the Prince of Peace, who supersedes the God of war.

The first books of the Old Testament, of which the Book of Joshua is the sixth, are the story of the Israelites as they slowly climbed their way to God. And Joshua himself rises up as one of the most optimistic figures in the unification of Canaan under God.

THE PROTÉGÉ OF MOSES

Joshua knew Moses from the time of his youth, for he was born in Goshen, Egypt, the son of Nun of the tribe of Ephraim, the twelfth generation from Joseph. Nothing else is known of his early life. He was thought to be about forty at the time of the Exodus. Through the wilderness wanderings, Joshua was inspired, molded, and ruled by the creative genius of Moses. With humble faith and spirited enthusiam he accepted every responsibility that Moses placed upon him.

When Moses went up to the sacred mountain and ascended to the heights and Joshua waited in the quietude of the lower area, he began to sense God's greatness. After this he ministered daily to Moses. It is said of Joshua that he "departed not out of the tabernacle," and that as he worked, he prayed for God to prepare him for the work of Moses.

When Moses sent him into Canaan with Caleb, Joshua returned and pronounced it "an exceeding good land." His real faith comes out in his words, "If the Lord delights in us, then he will bring us into this land and give it to us." He seemed to say that real victory in any battle is built not on a soldier's courage, but on fearlessness based on faith.

Joshua could not doubt when he lived under such assurance. He could not fail in an awesome task when he had been so well prepared. So it was that Joshua, through his long life, was compared with Moses. He was obeyed and exalted, as Moses was. He sanctified Israel, as Moses did. The angel spoke to Joshua before the fall of Jericho precisely as God addressed Moses from the burning bush. Like Moses, Joshua wrote laws on stone, both at Mount Ebal and Shechem, and he called the people together for the making of the covenant.

THE DAWN OF ANOTHER PROMISE

When the Israelites were ready to enter Canaan, Joshua stood with his troops on the banks of the Jordan River, where he heard

God say, "I was with Moses, so I will be with you . . . (Josh. 1:5). He was now prepared for the crossing, with water flooding each side.

Placing the priests with the Ark of the Covenant in front, Joshua went with his people to the very brink of the river. Before they crossed, Joshua commanded them, "Prepare your provisions; for within three days you are to pass over this Jordan, to take possession of the land which the Lord your God gives you to possess" (Josh. 1:11); "tomorrow the Lord will do wonders for you" (3:5). Joshua never lost sight of the wonders God had wrought and would still bring into the lives of his people. With their herds, their flocks, their tents, and scanty belongings, they now moved toward the Jordan unafraid. As they approached, the waters parted, first for the priests who bore the Ark of the Covenant of the Lord. Then "all the nation finished passing over the Jordan" (3:17).

And so they entered "a good land, a land of brooks of water, of fountains and springs, flowing forth in valleys and hills, a land of wheat and barley, of vines and fig trees and pomegranates, a land of olive trees and honey, a land in which [they found] bread without scarcity, a land of [no lack], a land whose stones are iron, and out of whose hills [in the time of Solomon] came copper" (Deut. 8:7–9).

Positive that the religion of their fathers must remain uppermost in their minds, especially after their miraculous deliverance, before the crossing, Joshua ordered that they take twelve stones, one from each tribe; and on the first night in their homeland they set up a memorial as a testimony to God for his goodness to the twelve tribes of Israel. When they first camped at Gilgal, which became the center for many activities in the conquest of Canaan by Joshua, the covenant of circumcision was fulfilled and the Passover kept. And when Joshua came over to Jericho, an unseen visitor told him that the place where he stood was holy. After this came the miraculous conquest of Jericho.

THE MILITARY STRATEGIST

Joshua's task, that of invading Canaan with forces made up of a small, poorly equipped group of nomads, now in Israel after their long desert wanderings, was difficult at best. But it was not hopeless. So Joshua went forward, believing that aid would come forth in a way never anticipated.

This became the basis for a hope that was to bring success from the unknown and unfamiliar. A new vitality, stimulated by expectation, gave Joshua the courage to chart the unexplored and to act in time of crisis. He waited for surprise, and it came forth in unexpected ways.

Joshua's nomadic force had something unique in its favor. Although it represented a loose confederacy, its people were held together by memories of a common past and a rich religious heritage under the leadership of Moses.

In the unification of Canaan, Joshua combined his religious perspective with military strategy. Even before he crossed the Jordan, he sent spies to Jericho to view the land, just as he had done under orders from Moses. Rahab, whose house was built on the walls of Jericho, this ancient "City of Palms," concealed the spies and further aided Joshua's army in the approaching battle with her own people. The Bible refers to Rahab as a harlot. Josephus calls her an innkeeper. Whatever she was, she became a friend to the invading army and accepted their God as her God too. By aiding and assisting the spies sent forward by Joshua, she made it possible for his army to march to Jericho after they entered Canaan.

During the six-day march around Jericho, Joshua sent seven priests blowing trumpets of rams' horns ahead with the Ark of the Covenant. This encompassed Jericho the night before the battle. The second day the armed men with the priests in front with the Ark, marched around the city again. This was repeated for six days. Finally on the seventh day the invaders arose at dawn and marched around seven times. Joshua commanded them, "Shout; for the Lord has given you the city . . . Keep yourselves from things devoted to destruction" (Josh. 6:16, 18). As they marched forward on this seventh day, the walls of Jericho miraculously "fell down flat" and Jericho was now in the hands of Israel.

Joshua's next invasion was at Ai, the precise location of which is not known. Here an easy victory was expected, but instead there was an unexpected defeat.

This could have clouded Joshua's hope but it did not. He raised his voice in prayer.

In all of his military exploits Joshua never failed to say to his people before battle, "Sanctify yourselves." This command was given after the defeat at Ai, as well as in the later conquest of Ai, also in the battle with the Amorites at Gibeon, and the later conquest of strategic centers in southern and northern Canaan.

Joshua is remembered as a great soldier who accomplished tremendous tasks, the most spectacular of which was the allocation of the Promised Land to the twelve tribes. In all of his achievements he exhibited the valor of a soldier, as well as the justice, forbearance, wisdom, and humility of an exemplary ruler.

His Last Years

Joshua is thought to have been about ninety years old when war and conquest ended. He now obtained for himself a modest inheritance in the hills with his own tribe of Ephraim. His last home was in the deep valley and rugged hills of Timnath-serah.

James Hastings in his book *The Greater Men and Women of the Bible* points out that "the twenty-fourth chapter of Joshua is a pathetic close to a book of battles. It is the confession of all true warriors that it is easier to win a battle than to fight against sin day by day; it is easier to capture the impregnable fort than to keep the heart pure to God . . .

"Joshua hears that more or less everywhere local sanctuaries are corrupting the disloyal conquerors and Jehovah is no longer the uncontested King of Israel. So the old soldier returns to fight one more battle—harder than all the rest. He convenes the great Israelite assembly at Shechem, and there, in a speech which recalls that of Moses in the plains of Moab or that of St. Paul taking leave of the Ephesian elders, Joshua rehearses the whole plan of God" (Vol. 2, p. 403).

He recalls Israel's blessings, its crimes and duties, and he musters all of his waning strength to remind his people that their future and salvation depend on their loyalty to God.

In this farewell message, which still echoes around the world, Joshua rises to supreme greatness when he faces the elders, the military leaders, the judges, and the scribes in a great assembly at Shechem, the site of Abraham's first altar. In this eloquent address (Josh. 24:1–15) he reviews God's dealings with Israel, from Abraham on through to the Exodus from Egypt and delivery in Canaan.

Then he says in part: "Now therefore fear the Lord, and serve him in sincerity and faithfulness; put away the gods which your fathers served beyond the River, and in Egypt, and serve the Lord. And if you be unwilling to serve the Lord, choose this day whom you will serve, whether the gods your fathers served in the region beyond the River, or the gods of the Amorites in whose land you dwell; but as for me and my house, we will serve the Lord" (vs. 14–15).

This public appearance closed the career of Joshua, who had toiled in the Egyptian quarries, who had crossed the sands of the Red Sea, who had climbed Mount Sinai, who had crossed the River Jordan, and who had fought battles up and down Canaan.

As Joshua was nearing death, he inspired his people with this hopeful message regarding his golden years: "And now I am about to go the way of all the earth, and you know in your hearts and souls, all of you, that not one thing has failed of all good things which the Lord your God promised concerning you; all have come to pass for you, not one of them has failed" (Josh. 23:14).

Joshua's confidence in God's goodness never faltered. Through his long career the flame of his hope remained unextinguishable, and this gave him a creative drive which enabled him to fight against dissolution, destruction, and despair.

At his death he was buried in his own inheritance in the hill country of Ephraim. The people continued to serve the Lord during the time of the elders trained by Joshua. They were far ahead of the generation which followed, "Who did not know God, nor yet the works which he had done for Israel" (Judg. 2:10).

CHAPTER 7

Samuel: His Hope—A Rulership Under God

He was dedicated to God in the temple at Shiloh and afterward ministered there. He dispensed justice and was the first prophet, the pioneer in the establishment of a religious monarchy, and one of early Israel's most revered men.

Although Samuel lived in the dark period of the eleventh century B.C., he saw beyond to a better age, and he helped to make this a reality when he established a government in Israel ruled by both a civil and a religious magistrate. This hope was destined later in its noblest exponents, first the prophets and then Christ, to transmute frenzy into the loftiest passion for righteousness the world has ever known.

When Israel's national situation appeared hopeless, Samuel, a man of high principle, became its religious magistrate and set about to deliver it. He actually founded the Hebrew monarchy, idealizing it at its inception and anointing first Saul and then David as the first kings. Later the monarchy was condemned, but in time of disillusionment Samuel never lost sight of Israel's destiny under God. Even amid bitter trials and disappointments, he confidently pressed forward to this better day.

Samuel's hope that his little country might recognize God as its supreme sovereign was both valid and firmly grounded. This did not spring from specific desires or expectations, such as fortresses or riches, but from clear-cut plans based on God's creative and sustaining power. He seemed to realize more than others that direct disobedience to the will of God destroys first a government and then a nation. His constructive objective marked a fresh beginning for Israel, its most aggressive religious step forward since the days of Moses.

Samuel did not see the realization of his lofty aspirations, but because he saw their possibilities from afar, he is included in the heroes of faith in Heb. 11:32–34, as one who "through faith enforced justice, received promises . . . and won strength out of weakness." At least his efforts carried Israel forward in his exalted example of what a rulership under God can mean.

With it all, his character so impressed itself upon his contemporaries that we still feel it, says Fleming James in his *Personalities in the Old Testament:* "There was about him an austere purity, an uncompromising simplicity and directness, a lofty way of looking at life, a sinking of self in the good of his people, a burning desire for Israel's welfare, a passionate advocacy of its cause before God, a faith, a perseverance, a continuance in service, a willingness in his old age to meet a new situation and to throw himself wholeheartedly into the support of a young man." These, continues James, "rank him with the chiefest of those men of God who were Israel's unique gift to the world" (p. 95).

A True Child of God

The child Samuel's noble destiny was apparent from his conception, and because his devout mother Hannah sensed this, she consecrated him before his birth in the song of praise she sang in the temple at Shiloh. Elkanah, who loved his wife, Hannah, was in accord with her dreams and desires, none of which was realized by the children of his other wife Peninnah.

Hannah not only petitioned God for a son, but she had the faith to believe that her son would serve God all the days of his life. When her prayers were answered, she named him Samuel, meaning "heard of God."

After she weaned him at her home at Ramah, a few miles from

Shiloh, she took him to the temple and left him there to be
educated by Eli, the priest in charge. The little Samuel slept near
the Ark of the Covenant, where the lamp of God burned day and
night. As he was a little boy, it probably became his duty to open
the door and let the sunlight filter into the temple corridors.

And "Samuel continued to grow both in stature and in favor
with the Lord and with men" (I Sam. 2:26). Even in his young
boyhood, his mother made for him a linen ephod (an apron like
that used by the high priest).

Samuel's story continues through two books named for him.
Originally, these were a single book.

HIS PRIESTHOOD

Having been reared in an atmosphere of Israel's highest religious
hopes and dreams, Samuel was receptive to God's call to minister
to the people. After Samuel served in the temple, he was sustained wherever he went as a magistrate and a prophet, with a
deep sense of God's character and being.

When Samuel learned as a youth that evil can exist anywhere,
even in a temple, young though he was, he was not afraid to speak
out against such evils as sexual immoralities, sacrilegious feasts,
and pagan fertility cults.

While ministering under the priest Eli, Samuel saw at first
hand some of the corrupt ways of Eli and his sons, Hophni and
Phinehas. Like other fathers too absorbed in their own duties,
Eli never sought to restrain his sons, even when he knew they
"treated the offering of the Lord with contempt" (I Sam. 2:17) or
when "they lay with women who served at the entrance to the
tent of meeting" (v. 22).

Samuel was grieved that these two evil brothers should reduce
Yahweh (God) to impotence and dishonor. It was not surprising
therefore that they afterward proved to be unworthy stewards of
the Ark of the Covenant, sheltered so long in the temple where
their father presided. Finally they were slain in battle as the Ark
of the Covenant, Israel's most cherished religious possession, was

seized by the Philistines. Their father, the priest Eli, died from a broken neck.

Despite the iniquities that he saw, Samuel loved the house of God and its place in his own life and that of his people, so much so that while there he three times heard God call him to his service.

A Prophet of God

Samuel, who was first of all a prophet, was being prepared at Shiloh to weld together the theocracy of Israel, a form of government recognizing God as the supreme ruler. The old way of governing was no longer adequate.

Samuel's word was respected throughout Israel. Not only did he foster prophecy in its early days but he set Israel forward on its development. Consequently, he is regarded as founder of the school of prophets, afterward to reach its fullness in the time of the great prophets of Israel, beginning with Elijah and Elisha and continuing through Isaiah and Jeremiah and other spokesmen for God.

As a prophet hearing the word of God, Samuel began early to prophesy to Israel, and "the Lord was with him." As he matured, Samuel developed wisdom, spiritual insight, and the ability to inspire others at a most critical period in Israel's development.

A Judge in Israel

Samuel was the last of the so-called judges. As long as he dispensed justice, according to a high code of ethics, Israel moved forward.

As a chief civil and spiritual magistrate of his little country, this necessitated a variety of duties, preaching, blessing, teaching, and ministering. Even in his later years he embodied such dignity in this office that the Bible describes him as "an old man wrapped in a robe."

From his birthplace and home at Ramah, in the territory of

Benjamin, Samuel performed his duties as a judge. From here he
made a circuit tour year by year to Bethel, Gilgal, and Mizpah. The
latter, a small village atop a high hill, was four miles northwest of
his home. Bethel was twelve miles northward, on the road to Shechem. Ancient Gilgal's location is uncertain, but it was thought
to be either near the Jordan, where the Hebrews first camped on
entering the country under Joshua's leadership, or in the highlands
of Ephraim. In all of these places Samuel administered justice,
and at Ramah, where he lived, he set up his own altar.

After he became a national priest and a judge, Samuel summoned the people to assemble at Mizpah and to discuss the
twenty-year encroachment of the Philistines. When he saw the
enemy pressing in upon his people, he sought to bring the scattered tribes of the highlands into a unity of faith. This had to
be achieved, if Hebrew hopes were to be realized.

Like other spiritually sensitive persons, Samuel knew that the
glory of Israel had departed when the Ark of God, the symbol of
their faith, was captured by the Philistines at Ebenezer. It had
to be retrieved from the Philistines, and when it was, seven months
later, Samuel set up a stone, calling it Ebenezer, to commemorate
the victory over the Philistines. Here he thanked God for bringing
the Ark of the Covenant back to Israel.

"Samuel judged Israel all the days of his life" (I Sam. 7:15).
When he grew old he named his sons—Joel, the first-born, and
Abijah, the second—as judges over Israel, but Samuel's high hopes
for his sons were defeated. Both took bribes and perverted justice
in the high office their father had so honored.

The people then demanded that Samuel appoint a king to rule
over them. Dismayed at this, Samuel warned them that a king
would take the best of their harvest, also their cattle and servants.
He would even force their sons to build and drive his chariots and
serve as horsemen in his stables. Other sons would be required to
plow the ground, reap the harvest, and make his implements of
war. Their daughters, Samuel said, would be forced to become
the king's cooks, bakers, and perfumers.

Still the people refused to listen to Samuel. They demanded a
king who could command their allegiance and unite them. But
Samuel never lost hope in his ideals for righteous government.

His Anointing of Saul as King

There came out of Benjamin a man named Saul, who was the son of Kish, a man of wealth. "There was not a man among the people of Israel more handsome than he; from his shoulders upward he was taller than any of the people" (I Sam. 9:2), not only great in stature but also in physical strength.

Samuel first anointed Saul secretly at Ramah and afterward publicly chose him as king. He impressed upon Saul that he was God's chosen and that he must conduct his office accordingly, that he was to rule over a new kingdom, not to be autocratic but theocratic. God would be the ruler of Israel and Saul his servant. After this Samuel gave up his office as judge, but continued to act as a religious counselor, accentuating such principles as these to the people: "Do not turn aside after vain things which cannot profit or save . . . only fear the Lord, and serve him faithfully with all your heart; for consider what great things he has done for you. But if you still do wickedly, you shall be swept away, both you and your king" (I Sam. 12:24–25).

King Saul's early involvements were in battles against the Philistines, in which he soon grew impatient and disobedient to God's demand. He ignored Samuel's position as the religious envoy during an unavoidable delay. Hurriedly usurping Samuel's priestly duties, Saul impatiently commanded the people to bring the burnt offering to him.

Saul had hardly finished these priestly duties when Samuel arrived. Upon learning that Saul had acted in his place, Samuel was agitated, for he foresaw that a king who tried to be both a ruler and a religious leader might be easily corrupted.

"You have done foolishly," Samuel told Saul. "You have not kept the commandment of the Lord your God . . . for now the Lord would have established your kingdom over Israel for ever. But now your kingdom shall not continue" (I Sam. 13:13–14). Samuel was grieved that he had made Saul king. He saw that selfishness and bad judgment were at the heart of Saul's hasty action. Saul repented, but the earlier close association of these two men was never resumed.

Samuel had moments of haunting sadness over his own disappointed hopes for Israel. But he also had moments of great joy, such as when he anointed David as the second king of Israel while he was yet a boy tending his father's sheep near Bethlehem. Now Samuel could only wait and hope for a more righteous king and a brighter age for Israel.

His Place in Hebrew History

Although Samuel's dreams for a God-ruled kingdom for Israel were something of a failure, he held out this hope until his death when "all Israel assembled and mourned for him" (I Sam. 25:1). Samuel, a real creative genius, had built a form of government that had never existed before. Though it had its weaknesses, he persistently fathered this religiously oriented government until his death at an old age.

In founding the school of prophets, Samuel succeeded in perpetuating Israel's greatness. As a magistrate he brought to his duties the highest code of ethics. In disputes the people knew that with Samuel as the judge they would receive justice.

At his death Israel still faced tremendous problems. But Samuel, who loved Israel, had started it on the road to a better future. He was held in honor for what he accomplished for his little country, for his incorruptible character, and for his highly ethical religion. It is no wonder that his contemporaries regarded him as a greater leader than any since Moses and that historians still exalt him as one of the foremost men in Hebrew history.

CHAPTER 8

David: Israel's Hopeful King of Destiny

*Israel's greatest king, also a soldier, prophet, poet-musician, shep-
herd, romantic friend, and tender father, is the forerunner of
Christ, the true king to come, as prophets proclaim.*

King David's hope in God is expressed in the Psalms, many
of which he inspired and some of which he wrote. In his great
prayer for deliverance in time of trouble (Ps. 39:7–13), David penitently asks "for what do I wait? My hope is in thee." Then he asks
God to deliver him from all transgressions and to give ear to his
prayer.

King David needed God's goodness and compassion, for he had
confidence in Israel's future and he knew he could not achieve
alone his destiny as its king. In a real sense he was founder of
the Hebrew nation. He gave it a government, a capital, court, and
royal residence, and a unity of purpose based upon a common
faith. Also he left an image of one who had concern for the poor,
the oppressed, and the persecuted. Furthermore, he prepared the
way for the development of the resources of empire, commerce,
and religion, all to be expanded by his son Solomon. And most of
all, he inspired the ideals of kingly justice for generations to come.

Is it any wonder then that David is acclaimed by so many of the
prophets—Nathan, Isaiah, Jeremiah, Ezekiel, and Hosea? All saw
in his confident leadership great expectations for the future.

When David was first anointed king, Nathan predicted that the
Lord had declared David's "throne shall be established for ever"
(II Sam. 7:16). Then, in prophesying when "the oppressor is no
more," Isaiah spoke,

> then a throne will be established in steadfast love
>> and on it will sit in faithfulness
>> in the tent of David
> one who judges and seeks justice
>> and is swift to do righteousness.
>>> (Isa. 16:5)

Jeremiah hopefully foresaw that "'the days are coming,' says the
Lord, 'when I will raise up for David a righteous Branch, and he
shall reign as king and deal wisely, and shall execute justice and
righteousness in the land'" (Jer. 23:5). Ezekiel prophesied that
the Messiah would be the new shepherd. Likewise, Hosea saw
that "a door of hope would open," as in the time of Moses and
Joshua, and Israel would be restored once again.

About one thousand years after David, during the appearance of
Christ, the true king, David's memory was so firmly etched upon
the people of Israel that the blind Bartimaeus, as Jesus passed,
cried out to him, "Jesus, son of David, have mercy on me!"
(Mark 10:47).

His Youthful Years

From his earliest years David, a Judean from Bethlehem, seemed
destined for glory. He was one of at least seven sons of Jesse, the
grandson of Ruth the Moabite and Boaz the Hebrew. A tender,
loving son, he served his father, a prosperous farmer, whose large
flocks grazed over the ancient fields of his ancestors. Three times
the King James Version says of the youthful David that "He be-
haved himself wisely."

David soon won high favor at King Saul's court, where he was first
chosen as an armor bearer and musician because he was "skilful
in playing, a man of valor, a man of war, prudent in speech, and
a man of good presence" (I Sam. 16:18).

He was loved by King Saul and by Saul's son Jonathan and daughter Michal, who lost her heart to him and became his first wife. Jonathan was so devoted to David that he took his part when his jealous father persecuted David unmercifully. For a time, the forgiving David took the lyre and played it; Saul was so refreshed that his evil spirit left him.

David, a young man of princely behavior and great physical strength, gained many admirers in King Saul's court. Their confidence in David gave him the courage to tackle the nine-foot Philistine giant Goliath.

For forty days, morning and night, Goliath, with a spear in his hand, had threatened David as the youth walked from Hebron to Bethlehem. Having been delivered from the paw of the lion and the bear molesting his father's herds and flocks when he sought to protect them, David had no fear of Goliath, giant though he was. Armed with only five smooth stones and his sling, David went forth in God's strength against Goliath, who held both a sword and a spear.

"This day the Lord will deliver you into my hand, and I will strike you down . . . that all the earth may know that there is a God in Israel" (I Sam. 17:46), David told Goliath. After he slew Goliath, the Israelites no longer feared the Philistines.

David's immense physical and intellectual energy, as well as his righteous wrath in the presence of evil, come to life in Michelangelo's famous sculpture, first called "The Giant" and afterward "David." Through the almost five centuries since the great Michelangelo sculptured this figure from a cold block of marble, it has been regarded as one of the remarkable art works of all time. Like the young David himself, it signifies power and manly strength.

As David grew more popular, Saul's jealousy increased, until finally David, with the help of his wife, Michal, had to flee from Saul. For a time David lived in a cave. Then he sought refuge in many places, during which he gathered around him over four hundred young men, some of whom he found in distress or in debt or in a state of rebellion.

During one of Saul's more serious threats, David sought the help of Jonathan, after first obtaining advice from Samuel at

Ramah. Jonathan pleaded with his father for David's life, but Saul was only angered at his son's intercession.

As time went on, "David grew stronger and stronger, while the house of Saul became weaker and weaker" (II Sam. 3:1). Actually, Saul became sicker and sicker with what was no doubt a mental illness. In desperation, Saul sought the help of a medium, the woman at Endor, who foretold his approaching death. Soon afterward, Saul and three of his sons, including the beloved Jonathan, were killed by the Philistines at the battle of Gilboa.

Holding neither hate nor a grudge against Saul, the warm-hearted David, overcome with grief, stood at the biers of Jonathan and Saul and spoke his famous elegy (II Sam. 1:19–27). This is regarded as one of the finest specimens of Hebrew poetry. David's magnanimity comes through all its words, but in none so strong as these,

> Saul and Jonathan, beloved and lovely!
> In life and in death they were not divided;
> they were swifter than eagles,
> they were stronger than lions.
>
> (v. 23)

The King of Judah and United Israel

After Saul's death, David was officially anointed king "of the house of Judah" (II Sam. 2:4). An earlier anointing took place at Hebron, when David was yet in his father's home (I Sam. 16:13). David had learned that the Lord does feed and guide his sheep, that he does restore one's soul and lead one in the paths of righteousness. And that for those who seek to dwell in the house of the Lord, there is an assurance of goodness and mercy, as affirmed in the Shepherd Psalm (23).

Now the time had come for David to take his place as the "shepherd of all Israel." After the anointing ceremony, David went into a quiet sanctuary to pray, during which time he rejoiced in the promise from God to bless his house "that it may continue for ever."

In his many wars David conquered the Philistines, the Moabites, the Aramean state of Zobah, north of Damascus, and the Edomites. When he became king, Judah stretched only about fifty-five miles from north to south and about thirty miles from east to west, an area smaller than today's average urban center, but King David rapidly expanded Judah into a modest empire, unique in the ancient world. Finally, David's kingdom reached to the Lebanon Mountains in the north and to the borders of Egypt in the south, and east and west of the Jordan.

David's victories brought immense wealth to Jerusalem for the most part. Iron, so long controlled by the Philistines, came into common use. The Ark of the Covenant also was brought back from Philistia to Jerusalem.

David achieved many economic reforms in his forty-year reign, seven and a half in Hebron and thirty-three in Jerusalem. But the most profound of his expectations were in the religious sphere, and it was largely because of his dreams that the Israelites survived as a people under God.

Historians and literary critics alike recognize that the Bible record of King David is one of the world's finest historical documents. This was largely due to his own pioneering efforts in employing a court recorder, who along with others included everything from his personal adventures, to a census of his generals and court officials, to a list of his wives and sons.

His name appears in the Old Testament about eight hundred times and in the New Testament sixty times. This record is largely in the two Books of Samuel and the first two chapters of the first Book of Kings, also in I Chron. 11–29, Ruth 4:18–22, and in Psalms. The narrative is minutely related by the Chronicler, and in the Books of Samuel, and although the several strands present divergent viewpoints, they provide one clear picture when taken as a whole.

THE CITY OF DAVID—JERUSALEM

King David inspired the development of one of the world's most historic cities, Jerusalem, overlooking the Hill of Moriah, where Abraham had nearly sacrificed Isaac. There too was the historic threshing floor David had bought from the Jebusite landsman Araunah.

Jerusalem, also called Zion, was at a pivotal point, near Beersheba, Hebron, Bethlehem, Shiloh, and Shechem, where David's forefathers set up their first altars.

Jerusalem had its own natural beauty, the Judean hills fanned by the afternoon breeze from the Mediterranean and trees and flowers that were luxuriant because the land lay in a watershed between the desert and sea. The location was blessed, too, with an excellent water supply from the ever-flowing Gibeon spring.

But even in his fondest imagination, David could not have dreamed that Jerusalem would become such a historic city, the capital for almost four centuries of the kings of Judah and the home of many of the prophets. Nor could he have visualized the beauty of the great white temple to come. It would stand there, twenty-four hundred feet above sea level and look east to where the sun rises over the Mount of Olives.

In Jerusalem, too, the life and miracles of Jesus unfolded. It is probable also that Jesus preached a part of the Sermon on the Mount there, although Galilee is also a possibility. Here, too, Paul was educated under Gamaliel, the pentecostal revival of the New Testament Church took place, and Stephen was stoned. Jerusalem became holy to three world religions—Judaism, Christianity, and Islam.

It is no wonder that this Psalm and other immortal works related to this Holy City of David still exhilarate:

> I was glad when they said to me,
>   "Let us go to the house of the Lord!"
> Our feet have been standing
>   within your gates, O Jerusalem!
>   (Ps. 122:1–2)

His Religious Leadership

King David was the only man of his time to appreciate fully Israel's religious history. His great influence on ecclesiastical matters continues to this day, for it was he who organized the tabernacle service.

During the time of the census, a pestilence struck down thousands and threatened the wheat harvest. David then set up an altar on the threshing floor he had bought from a Jebusite farmer. In three days the pestilence subsided.

No wonder it is written, "The Lord gave victory to David wherever he went" (II Chron. 18:6). "David reigned over all Israel and he administered justice and equity to all his people" (v. 14). But David took none of these honors to himself.

Although David had great fervor for God, his primitive traits often came into the foreground in religious matters. To him the Ark of the Covenant represented the sacramental presence of God, and so, as he brought it back to Jerusalem from the Philistines, who had captured it as war booty, he wore a priestly ephod rather than a regal robe. On returning through the streets of Jerusalem with the Ark, he led the procession, joyously shouting and dancing to the sound of the horn, trumpet, cymbal, harp, and lyre. His wife, Michal, looking down upon him from her cedar palace window, upbraided him because of his scanty attire and his emotional outburst, not befitting a king.

But in this moment of religious zeal, David forgot everything else, including his kingly role and his wife's opinion. He had one objective and that was to bring the Ark back from former enemy territory to Jerusalem, where it belonged. He lamented to the prophet Nathan, "See now, I dwell in a house of cedar, but the Ark of God dwells in a tent" (II Sam. 7:2). This launched David on his dream of building a magnificent temple to the Lord, afterward accomplished by his son Solomon.

David was never nobler or more far-seeing than in the moments when he was planning the temple at Jerusalem. Humbly he went before the Lord in worship, to ask, "Who am I, O Lord God, and what is my house that thou has brought me thus far? . . . Because of thy promise . . . thou hast wrought all this greatness, to make thy servant know it. Therefore thou art great, O Lord God; for there is none like thee, and there is no God besides thee" (II Sam. 7:18, 21–22).

Because he had spilled too much blood in war, David knew he

was not worthy to build the temple, but he marked out its course. He had the stonecutters dress much of the stone. He stored this and the iron for the nails. He had bronze weighed in quantities and set this aside with huge cedar timbers.

Finally, David turned over to Solomon plans for the vestibule of the temple, also its treasuries, upper rooms, and inner chambers. "He [God] will not fail you or forsake you until this magnificent temple is finished," he promised Solomon.

David thus fulfilled his expectations for a religious capital and temple, where God would reign.

His Faults and Virtues

More is known about David, his good points and his bad ones, his successes and his failures, than about any other man in the Old Testament.

From the time he was a shepherd boy until he made his way into King Saul's court and afterward became king, David displayed the same charisma. Everyone, friends and enemies alike, seemed to sense his irresistible charm. He could love devotedly, and he possessed an amazing power to be loved.

He was talented, too, in things as far removed from each other as leading a war and playing a lyre. He was also generous to a fault, courageous, patriotic, resourceful, and he possessed an amazing power to win men's trust, even as a youth.

When Samuel was looking for a king, he had the seven sons of Jesse pass before him. "And Samuel said to Jesse, 'The Lord has not chosen these.' And Samuel said to Jesse, 'Are all your sons here?' And he said, 'There remains yet the youngest, but behold, he is keeping the sheep.' And Samuel said to Jesse, 'Send and fetch him.' . . . And he sent and brought him in. Now he was ruddy, and had beautiful eyes, and was handsome. And the Lord said, 'Arise, anoint him; for this is he'" (I Sam. 16:10–12).

King David's faults were those of a versatile genius in face of powerful temptation. Yet if he sinned against God, he had the willingness to say, "I have sinned," and then he begged God's forgiveness. While he might win men's trust he also could abuse it. (The wonder of the Bible is that it never glosses over the character of one of its heroes like David).

A man of polygamous times, David is presented exactly as he was, one who could conquer a nation but not his own passion. To him sensuality was quite legitimate, so he took many wives and concubines.

HIS FAMILY RELATIONSHIPS

Harem intrigue created family conflicts that brought out the worst qualities in David—folly, presumption, disobedience. But in these moments of wrongdoing his profound religious emotion came into the ascendancy, and in his innate love for God he sought to conquer them.

David had eight wives, Michal already mentioned, Abigail, Bathsheba, Ahinoam, Maacah, Haggith, Abital, and Eglah; also numerous concubines, ten of whom he left behind to look after his house when he fled Mahanaim during his son Absalom's rebellion.

David's best known concubine was the beautiful Abishag, who came to him as a nurse in his feeble years. His son Adonijah asked her hand in marriage, but the request was denied, and he was punished by King Solomon for his designs on the throne.

David had no children by Michal, but several by Bathsheba, one of whom was Solomon. Maacah, the daughter of the king of Geshur, was the mother of David's daughter Tamar and also of his most beloved son, Absalom.

Never was David greater than at the bier of Absalom, who had organized a plot to seize the throne from his father. At Absalom's accidental death, David forgot this and indulged in heartbreaking grief known only to a devoted father. "O my son Absalom, my son, my son Absalom!" he sobbed out loud. "Would I had died instead of you, O Absalom, my son, my son!" (II Sam. 18:33).

David had many sons, at least nineteen, most of whom are named. Only two daughters are mentioned. A tender and indulgent father, David spoiled his children. Of Adonijah it is said, "His father had never at any time displeased him by asking, 'Why have you done thus and so?'" (I Kings 1:6). What an indictment against a father's lack of discipline of his son! And even though David lost his temper when Amnon, the son of Ahinoam, committed incest with his sister Tamar, he did not punish Amnon.

The best known of all David's wives and probably the one he loved best was Bathsheba. When David first saw her bathing on her roof top, he was promenading on his adjoining roof garden. She was then the wife of Uriah, a soldier in David's army. Enamored with the beautiful Bathsheba, David ordered his messenger to bring her to his palace, a king's privilege in that uncouth age.

He had an adulterous union with Bathsheba, and when he found that she was with child—his child—he wrote out an order for her strong and faithful husband, Uriah, to be placed in the forefront of battle, where he was killed. David then made Bathsheba his wife.

When the child of their adulterous union died soon after birth, David comforted Bathsheba, but he was so griefstricken over his own iniquity and the loss of his child that he went to God, and in his penitential prayer, begged, "Create in me a clean heart, O God, and put a new and right spirit within me" (Ps. 51:10). Later the grief-stricken David poignantly lamented, "I shall go to him but he will not return to me" (II Sam. 12:23).

While David spoiled his children, he looked down on women and their rights. He was harsh and unforgiving with Michal when she derided him for being undignified. On the other hand, he showed great tenderness to the lovely and wise Abigail, who had come to him when he was a shepherd hiding from Saul in the wilderness of Paran with his bodyguard. Abigail went before David to assuage his anger against her husband Nabal, described as rich, churlish, and ill-behaved. The wealthy Nabal had insulted David when he and his men, who had protected Nabal's herdsmen, were hungry.

When they asked for food while Nabal was giving a feast, Nabal refused them. When Abigail learned of her husband's insult to David, she and her maids took food to David. She alighted from her ass and kneeled before David to make amends for the insult of her drinking husband, and she predicted that David would be prince over Israel and in the care of the Lord his God.

David did not forget the wise and understanding Abigail, who had saved him from probable tragedy and had inspired him to be prince over Israel. After Nabal's death, King David sent his messenger for Abigail to be his wife, probably his third.

In all of his family experiences, which ran the gamut of every human emotion, David never resorted to hopelessness. And though often in the wrong, he never failed to admit his worst errors and faults.

HIS LAST YEARS AND DEATH

David's men loved him until the end. When his strength was waning, Abishai, David's nephew, said to him, "You shall no more go out with us to battle, lest you quench the lamp of Israel" (II Sam. 21:17). But Israel's light would soon go out anyway. The hardships of David's youth and the self-indulgences of his polygamy had weakened his constitution. He slowly sank to his death when he was nearing seventy, according to Josephus, the first-century Jewish historian.

In a poetical passage of David's last words (II Sam. 23:1–7), David presents the ideals he tried to live by as a ruler. He says in part:

> The Spirit of the Lord speaks by me,
>> his word is upon my tongue . . .
> When one rules justly over men,
>> ruling in the fear of God,
> he dawns on them like the morning light,
>> like the sun shining forth upon a cloudless morning,
> like rain that makes grass to sprout from the earth.
>> Yea, does not my house stand so with God?
> For he has made with me an everlasting covenant,
>> Ordered in all things and secure

(vs. 2–5)

David gave his last orders to his followers and spoke his final words to Solomon, now king. "I am about to go the way of all the earth." He was buried in Jerusalem.

On the day of Pentecost, Peter alluded to David's sepulcher as "with us to this day" (Acts 2:29). Then Peter paid David the greatest compliment of all: "Being therefore a prophet, and knowing that God had sworn with an oath to him that he would set one of his descendants upon his throne, he foresaw and spoke of the resurrection of the Christ" (vs. 30–31).

Afterward, on his first ministry in Perga and Antioch, Paul spoke of how when Saul was removed as king, God had said, " 'I have found in David the son of Jesse a man after my heart, who will do all my will.' Of this man's posterity God has brought to Israel a Savior, Jesus, as he promised" (Acts 13:22–23). This promise, a part of the Davidic Covenant (II Sam. 7:4–16), foretold that David's kingdom would endure forever. Christ it was who was exalted to supreme ruler over the kingdom of God foretold to his mother Mary in the Annunciation (Luke 1:32–33).

All of the Davidic expectations were miraculously fulfilled in the predictions by the prophets, the eulogies of Peter and Paul, and the inclusion of David in Christ's genealogy.

CHAPTER 9

Solomon: From God to Mammon

Far-famed for his wisdom, wealth, and splendor, Solomon became known all over the ancient world as its most brilliant king and industrialist.

When King Solomon kept his hope in God, he "excelled all the kings of the earth in riches and wisdom. And the whole earth sought the presence of Solomon to hear his wisdom, which God had put into his mind" (I Kings 10:23-24).

The splendor of his reign ushered in the golden age of Israel's political history, first set in motion by his brilliant legacy from his father, David. Then Solomon, with high hopes, asked God for an understanding heart to rule the people. His fortitude, fearlessness, and his love of God, all inbred in him by his father, became the very dynamics of his driving force in his early years as king.

His kingdom was like a fanciful dream. "The brilliant spectacle of the court, the prancing of the war-horses, the flash of many chariot wheels, the coming and going of embassies, the visits of foreign dignitaries, all contributed to make the Israelite feel that now at last his king was taking a place among the great ones of the earth. At the center of the splendor, spinning it about himself tirelessly, exulted its royal creator," says Fleming James in his *Personalities of the Old Testament* (p. 158).

But when Solomon began to glory too much in gold, great

houses, fortifications, and other indulgences, especially marriages
into many foreign cults—everything the prophets were later to
condemn—Israel eventually paid the price in high taxes, foreign
debts, and oppression, including forced labor. And the people
were filled with despair and hopelessness.

Despite his faults King Solomon made two distinct contribu-
tions to Israel: first, the construction and dedication of the magnificent temple at Jerusalem; next, the gift of wisdom.

The narrative of King Solomon's forty-year reign runs through
the First Book of Kings, chapters 3 through 11, and the Second
Book of Chronicles, chapters 1 through 9. The central theme is
Solomon's glorious victory when he remained obedient to God.
Then his hopes became realities; but when he turned from God,
his earlier hopes were lost dreams.

The Wise, Grandiose King

Solomon was the favorite of his mother Bathsheba, who had
three other sons by David. When King David was old and ill, she
pleaded with him to name Solomon as his successor, and he did.
Solomon was a mere youth (probably under eighteen) at the time
he was conducted on his father's mule to Gibeon, the sacred spring
near Jerusalem, where he was anointed king by the priests Zadok
and Nathan.

Solomon was now humble, because he knew he had come to
the throne over the rights of others, especially Adonijah, his half-
brother by Haggith, one of his father's eight wives. After he gained
power, he put to death three men in his way. The first was Adonijah and then Joab, who had sided with Adonijah. The third was
Shimei, his father's enemy, who also stood in the way of his own
royal power.

Penitently, Solomon later went to offer a sacrifice at Gibeon.
He knew he needed God because his right to rule was founded
upon intrigue and treachery. In his exalting dialogue with God
(I Kings 3:5–15), Solomon admitted that he was unskilled in
leadership, and then he asked for "an understanding mind to gov-
ern the people" (v. 9). Pleased with his noble objective, God, in

a dream, promised Solomon not only an understanding heart but riches, glory, and a long life.

We see King Solomon, like a grandiose actor, striding dramatically into the ancient world as its wisest and most powerful potentate. In his gold-woven robes adorned with precious jewels, he suggests a commanding actor wrapped in a haze of romance. Again, like a conspicuous actor, one sees him moving about an impressive stage, from his ivory and gold-trimmed throne, to a group of imposing buildings leading up Jerusalem's Hill of Moriah, where stood at its highest point the Holy Temple. On terraces below were his court buildings, including his palace, the Hall of the Forest of Lebanon, the Hall of Pillars, and the Hall of Justice. Other palatial structures were added for his wives and concubines.

And so his early hopes and dreams, deeply rooted in moral integrity and spiritual discernment, were miraculously accomplished.

In order to strengthen the achievements of his father, Solomon expanded the system of national organization. He appointed an adjutant general, a secretary of state, a commander of the army, two priests, a superintendent of regional governors, a comptroller of the household, a superintendent of the forced levy, two regional governors, and one governor over all the government, all named in I Kings 4:1–19. King Solomon remained in supreme authority over all of them.

The Temple Builder

His construction of the temple, atop the Hill of Moriah, helped to unify Israel as well as to dignify its religious heritage. He built two houses, as they are called in the Bible, one for the Lord and the other for himself. It took him about seven and a half years to finish the temple, begun in the fourth year of his reign, about 975 B.C. but about thirteen years to finish his own palace, so extensive were its many parts.

The temple was built of elegant white stone finished by thousands of Hebrew and Phoenician laborers. The interior was wainscoted with cedar from Lebanon.

The task of building this magnificent structure is described in detail in the sixth chapter of I Kings. This tells of the interior furnishings, many trimmed with gold. Even the floor and doors were plated with gold. In the center of the inner chamber stood the large cherubs of olive wood. Tall sandalwood pilasters, carved with trees, added dignity. Hiram, the Phoenician architect and artist, cast the bronze (copper) pillars and other temple furnishings.

The temple had so much gold that it must have shone in the light, even inside, for the altar, the table for the Bread of the Presence, and the lampstands were of pure gold, as well as the cups, snuffers, basins, dishes for incense, and firepans. And Solomon added to these the treasuries of the house of the Lord assembled by his father.

After the temple was completed, Solomon had the Ark of the Covenant placed in the inner sanctuary amid great ceremony and music. The procession, led by Solomon and the elders and priests, ascended the Hill of Moriah, crossed the temple court, and entered the main sanctuary between handsome bronze pillars. And the throngs of onlookers sensed the presence of the Lord when Solomon arose to say:

> The Lord has set the sun in the heavens,
>> but has said that he would dwell in thick darkness.
> I have built thee an exalted house,
>> a place for thee to dwell in for ever.
>> (I Kings 8:12–13)

His dedicatory address includes a long prayer (I Kings 8:22–61). In his benediction he begs God not to forsake his people . . . "that all the people of the earth may know that the Lord is God; there is no other" (v. 60).

King Solomon spoke as one with noble objectives. Demanding continuing obedience, God said to Solomon, "If you turn aside from following me, you or your children, and do not keep my commandments and my statutes which I have set before you, but go and serve other gods and worship them, then I will cut off Israel from the land which I have given them; and the house which I have consecrated for my name, I will cast out of my sight . . . And this house will become a heap of ruins" (I Kings 9:6–8). This dialogue shows that the Israelites believed that God takes the destiny of mortals in his hand, even so great a potentate as Solomon.

For the first years this magnificent temple gave stability to the religious life of Israel. The structure itself stood for more than four centuries, until destroyed by the Babylonians, but was afterward rebuilt by Zerubbabel in 516 B.C., in a much shabbier form, after the return of the exiles from Babylonia. Herod's temple later was erected on the same site, and this was the temple Jesus knew.

But the account of when "a cloud filled the house of the Lord" (I Kings 8:10–11) makes the reader know that Mount Moriah was never such a beacon of hope to Israel as on that day when Solomon dedicated its great temple.

The Father of Wisdom

Israel began to marvel at King Solomon's wisdom, the fame of which reached all over the world. One of his early cases was that of the two prostitutes dwelling in the same house, each of whom gave birth to babies born within three days of each other. One baby died in the night when its mother, in her sleep, lay over it. The real mother of the child made this explanation to King Solomon:

"And in the middle of the night she got up and took my son from beside me while your servant was asleep; she put him to her breast and put her own dead son to mine. When I got up to suckle my child, there he was, dead. But in the morning I looked at him carefully, and he was not the child I had borne at all." Then the other woman spoke. "That is not true! Your son is the dead one, mine is the live one." And so they wrangled before the king." . . . "Bring me a sword," said the king; "Cut the living child in two . . . and give half to one, half to the other." At this the woman who was the mother of the living child addressed the king, for she burned with pity for her son. "If it please you, my lord," she said, "let them give her the child; only do not let them think of killing it." But the other said, "He shall belong to neither of

us. Cut him up." Then the king gave his decision. "Give the
child to the first woman . . . and do not kill him. She is his
mother."

(I Kings 3:19–28, JB)

Onlookers were awed at Solomon's wisdom, his innate knowledge of human nature, and his sense of justice.

The Book of Wisdom in the Apocrypha, although not written
until around 50 or 100 B.C., was called by its authors, "The Wisdom of Solomon." Solomon was thought to have provided certain
maxims for that book, as well as for the Book of Proverbs and the
Song of Songs. But today's scholars regard Solomon as the fountainhead of wisdom, not the author. It is their opinion that the
Book of Proverbs was attributed to King Solomon only as a courtesy, that it was probably written during the fifth and fourth
pre-Christian centuries by masters in the academies as study books
for the young men of the more affluent families.

THE GREAT INDUSTRIALIST

God, who had come into Solomon's life as silently as light,
seemed to be the center of great wonders. King Solomon's sa-
gacity, cosmopolitanism, power, and administrative ability brought
great prosperity to Israel.

On the level below the temple he built the beautiful buildings
of state described in I Kings 7.

Solomon's vast shipping and mining interests were greater than
any known then. He is still called the "ancient world's copper
king." The copper had been there all the time but it took the
genius of Solomon to mine it. Much earlier, the Deuteronomist
confirmed that Israel was "a land whose stones are iron, and out
of whose hills you can dig copper" (Deut. 8).

Archaeologists have found the remains of Solomon's extensive
complex of huge copper and iron smelters around the Dead Sea
and Gulf of Aqaba. At the latter place, in 1938–40, the late Nelson
Glueck found a refinery.

Here on this gulf Solomon built a large seaport, with ample
storage facilities for his vast shipping interests, carried on by his

fleet of ships sailing the seas as far as Ophir (perhaps near Bombay, India?). From there his fleet is thought to have brought back the gold used for furnishings in the Hall of the Forest of Lebanon and also the temple.

His needs for gold were many. His gold throne has been described as unlike that in any part of the world. His drinking vessels were of pure gold, too.

Silver was as common as stone and cedar as plentiful as the sycamore of the lowlands. Each ship returning from other parts of the world brought more gold and silver, robes, armor, spices, horses, and mules. Great cargoes also were loaded with precious stones and almug wood. In I Kings 9:26–28, a description is given of King Solomon's fleets returning to Ezion-geber, on the shore of the Red Sea. There the great treasures from many places, amounting to what would be millions of dollars annually, were loaded and carried overland to Jerusalem.

King Solomon's twelve thousand horses came from Que in Syria, and his fourteen hundred chariots were imported from Egypt. He also built the Millo, probably a fortress on the wall of Jerusalem, and repaired this wall built by his father. He is credited with building new cities, too, Hazor, Megiddo, Gezer, as well as storage cities for his chariots and cavalry.

A great lover of nature, he designed pools and extensive gardens and brought in peacocks to add to the beauty of the latter. His orchard, too, produced fruits of many kinds.

It is no wonder the whole world sought audience with him. When the queen of Sheba came with her large caravan from what is thought to have been southern Arabia, she said to Solomon, "The report was true which I heard in my own land of your affairs and your wisdom, but I did not believe the reports until I came and my own eyes had seen it; and behold, the half was not told me; your wisdom and prosperity surpass the report which I heard" (I Kings 10:6–7).

She came to see his great display of gold from Ophir, silver (probably) from Spain and Asia Minor, precious stones and spices from Arabia, and cedar from Lebanon. She was so impressed with his array of servants and cup bearers, the rich cuisine of his table, the gold vessels with which it was set, the fine clothing of

the officers, the courtiers, and the princes who came from far and
wide to pay tribute to him that she declared there was no king like
him.

HIS MANY WIVES AND CONCUBINES

In the early part of his reign King Solomon made an alliance
with the pharaoh of Egypt to marry his daughter, and she brought
with her as dowry rights the old Philistine city of Gezer. Solomon
built for her a palace fashioned of the same costly stones as the
temple, which could be viewed from it.

Solomon began to draw up alliances with other rulers in foreign
lands for their daughters in marriage. The Bible tells us that Solomon "clung to them in love"—Moabite, Ammonite, Edomite,
Sidonian, and Hittite women. Solomon had in all seven hundred
wives, princesses, and three hundred concubines, "and his wives
turned away his heart, after other gods" according to I Kings
11:3–4. "And the Lord was angry with Solomon, because his heart
had turned away from the Lord" (v. 9).

In order to please his many wives Solomon built shrines to their
gods: to Asherah, the goddess of the Sidonians; to Milcom, the
god of the Ammonites; to Chemosh, the god of Moab. Solomon
offered sacrifices to these gods with his foreign wives, until pagan
temples were now competing with the Temple of God.

More than four centuries later, Nehemiah, after his return with
the exiles from Babylonia, would ask, "Did not Solomon, King of
Israel, sin on account of such women?" (Neh. 13:26).

These pagan temples were allowed to remain until Josiah's
reformation nearly four hundred years later. Silent testimonials
they were to Solomon's apostasy during the years of the divided
kingdom under the monarchy, which began after the reign of Solomon's son Rehoboam.

It is easy to imagine the tremendous costs to Israel of maintaining such a harem as Solomon had. The palace had to be enlarged. More chariots and horses were needed. More costly attire
had to be made. From this harem, naturally, came many children,
only a few of whom are named.

Such a harem also would be filled with jealousy and discontent. How could it fail to set a bad example and create ever increasing problems for the people of Israel?

With all his wisdom, Solomon did not look ahead when he gave himself up to the pursuit of luxury and splendor. Naturally, his costly way of life nearly wrecked the government and threw the people into a mood of despair and hopelessness about the future.

His Worldly Hopes in Ashes

The high noon of Hebrew national and religious life passed, and with it Solomon's glory, like the brilliance of the setting sun. Then came sudden darkness.

The treasury was impoverished. The empire was tottering. The people were so discontented that they began to rebel more and more at the cost of maintaining Solomon's bureaucracy and his large harem, all enormously expensive to support. They saw no way out of higher and higher taxes and other growing complications in Solomon's great industrial empire and luxurious court. Like many absolute monarchs, King Solomon became incredibly selfish and personally ambitious. Motivated more and more by his love of pleasure, splendor, wealth, and fame, and of many women, Solomon had less and less time for God when his hopes were centered on materiality and sensuality.

Solomon, who had once possessed so many of the cardinal virtues—wisdom, justice, temperance, and hope—was now ruled by the deadly sins of pride, avarice, lust, and greed. No longer could he wisely resolve his problems. He had lost friends and was approaching old age, worn out by his many indulgences.

Hiram, head of the king's large building enterprises, foreclosed on him. To settle this debt, Solomon deeded to Hiram twenty cities of Galilee. But even this was not enough to satisfy Hiram's losses.

New adversaries arose. One was Hadad, who began to get a stranglehold on Israel when he became king of Edom. Another was Rezon, captain of the freebooters, who occupied Damascus.

So it was with King Solomon. His material kingdom had sprung up like a mushroom. Then it disappeared like the wind. The brokenness and emptiness of his life at the end, the vanity of his pleasure and wealth mirrored his earlier worldly hopes so soon turned to ashes.

The first two chapters of Ecclesiastes, a kind of literary fiction, sum up the thoughts of Solomon in his later years. Although it is not thought that Solomon was the author, the writer, Qoheleth (Ecclesiastes), assumes the role of Solomon in these reflections on the great king's life.

"Vanity of Vanities, All Is Vanity!"

I did great things: built myself palaces, planted vineyards; made myself gardens and orchards, planting every kind of fruit tree in them. I had pools made for watering the plantations; bought men slaves, women slaves; had home-born slaves as well; herds and flocks I had too, more than anyone in Jerusalem before me. I amassed silver and gold, the treasures of kings and provinces; acquired singing men and singing women and every human luxury, chest on chest of it. So I grew great, greater than anyone in Jerusalem before me; nor did my wisdom leave me. I denied my eyes nothing they desired, refused my heart no pleasure, a heart that found all my hard work a pleasure; such was the return I got for all my efforts. I then reflected on all that my hands had achieved and on all the effort I had put into its achieving. What vanity it all is, and chasing of the wind! . . .

All I have toiled for and now bequeath to my successor [Solomon's son, the unworthy Rehoboam] I have come to hate; who knows whether he will be a wise man or a fool? Yet he will be master of all the work into which I have put my efforts and wisdom under the sun. That, too, is vanity. And hence I have come to despair of all the efforts I have expended under the sun. For so it is that a man who has laboured wisely, skilfully and successfully must leave what is his own to someone who has not toiled for it at all. This, too, is vanity and great injustice; for what does he gain for all the toil and strain . . . What of all his laborious days, his cares of office, his restless nights? This, too, is vanity."

(Ecc. 2:4–11, 19–23, JB)

The famous lines on "A season for everything, a time for every occupation under heaven" (Ecc. 3, JB) follow. The final question is "Who then can bring him to see what is to happen after his time?" (v. 22, JB).

King Solomon's forty-year reign ended abruptly in his sudden death. He was buried in Jerusalem. Soon after his son Rehoboam was crowned king, the people complained to him, "Your father gave us a heavy burden to bear; lighten your father's harsh tyranny now, and the weight of the burden he laid on us, and we will serve you . . ." (I Kings 12:4, JB). Rehoboam, refusing to counsel with the older men, answered, "My father made you bear a heavy burden but I will make it heavier still. My father beat you with whips; I am going to beat you with loaded scourges" (v. 14).

The New Hope in Simpler Living

Rehoboam's haughty attitude and cruel words alienated the people; Solomon's kingdom, now torn by political and religious schisms, was soon in a state of revolt and decay.

"King Rehoboam lived and died a monument to his father's sin and of his mother Naamah's hatred for the God of the Israelites" (*All of the Women of the Bible*, p. 285).

Centuries later Christ walked in the temple ruins, where only a part of Solomon's portico stood. With the coming of Christ (one greater than Solomon), hope in a simpler way of life evolved. In speaking of the lilies of the field, the same lilies poetically described in the Song of Solomon, Christ told his listeners in his Sermon on the Mount that "Solomon in all his glory was not arrayed like one of these."

SECTION THREE

In Time of Despair
Hope

"The pain of despair surely lies in the fact that a hope is there, but no way opens toward its fulfillment," says Jurgen Moltmann in his *Theology of Hope* (p. 23). So it was with the great men of hope in this section, covering a period of about seven hundred years, from about 900–200 B.C. Although they lived in an era of despair, hope runs through their lives like a scarlet thread.

Elijah and Elisha, the great prophets of the ninth century B.C., fought against a world filled with evil, but in their trials and tribulations, they were willing to wait for a better day, a fact central to hope.

These two prophets were forerunners of those divinely inspired spokesmen for God, the Major and the Minor Prophets. Amos gave the universal passport to a future with hope when he declared, "Seek good and not evil."

The Book of Job, built around its central character, is a story of one man's struggle for survival against tremendous obstacles. Job reasons that God is not at man's disposal, but in the final analysis, he says, man not only must believe in God's goodness and wisdom but also that he stands on his promises.

Scholars do not agree on the time and locale of Job. Some today think Job lived probably as late as 400 B.C.; however, his secure place in the Bible is before the prophets.

While hope in the Old Testament signified social regeneration, national well-being, and so on, with the prophets it advanced into grandeur and spirituality. They lived and wrote of a period during and after the rulership of kings, most of them wicked. God was dead to most of the kings and many of their subjects because all were lost in idolatry, dishonesty and injustice. Consequently they oftentimes were desperate and desolate but did not know why.

It might appear God had abandoned Israel. He had not. By virtue of divine love his covenant with Israel was unbreakable. What had been broken was the people's faith in God. Their sin, as one writer analyzed it, "had turned creation upside down." In the preservation of that righteous remnant, inspired by the prophets, lay the hope of Israel, the nation that was supposed to be a witness to all nations.

Centuries had passed since the Exodus. The new generations had forgotten that new conflicts and defeats were always demanded as man crawls his way to godliness, the lighted frontier for a hopeful future.

CHAPTER 10

Elijah: Hope for the Righteous Remnant

A champion of justice and morality, Elijah is a prophet, a healer, and the forerunner of the classical prophets.

Elijah, one of the most amazing characters in the Old Testament, seemed to come out of nowhere, a plain man wearing the skin of some animal but also bearing the mantle of the prophetic office. Rugged, stern, solitary, inflexible, he attracted attention not by his demeanor but by the suddenness with which he came, his supernatural fleetness of foot, and the authority with which he spoke out against the idolatry, immorality, and ruthlessness of the kings of Judah like Ahab and his hated wife, Jezebel, Elijah's own contemporaries.

Elijah could see moral decay everywhere. The people had confused materialism with idealism. They loved things more than high principles. They had forgotten the Holy Law that had been written into their constitution, also the Ten Commandments, their "Bill of Rights" and their "declaration of dependence" upon God, their king and sovereign ruler.

Better than any man of his time, Elijah knew that obedience to the law of righteousness was the only foundation for national greatness, liberty, and security, that righteousness alone, not material prosperity, blessed a nation.

A man with fervent hope and faith in a God of Righteousness,

Elijah was willing to bear his crosses for the things he believed in. And he had the courage and the fire to lash out against injustice, lawlessness, falsehood, and hypocrisy.

Fearlessly, Elijah went before King Ahab, whose wife, Jezebel, had "stirred him up to do evil." Violently, Elijah denounced Baal, the false fertility god, and his goddess Asherah, the worship of whom Jezebel brought with her from her native Sidon. Hopefully, Elijah set about to destroy them.

Naturally, Elijah had moments of despair, but he arose and went to pray by a broom tree, or by a brook, or in a cave, or on a mountaintop when he was faced with tremendous obstacles.

Because he was divinely inspired and learned how to deal intuitively with the will of God for high standards of conduct in all the relationships of life, he accomplished the impossible.

Consequently, Elijah takes his place as the spokesman for the righteous remnant of Israel, who had faith in the covenant God of the patriarchs and their descendants and the religion set up by Moses. As such, Elijah was the pioneer of the school of prophets, and he helped to prepare the way for those mighty prophets to come, who would sustain Israel by hopes and promises before unknown.

His Struggle for the Common Man

Elijah is described as a Tishbite, a poor man, who came out of Gilead. From there he no doubt could see the ivory-decorated palace of King Ahab and Queen Jezebel which stood on the four hundred-foot hill of Jezreel, the royal city of Israel's kings. Perhaps Elijah had often passed the palace and had become incensed when he saw the pagan prophets of Baal coming in and out of the palace gardens to the grove down below where they lived and he knew that they were practicing their voluptuous ceremonies to Baal in the groves below the palace.

A magnificent temple to Baal had arisen in Samaria, and there was another to his goddess, Asherah, in Jezreel.

The merciless Jezebel had issued an order to exterminate the prophets of the Lord who roamed the countryside or were attached to various shrines. And the country was defiled with blood and corruption. Some of the Lord's prophets had been cut off, some hidden, others impoverished. Altars of the Lord had been destroyed and those who worshiped at them had been driven into obscurity.

This idolatrous current, begun in the time of Solomon, was like a badly polluted stream. And it was visible everywhere.

Elijah was so filled with impatience and indignation at what he saw that he became fearless of his own safety and willing to suffer many things. Finally he became so incensed at the idolatrous court that he went boldly forth to the palace in his garment of coarse hair, girt with a leather belt, and bluntly announced to the king that there would be neither dew nor rain in the coming years.

While Elijah was in hiding in a cave near the brook of Cherith and fed by the ravens, King Ahab and Queen Jezebel became so drought-conscious that they coveted the land owned by their neighbor Naboth, a common man. They wanted it for a vineyard for themselves.

When Naboth refused to sell, the fierce and stern Jezebel plotted to have him stoned to death. Taking her husband's kingly seal in hand, she wrote letters to officials in his name. In these she falsely accused Naboth of blasphemy against God and treason against the king. Orders were issued for Naboth to be stoned to death, and after he was stoned, Jezebel, the ablest and most determined enemy of the Hebrew religion, went triumphantly before her husband and declared, "Arise, take possession of the vineyard of Naboth . . . for Naboth is not alive, but dead" (I Kings 21:15).

Jezebel's highhanded action aroused the religious zeal and democratic fervor of Elijah. Taking grave exception to what Jezebel had done, he set forth for Naboth's vineyard and found there Ahab, who had come to seize Naboth's land.

Fearlessly, Elijah demanded of Ahab, "Have you killed, and also taken possession?" (I Kings 21:19). Elijah was so outraged that he prophesied, "In the place where dogs licked up the blood of Naboth shall dogs lick up your own blood" (v. 19). This prophecy later came to pass when Jezebel met a horrible death in this same field.

No wonder it is written that "Ahab did more to provoke the Lord, the God of Israel, to anger than all the kings of Israel who were before him" (I Kings 16:33). And it was all at the instigation of Jezebel, who turned Israel into a vast moral wilderness.

The ascetic Elijah, just as stern in his fight for right as Jezebel was in her fight for wrong, miraculously emerged as "the personified conscience" of God's people. And as he waged a long fight for the rights of the common man, he achieved a successful revolution against Ahab and Jezebel. After their death, their son Ahaziah continued to fight Elijah with all his might, but in a few months he died a violent death and the rulership of this wicked line was soon on its way out.

A POOR WIDOW AND HER EMPTY CUPBOARD

Before his confrontation with Ahab over Naboth, Elijah began his many services to the poor. None seemed more needy than the impoverished widow with no food for herself or her son. When the brook of Cherith, east of the Jordan, dried up, Elijah trudged on from there to Zarephath, in Phoenicia, in search of food and water for himself.

Soon he came upon this widow outside her house gathering some sticks for a fire on which to cook her last food. When Elijah asked her for a little food, she told him she had only a handful of meal and a little oil with which to make her last bread. "Fear not; go and do as you have said, but first make me a little cake . . . the jar of meal shall not be spent, and the cruse of oil shall not fail, until the day that the Lord sends rain upon the earth," Elijah said to her (I Kings 17:13–14).

With the Lord's help, Elijah taught this impoverished widow how to bring abundance out of lack. Later, when her son died, probably from malnutrition suffered earlier, Elijah took him into an upper room and stretched himself upon the child three times, the same method used in modern mouth-to-mouth resuscitation. But Elijah went one step farther. Fervently he prayed: "O Lord my God, let this child's soul come into him again" (I Kings 17:22). The Lord heard Elijah's cry, "And the soul of the child returned to the child's body, and he revived" (v. 22). Elijah took the well child to his mother, who said to the rough-clad prophet, "Now I know that you are a man of God, and that the word of the Lord in your mouth is truth" (v. 24).

Elijah proved to this widow and her son that God reveals himself to those with the hope and faith to believe in his promises. In turn, the widow set a marvelous example in her willingness to accept God, as revealed by Elijah. What a contrast in this poor widow and Jezebel, who would go down to her death fighting God.

His Confrontation with Baal

Famine was at its height during the third year of the drought, and King Ahab and his chief steward Obadiah were searching for patches of green grass to feed the king's horses and mules. Elijah appeared before Obadiah, who had hidden one hundred prophets of the Lord in caves, and now requested an interview with the king.

This time, when Elijah appeared, Ahab turned and said to him, "Is it you, you troubler of Israel?" (I Kings 18:17). Elijah answered, "I have not troubled Israel; but you have and your father's house, because you have forsaken the commandments of the Lord and followed the Baals" (v. 18). Then Elijah boldly ordered the king to summon the four hundred and fifty prophets of Baal and the four hundred prophets of Asherah, who, as Jezebel's pensioners, were being fed on the bounty of the palace in the midst of drought when the poor people had no food.

When these prophets and the Israelites assembled on Mount Carmel, the fearless Elijah shouted out, "How long will you go limping with two different opinions? If the Lord is God, follow him. But if Baal, then follow him" (I Kings 18:21–22). The people had no answer to these impassioned words with blades in them. Now Elijah, this confident prophet of God, stood alone in this trial by fire against the prophets of Baal. This was a day of destiny, a day of decision. It had to be God or Baal, either on one side or the other. "Whom will we serve?" the fiery Elijah asked.

Afterward the followers of Baal, the nature god, danced before their idol's altar, invoking him to save them from famine.

Mocking them, Elijah roared, "Cry aloud, for he is a god; either he is musing, or he has gone aside, or he is on a journey, or perhaps he is asleep and must be awakened" (v. 27). What a god, one who is too deep in thought to hear the cries of his people, or too busy to listen, or on a journey, or so sound asleep that he has to be awakened!

Elijah called the people to him after the prophets of Baal had raved and ranted before their powerless god. And they looked on as he repaired the altar to God that had been torn down, a simple one of twelve stones. And there Elijah came near and said, "O Lord, God of Abraham, Isaac, and Israel, let it be known this day that thou art God in Israel, and that I am thy servant, and that I have done all these things at thy word. Answer me, O Lord, answer me, that this people may know that thou, O Lord, art God, and that thou hast turned their hearts back." (I Kings 18:36–37). After that the miracle happened. "The fire of the Lord fell, and consumed the burnt offering, and the wood, and the stones, and the dust, and licked up the water that was in the trench. And when all of the people saw it, they fell on their faces; and they said, 'The Lord, he is God; the Lord, he is God'" (vs. 38–39). And after that Elijah killed the false prophets, who were destroying Israel.

Later Elijah climbed again to the top of Mount Carmel and "there he bowed himself down upon the earth, and put his face between his knees and began to pray" (v. 42). Soon the sky grew black with clouds and wind, and there was a great rain. And Ahab was forced to drive to Jezreel facing black clouds and rain. Like a courier, Elijah walked ahead of Ahab's prancing steeds, as far as the gates of Jezreel, a distance of about eighteen miles.

The Prophet's Flight to Mount Horeb

When Jezebel learned from Ahab that all of her prophets of Baal had been slain, she became so incensed that she threatened Elijah's life. He might quail for a moment at Queen Jezebel, powerful as she was. But she was not omnipotent—God was.

A second time he fled into the wilderness, where he rested under a broom tree. Again he was miraculously fed, this time by an angel; and when he had eaten he arose and walked for forty days and nights until he reached the summit of Mount Horeb (Mount Sinai), where Moses had his mystical experiences.

We come to know God better because of Elijah's experience on Mount Horeb. It is revealed in one of the more remarkable passages in the Old Testament:

> And behold, the Lord passed by, and a great and strong wind rent the mountains, and broke in pieces the rocks . . . but the Lord was not in the wind; and after the wind an earthquake, but the Lord was not in the earthquake; and after the earthquake a fire, but the Lord was not in the fire; and after the fire a still small voice. And when Elijah heard it, he wrapped his face in his mantle and went out and stood at the entrance of the cave. And behold, there came a voice to him, and said, "What are you doing here, Elijah?"
>
> (I Kings 19:11–13)

Like Elijah, we too can know better a God who laid the foundations of the earth and all the planets that revolve around it and whose voice is the "still small voice" within each soul, a power beside which all the elements of nature are as nothing. And we come to understand more clearly, too, that "the road to God is in the soul of every man." Or, as the wise man puts it so well, "The spirit of man is the lamp of the Lord" (Prov. 20:27).

When Elijah understood the meaning of that voice and answered back that he was on the mountaintop because of his zeal for God, the elemental power of God seemed to burst afresh into humanity. Earlier Elijah had been troubled because the people had forsaken God's covenant, torn down his altars, and put his prophets to death, but now he was renewed in spirit and at God's command ready to go to the wilderness of Damascus to be an active participant again; there he would anoint a prophet (Elisha) as his successor.

FIRE AND A CHARIOT FROM HEAVEN

One of Elijah's first duties was to cast his cloak on the young Elisha as he came upon him plowing in his father's field with a team of twelve oxen. Sensing Elijah's greatness, the young Elisha walked away from his oxen, kissed his mother and father goodbye, and went with Elijah and ministered to him.

Some time after that, Elijah and Elisha set forth for Bethel, where they were met by the sons of the prophets. One of them asked Elisha, "Do you know that today the Lord will take away your master?" (II Kings 2:3). Elisha already had a premonition of this. As the two of them crossed the Jordan near Jericho, Elijah asked Elisha what he could do for him before "I am taken from you." Elisha humbly answered " 'I pray you, let me inherit a double share of your spirit.' And [Elijah] said, 'You have asked a hard thing; yet, if you see me as I am being taken from you, it shall be so for you; but if you do not see me, it shall not be so' " (vs. 9–10).

As they talked, a "chariot of fire and horses of fire," as they are described, separated the two of them. And Elijah disappeared in a "whirlwind into heaven." Could this be the ancient's way of describing a celestial vehicle, which like today's space ship, stirred up a whirlwind when its motors were fired?

Illumined by this miraculous scene, the young prophet Elisha seemed to understand that the older prophet Elijah had experienced a miraculous and unexplainable change in consciousness.

Elijah's translation, one of the great miracles of the Old Testament, takes on more significance at Christ's transfiguration. It is recorded in the first three Gospels that Peter and James and John saw Moses, the founder of the religion of Israel, and Elijah, who had given it new impetus, talking with Jesus, the founder of Christianity.

Paul compares the remnant of believers in his time to that remnant who did not worship Baal in Elijah's time. So, too, at the present time, Paul added, "there is a remnant, chosen by grace" (Rom. 11:5). Elijah had demonstrated that in that righteous remnant there is unremitting hope for future salvation.

CHAPTER 11

Elisha: A Man of Wonder

Like his predecessor, Elisha fought every kind of evil in Israel. He served more than half a century, reaching out to kings and people alike.

Elisha was the amazing prophet of the populace and the court, while Elijah had been the lone prophet of the wilderness. Elisha quietly emerged from a well-established farm family, while Elijah had suddenly appeared out of poverty from an unknown family background. Elisha was a prophet of mercy and restoration, while Elijah had been a prophet of fire—fierce and overwhelming.

Elisha's miraculous place in Old Testament history is poetically described in the Apocrypha:

> Nothing was beyond his power;
> > beneath him flesh was brought
> > back into life.
> In life he performed wonders,
> > and after death, marvelous
> > deeds.
> > > (Ecclesiasticus [Sirach] 48:13–14, NAB)

Each prophet blessed the other in a different way. In a moment of despair Elijah had scarcely uttered his burning words, "I, even I only, am left; and they [the people] seek my life to take it away" (I Kings 19:14). Filled with awe and meekness at Elijah's sudden appearance, Elisha poured water on the old man's hands, as an expression of his willingness to be his servant. Elijah was comforted when Elisha, like a first-born son, asked not for material possessions—the old man had none—but for a double portion of his marvelous spirit, which encompassed a knowledge of God and his miraculous power.

When Elijah was removed from the earth to the heavenly state, without the intervening experience of death, as related in the preceding chapter, Elisha took up the old prophet's mantle for his own and retraced his steps to the Jordan where he smote the waters, and as they parted, he walked forward on dry land. And then he set forth on his far-reaching ministry. Wherever he went, mostly on foot, from Bethel to Jericho to Dothan to Gilgal, he carried an ordinary staff which came to symbolize his wonder-working miracles.

His story embraces a good part of the first thirteen chapters of II Kings, and nearly all of the narrative is filled with miracles illustrating his wonder-working power and showing the history of Israel as progressing, moving, and changing, according to the promises of God. And Elisha, who often changed history, came to be known as a man who could suspend the laws of nature, accurately predict the future, and divine the needs of others.

His Concern for Others

The kind prophet would ask others, "What may I do for you?" So, like a golden thread, human helpfulness is woven into the tapestry of his life. Amid the anxieties and struggles, sorrows and joys of others, especially everyday folk, he managed to bring to them a holy, soothing beneficence.

Although he accepted free-will offerings occasionally, he shared them with others; but when he healed, he refused gifts in return. Through him, others came to see that doing good for others represents religion at its best.

As Elisha went on prophetic missions, his favorite retreat was in the rich grain field country of Shunem, where lived the wealthy and influential woman known as the "Shunammite." Seeing Elisha pass by one day, the woman said to her husband, "I perceive that this is a holy man . . . Let us make a small roof chamber . . . for him" (II Kings 4:9–10).

So she set up a small room, furnishing it with a bed, a table, a chair, and a saucer lamp fed by olive oil from a wick of hemp. One day Elisha asked his thoughtful hostess what he could do to repay her. She made it clear that she sought neither honors nor favors from him. Later, in discussing the matter with his servant Gehazi, Elisha learned that the woman had no son, the sacred desire of every hopeful wife in Israel.

Elisha told Gehazi to call the woman, and when she stood in the doorway of the guest chamber, he told her that in the spring she would embrace her own son. When that time arrived, this joyful woman gave birth to the son she had so long desired.

Later, probably ten or twelve years, Elisha raised this woman's son from the dead. His father had brought his lifeless form to the mother, from the field where it is quite possible he had suffered a heat stroke. She rushed to Elisha for help and he went to the child and revived him with the same method of mouth-to-mouth resuscitation that Elijah had used on the impoverished widow's son. Then Elisha called to the child's mother to come and take her son, who was well and whole again. This prophet, "who had lived in a spirit of victory, had given her a wonderful demonstration of spiritual victory" (*All of the Women of the Bible*, p. 139).

Like Elijah, Elisha "befriended a poor widow" (II Kings 4:1–7). She had no food, only a jar of oil. Her husband had left so many debts that his creditors had come to demand that her two sons be given as slaves in payment of the debts. At Elisha's direction this woman borrowed jars from her neighbors and then went into the house, shut the door, and began to fill them with oil that now flowed so plentifully that she had enough to sell and pay all of her debts.

This permanent relief to this destitute family, provided by the kindly Elisha brought new hope to this widow, who only a short time before had faced debt, hunger, slavery, and early death.

Another time Elisha saw that one hundred hungry men were miraculously fed from only twenty loaves of barley and a few fresh ears of corn (II Kings 4:42–44). This suggests the later miracle of

Jesus when he multiplied the five loaves of bread and a few fish for the five thousand at the Sea of Galilee.

HIS MINISTRY TO THOSE IN HIGH PLACES

Elisha's prophetic service was linked to the political and military affairs of his country. Although he fought the idolatrous practices of some of Israel's kings, he still was ready to help them in time of his country's need.

One of his first political moves was to anoint Hazael, king of Syria after the death of Benhadad (II Kings 8:7–15). Elisha also continued the rebellion begun by Elijah against the Omri dynasty as represented by Ahab and his wife, Jezebel, and their sons Joram and Ahaziah, all of whom committed much evil. Finally, Elisha commissioned Jehu to overthrow the throne of Israel, and when he did, Elisha sent one of the sons of the prophets to anoint Jehu as king. Jehu's bloody method of obtaining the throne later was deplored by Hosea (Hos. 1:4).

Elisha's service to Naaman, captain of the host of the king of Syria, was one of his most admirable services to one in a high place. When Naaman was stricken with leprosy, his wife's little Hebrew maid told him about the miracles of Elisha. Taking along a letter from the king of Syria to Joram, king of Israel, as well as ten festal robes, ten talents of silver, and six thousand shekels of gold (amounting to tens of thousands of dollars), Naaman made haste from Damascus to Israel in his chariot drawn by fast-stepping horses. When Elisha heard that the king had given Naaman no co-operation, he sent word to the king, saying, "Let him come now to me, that he may know that there is a prophet in Israel" (II Kings 5:8). When Naaman arrived at Elisha's door, Elisha sent a messenger to tell Naaman to bathe in the Jordan seven times. There his flesh would be restored, Elisha promised. After bathing as Elisha had directed, Naaman's flesh became "like the flesh of a little child" (v. 14). Elisha would accept nothing for this healing, which was God's, not his.

Naaman turned homeward, a convert to the God of Israel, taking back with him his gold and silver and something else of greater significance, a little earth from Israel to build in Syria an altar to the Lord God of Israel. Although Naaman was returning to an idol-worshiping country, Elisha seemed to perceive that the God who had healed Naaman would continue to bless him and others who saw the leprosy was gone.

In times of despair in Israel, even when a powerful enemy had the upper hand, Elisha had hope for Israel. One morning his servant discovered the Syrian army on Israel territory. A messenger came to seize Elisha, because they feared his power. Undisturbed, Elisha told his servant, "'Fear not, for those who are with us are more than those who are with them.' Then Elisha prayed, and said, 'O Lord, I pray thee, open his eyes that he may see'" (II Kings 6:16-17). And as he did, the messenger dreamed of a mountain full of horses and chariots of fire round about Elisha.

When the Syrian army came down, Elisha prayed God to send them an illusion so that they might be misled. The Syrian army came into Dothan, and suddenly they found themselves at the mercy of Israel's King Joram and his troops. Elisha shamed his own king when he asked "Would you kill those you have taken captive?" Instead, they were given a bountiful meal, dismissed, and they then returned home.

Later, the ungrateful and greedy Syrian king came with a great force to fight Israel. This time Elisha advised the army of Israel to resist the enemy to the bitter end, showing he could be realistic as well as helpful.

During Joram's war against the kingdom of Moab, Elisha advised the coalition leaders of Israel, Judah, and Edom to dig irrigation trenches to channel the rainfall of the uplands into the wadis of Edom. As the king's minstrel played, "the power of the Lord came upon him [Elisha]." And he declared that the Lord would fill the dry stream with water. And there was an abundance for all the people and their cattle, even the soldiers and animals of the allied troops. Once more the people believed.

AID TO THE SONS OF THE PROPHETS

Elisha, the beloved leader of the sons of the prophets, won their reverence from the time a group of them, some fifty, stood from a high point and saw the waters of the Jordan part before

him. In his long ministry of more than half a century, he befriended them again and again. Although he did not participate in
their communal life, he looked after their food supplies, provided for their widows and orphans, and helped them in other
difficulties.

Once he saved them from death during a famine when food
was so scarce that one of them went to gather several wild plants,
among which were gourds, which, when cooked and sampled,
turned out to be poisonous. The sons of the prophets called out
to Elisha, " 'O man of God, there is death in the pot.' And they
could not eat it. He said, 'Then bring meal.' " (II Kings 4:40–41).
And with that, Elisha neutralized the pottage.

Another time when the sons of the prophets resolved to build
a larger dwelling by the Jordan, and when they went out to cut
the trees, one of the sons of the prophets dropped the iron head
of a borrowed ax, which fell into the water. Elisha broke off a
stick, cast it into the stream, the iron rose to the surface, and the
ax was restored to its owner.

After Elisha's death at an old age, probably a century after his
death, the sons of the prophets wrote the story of the miraculous
Elisha, this holy man of God who had done great things—healed
the sick, fed the starving, brought confidence to a defeated army,
and performed other wonders that only a prophet with spiritual
power could accomplish.

Although much legend centers around some of Elisha's miracles
—and modern scholars do not accept all of them—Elisha's greatness has survived some of the so-called legends, even the miracles
at his tomb (II Kings 13:20).

God-loving people reverence the name of Elisha as the prophet
who had the hope and the faith to bring the possible from the impossible and the inspiring influence to create belief among disbelievers, confidence among the fearful, and cheer among the
disconsolate.

CHAPTER 12

Job: "Where Is Now My Hope?"

A righteous man, Job endures undeserved affliction with fortitude and hope. God's talk with Job at the conclusion is one of the great literary treatises on the Creator's handiwork.

Job endured the most prolonged human suffering conceivable—the death of all of his children, seven sons and three daughters, and the loss of his wealth and health. A native of ancient Uz, probably east of the territory now occupied by Israel, he was considered a wealthy man for his time. His possessions included seven thousand sheep, three thousand camels, five hundred yoke of oxen, five hundred she-asses, and many servants.

In one day his children and all of his possessions were destroyed. A whirlwind struck the four corners of a son's house, where all of his children were feasting. They were killed instantly. Three bands of Chaldeans raided his fields and took his camels. The Sabeans killed his herdsmen and seized his oxen and asses.

Afterward Job developed a loathsome disease, perhaps elephantiasis, marked by swellings and ulcers, over his entire body. He endured such unbearable itching that finally, as he sat on the village junk heap, he picked up a piece of broken pottery and scratched his sores.

His impatient, rebellious wife urged him to "Curse God, and die." But Job, who loved God with all his heart, turned to ask her,

"Shall we receive good at the hand of God, and shall we not receive evil?" (Job 2:10).

Although Job questioned, agonized, grieved, and lamented over his tribulations when all of his problems remained unsolved, he battled on through his long ordeal, all the while accepting God's will in his life, knowing that the answers to things he did not understand lay beyond time and place. Never did he lose his intellectual honesty as he tried to unravel the meaning of his cruel fate.

The Bible's Literary Masterpiece

The Book of Job is a spiritual epic written by an unnamed author, probably between 600 and 400 B.C., but it has all the characteristics of a much older folk tale. Scholars call it the "literary masterpiece of the Bible"; they also regard it as perhaps the most original work in literature.

In her preface to a special edition of the King James Version of the Book of Job published by the Heritage Press in 1946, Mary Ellen Chase, essayist and educator, ranks the Book of Job with Dante's *Divine Comedy*, Milton's *Paradise Lost*, the great Greek tragedies, Shakespeare, and other literary masterpieces.

"With them," she says, "it [the Book of Job] shares the qualities of all complete and perfect art in its noble and exalted conceptions, its superb style, its sensitive apperception of the physical work, its profound thoughts, its compassionate illumination of human experience" (p. 5).

The Book of Job has five well defined parts. The prologue and the epilogue are both in prose; the second, third, and fourth parts are in poetry. It is in the fourth part that Job proclaims not only his faith but his hope that after his death he may be vindicated by God, for he knows his Redeemer liveth, and that he shall stand victorious in the last days of the earth.

The Meaning of Human Suffering

Written because a poet-philosopher could not justify the ancient world's belief that sin is always the cause of human suffering, it graphically delineates Job's trials and heartaches. One of the conclusions drawn is that human suffering is not always God's punishment for sin. God is testing the sincerity of Job, who reasons that a moral order guides the destinies of man; and so he resigns himself to God's wisdom, which is both undeniable and incomprehensible.

The book, an unconditional release for those who live by the old retribution dogma, concludes with the theme that no innocent man ever perishes through affliction. Whatever suffering comes to the pure in heart must be endured, because one's own conscience provides one's own happiness and is the surest way to find peace in God.

Philosophical and theological problems become of far more significance than the simple folk tale itself. Some of the other conclusions drawn are still debated by scholars. One is that prosperity is not connected with goodness any more than adversity is linked with sin, for man's conduct and his fate are not correlated. God does not dispense rewards or punishments.

Actually, there are no specific answers to the vast and dark problem of human suffering and the presence of evil and injustice. Although the question, "Why must the righteous suffer?" is foremost, Job never asks it. Willing to accept with great love whatever suffering falls his lot, he is not interested in the answer. Despite his own heartaches and hardships, he holds to the belief that God is omnipotent and just.

His Honesty and Humility

Called "blameless and upright, one who feared God and turned away from evil" (Job 1:1), Job exhibits the highest ethical standards in matters of sexual morality and purity of act and motivation, as high as that of any character in the Old Testament.

In his vindication of himself in Chapter 31, he presents a declaration of his ethical standards; in this he confesses he has not taken or given bribes, or ill-treated his servants, or engaged in idolatry. He also has sought, he says, to use his money wisely, both in his good works and in his personal expenditures.

He did not raise, he says, his hand against the fatherless or cause the widow to suffer. He did not countenance falsehood or deceit in himself. He did not trust in gold or conceal his iniquities. He sought to have a tolerant attitude toward his enemies and never rejoiced when evil overtook those who hated and hurt him.

All through his frank analysis of himself, Job is completely honest and humble before God. What he seems to desire most is a restoration of his fellowship with God, his creator and friend. The only time Job falters in his faith is when his heart bleeds for his children and his home.

THE GREAT DIALOGUE

One of the most remarkable phases of the story is the dialogue between Job and three friends. This is called one of the most profound discussions on theological and philosophical problems in literature. Although the story probably dates to early antiquity, the questions are the same as those that might be asked today by well-meaning friends, who try to delve into the answers of why a seemingly good person has so many trials and tribulations.

The dialogue is in three cycles. At first it seems that Job's friends are unkind. Actually, they are so courteous that they only hint at his guilt. As Job cries out at the chastisements and calamities which have befallen him, his friends become more vehement in their argument, but Job still maintains he does not believe that God has singled him out to suffer.

The three friends are Eliphaz, Bildad, and Zophar, who seem to have come from northern Arabia. First, Eliphaz says that God does not punish the righteous, so he implores Job to seek God.

Job then asks for evidences of his sins and concludes by praying for understanding in his distress.

Bildad calls Job a hypocrite and urges him to repent. But Job acclaims God's goodness and acknowledges him as his creator and preserver. Zophar also accuses Job of lies and hypocrisy. Job denies this accusation and enlarges on God's providence again.

As the spiritual and mental gulf widens between Job and his friends, he seems to resent their intrusion, and laments,

> Man that is born of a woman
>   is of few days, and full of trouble.
> He comes forth like a flower, and withers;
>   he flees like a shadow, and continues not.
>   (Job 14:1–2)

In the third cycle of speeches the disgust and anger of the three friends become more pronounced. Overlooking their accusations, Job concerns himself with profounder matters.

A fourth friend, Elihu, angered at Job for his justification of self, enters into the dialogue. Seeing that his three friends have not won the argument, Elihu contends they have defended too narrow a viewpoint.

Elihu's thesis is that God is never unjust, that he uses pain to chasten. His ways are inscrutable, for he is infinite and all-powerful. Job's tribulations continue, Elihu says, so that he might become more like God's image.

Elihu adds nothing new to the dialogue and reiterates the old arguments rather badly, intimating that Job will suffer in the future more than he has in the past.

Amid all his suffering and questioning, Job arouses little sympathy in his acquaintances, much less in his friends. Some abhor him. Others keep aloof from him. Others make sport of him. Not only does his affliction continue to follow him, but his honor is pursued as by a wind. He is in pain and can not rest. When he looks for good, evil persists. When he seeks light, he finds darkness.

Job's poignant heartaches and afflictions show us how wrong we are to condemn others when they are under the stress of pain. He only wanted time to reason out his difficulties honestly himself, for he seemed to know he must accept what he could not change.

HOPE IN GOD'S MAJESTY

Occasionally Job argues against hope, saying, "My days are swifter than a weaver's shuttle, and come to their end without hope" (Job 7:6). Another time he says, "I have no hope; yet I will defend my ways to his [God's] face" (13:15).

But again, when Job speaks to God he compares his condition to that of a tree: ". . . there is hope for a tree, if it be cut down . . . it will sprout again . . . its shoots will not cease" (14:7). Afterward he talks to God about the mountains falling and crumbling away, of the forests washing away the soil of the earth. In his dialogue with God, Job, in a fleeting moment then wonders about "the hope of man."

Once more he tells Bildad, "He [God] breaks me down on every side, and I am gone, and my hope has he pulled up like a tree" (Job 19:10). Though Job recognizes that man often is disappointed in his material hopes, yet he still retains his hope in God's majesty and might.

Job's well-meaning friends continue to try to restore his hope, which they were sure had vanished amid his trials. Eliphaz first asks him, "Is not your fear of God your confidence, and the integrity of your ways your hope?" (Job 4:6). Persistently continuing his argument, Eliphaz implores Job to seek God. In a heavyhearted moment, Job momentarily argues against hope. Human nature impels him to, but he is only human. When his "flesh is clothed with worms and dirt" (7:5), why wouldn't he experience moments of despair?

The second friend, Bildad, reasons with Job in much the same tone as Eliphaz. So does Zophar, the third friend, who concludes that the hope of the wicked is "to breathe their last" (Job 11:20). Despondent again, but only for a fleeting moment, Job turns his thoughts back to God, acclaiming his wisdom and might, his counsel and understanding. In appealing to God against the verdict of his friends, Job asks, "Where then is my hope? Who will see my hope?" (17:15).

After the repentant Job has wavered between hope and hope-

lessness and declared that he knows the greatness and majesty of
God and how and where true wisdom is to be acquired, he sums
up his earlier life nostalgically:

> Oh that I were as in months past, as in
>   the days when God preserved me;
> When his candle shined upon my head, and when by his
>   light I walked through darkness;
> As I was in the days of my youth, when the secret of God
>   was upon my tabernacle;
> When the Almighty was yet with me,
>   when my children were about me;
> When I washed my steps with butter, and
>   the rock poured me out rivers of oil. . . .
> Then I said, I shall die in my nest, and I
>   shall multiply my days as the sand.
>
> (Job 29:2–6, 18, KJV)

God in All His Wonder

Then comes the triumphant conclusion in which the voice of
God sounds in a whirlwind and says to Job, "Brace yourself and
stand up like a man; I will ask questions and you will answer"
(Job 38:3, NEB). This superb poem (Chapters 38–41) on the
wonders of heaven and earth has no equal in Genesis or any other
book of the Bible. Beginning with God's creation, it says in part,

> Where were you when I [God] laid the foundation of the
>   earth?
>   Tell me, if you have understanding.
> Who determined its measurements—surely you know!
>   Or who stretched the line upon it?
> On what were its bases sunk,
>   or who laid its cornerstone,
> when the morning stars sang together,
>   and all the sons of God shouted for joy?
>
> Or who shut in the sea with doors,
>   when it burst forth from the womb;
> when I made clouds its garment,
>   and thick darkness its swaddling band,

and prescribed bounds for it,
    and set bars and doors,
and said, "Thus far shall you come, and no farther,
    and here shall your proud waves be stayed?"
Have you commanded the morning since your days began,
    and caused the dawn to know its place,
that it might take hold of the skirts of the earth,
    and the wicked be shaken out of it?
It is changed like clay under the seal,
    and it is dyed like a garment.
From the wicked their light is withheld,
    and their uplifted arm is broken.

                                    (38:4-15)

Like Job, the reader is immediately awed with the mystery of God's creation: the proud waves of the sea, the illimitable dwelling place of darkness and light, the phenomena of the cosmos: clouds, sky, snow, hail, fog, wind, rain, thunder, mists, and drops of dew.

There is marvelous beauty, too, in the mysteries of the earth: animal and plant life; the wildness of the mountain ass; the gorgeous wings of the peacock; the wings and feathers of the ostrich, who leaves her eggs in the earth and warms them in the dust; the horse with its strong neck and glorious nostrils; the lion in its den; the hawk as it spreads its wings toward the south, the eagle nesting on high. These and other vivid pictures appear in a fast-moving panorama.

THE VICTORIOUS JOB

Finally, Job is so overawed he begins to understand God's purpose in all his suffering. At first the wonder of God's words has reduced Job to complete silence, but now the acquiescent Job arrives at this triumphant reasoning, showing that he thoroughly perceives God's purposes:

I know that you can do all
    things,
and that no purpose of yours
    can be hindered.

> I have dealt with great things
>   that I do not understand;
>   things too wonderful for me,
>   which I cannot know.
> I had heard of you by word of
>   mouth,
> but now my eye has seen you.
> Therefore I disown [retract] what I have
>   said,
> and repent in dust and ashes.
>   (42:2–6, NAB)

Job now experiences a great change. He is completely vindicated and has twice as many material possessions as he had in the beginning. Another seven sons and three fair daughters are born to him. He lives a long, full life in the enjoyment of his children and grandchildren. Amid all his joys, he is more thankful than ever for God's abundance.

No longer does Job ask for answers to the unexplainable questions of this earth, for now he comprehends God's wisdom, the order of his cosmos, the creation of his creatures. At last his own spirit is exalted and free and his own hope is renewed in all of its fervor.

CHAPTER 13

The Three Major Prophets: "The Lord the Hope of His People"

As spokesmen for God, for almost two centuries the Major Prophets fought evil in every form. The God-loving will not let die the words of these hopeful men, who like the twelve Minor Prophets in the succeeding chapter, are unique in history.

All fifteen prophets (750–300 B.C.), of which the three Major Prophets come first in the Bible, represent a religious regeneration of world-wide significance, unparalleled in history. This succession of creative personalities proclaims values that never change. In unison, the prophets speak primarily to the spiritually indifferent on one theme, the centrality of God.

All are bold, penetrating spokesmen, voicing a strange, recurrent conviction that somehow a full association between God and man will be established. Amid all the evil that they saw, they echo the voice of hope again and again, as does Joel (Joel 3:16, KJV) in the words quoted in the title above. They see God as the one who guides mankind, according to promises he made and will not break, and they look hopefully toward a golden age when all nations will enjoy the divine blessing.

Their motivating purpose is to interpret the mind of God to man. They are sure in their sense of values and their hope is for a new birth in righteousness, social justice, and leadership. Their expectancy for humanity is so filled with wondrous spiritual truths that what they say and the way they say it are as relevant today as in the past and future.

The three Major Prophets, Isaiah, Jeremiah, and Ezekiel— major largely in the length of their messages—are highlighted in the latter part of this chapter and followed in the next chapter by the twelve so-called "Minor Prophets," minor only in their brevity. The latter twelve are: Hosea, Joel, Amos, Obadiah, Jonah, Micah, Nahum, Habakkuk, Zephaniah, Haggai, Zechariah, and Malachi. In some of the earlier manuscripts, these twelve follow a different sequence.

Confusion arises over their chronological sequence, and there is much diversity of opinion about them among Bible scholars. Some of the more recent scholars are of the opinion that Isaiah 1–39 was written between 740–700 B.C., while Isaiah 40–66, covering a period following 550 B.C., was the work of Isaiah's later disciples, who sought to make his message relevant for a later day. The writings of Zechariah, like Isaiah's, spread over a long range of time. Chapters 9–14 of Zechariah are regarded as later additions to the book. No matter how many editorial hands touched the text or how many disagreements there are about them, their message and inspiration are never lost.

THE PROPHETS AND THEIR TIMES

These passionate reformers began during the period of the divided monarchy of Judah and Israel, after about a century of rule under wicked kings, among whom was Ahab, violently denounced by Elijah, as cited in an earlier chapter.

Although Amos is not listed in the Bible as the first among the prophets, he was actually the first of them in point of time. Like Amos, the other prophets spoke and wrote in the darkest days of Israel's history. This encompassed the period of the Hebrew monarchy, the fall of Jerusalem, the exile in Babylonia, and the return to Jerusalem, much of which had been destroyed.

Through the many vicissitudes of these times, the prophets were the inspiration of the God-loving. No matter how ominous the fate of Israel seemed in terms of its survival as a nation, these hopeful men maintained a faith both fervid and lofty. Their leadership, always practical, was based on God's laws, and they stressed that obedience to these laws represented glorious hope for Israel.

So central is their message to righteousness and social justice that it is often hard to identify what they said with any specific period. What is of greater significance is the timeless quality of their teaching. This has given them an immortality.

These great spokesmen for God are similar but distinctive. Even though they discoursed at length more than twenty centuries ago, and their contemporaries were too often absorbed in material pursuits to listen to them, their acts and words continue to inspire and uplift.

So certain were they that God had called them to speak, that their messages state "Thus spoke the Lord" more than three hundred times. It is no wonder that their words have soared to the realm of the spirit and that the full impact of what they said has gained momentum with time.

LONELY SOULS WITH HOPE

In his book *The Goodly Fellowship of the Prophets,* John Paterson, a Hebrew and Old Testament scholar, calls the prophets "lonely souls who stand on heights which lesser men dare not, or will not climb" (p. 272). In her *Spokesmen For God,* Edith Hamilton, the classical scholar, calls them "lonely men, who made their way to God alone." She is sure that "each had a spiritual experience so actual, so vivid, it was like sight and sound, like the touch of a hand, like contact with a burning coal. The reality of it they proved is the only way any experience can be proved real, by the way they acted upon it" (p. 238).

The prophets knew that they must uphold beauty and love, goodness and faithfulness, meekness and self-control. Like spokesmen for God today, they often received a storm of protest from the ungodly. The writer in Isaiah 50:6 tells of people spitting in his face and pulling out his beard. But this great prophet was not confounded. "Therefore I have set my face like a flint," he says, "and I know that I shall not be put to shame; he who vindicates me is near" (v. 7).

Trusting a God big enough to transform the world, the fearless Isaiah spoke against the cynical, despairing, oftentimes violent people. He did not reshape Israel, but he set a high standard that has continued to strengthen the understanding of God in history.

WHAT IS A PROPHET?

In the Book of Isaiah is this poetic description of a prophet:

> The Lord God has given me
>   the tongue of a teacher
> and skill to console the weary
>   with a word in the morning;
> he sharpened my hearing,
>   that I might listen like one who is taught.
>   (Isa. 50:4, NEB)

Amos was sure "the Lord God does nothing, without revealing his secret to his servants the prophets" (Amos 3:7).

Writing after the appearance of Jesus, the greatest of all prophets in the Bible, it was Peter who later explained, "First of all you must understand this, that no prophecy of scripture is a matter of one's own interpretation, because no prophecy ever came by the impulse of man, but men moved by the Holy Spirit spoke from God" (II Peter 1:20–21).

At the outset the prophets viewed Israel as God's chosen, but "they finally learned that Israel was God's servant, whose sufferings would show the nations the consequences of sin, and cause them to turn with grateful hearts to the God of all nations" (*Harper's Bible Dictionary*, p. 584).

Intensely patriotic men, the prophets were certain that Israel was God's testing ground and that for this reason their little country must serve as an example to the nations of the world. Here their spiritual identity came into being. Here they wrote the Bible. From here its message spread to the world.

THEIR BATTLE WITH EVIL

When the three Major Prophets first began speaking, the masses of the people did not know good from evil. Drunken priests ministered to shallow, heartless audiences. A man and his father went in to the same maiden. Merchants falsified weights. Bribery was common. Judges could be easily bought. Religious shrines were no longer God's but Baal's, and drinking was common in the House of the Lord.

Greed, arrogance, and hypocrisy filled the hearts of many of the rich. The women thought more about what they wore than the standards they lived by. Some of the kings called good evil and evil, good. Banqueting, feasting, and drinking lasted all night during which revelers made heroes of those who drank strong wine to excess and called valiant the men who knew how to mix strong drink.

Judah, said Isaiah, was guilty of eight sins, namely, selfish greed, self-indulgence, cynical materialism, intellectual pride, self-sufficiency, intemperance, dishonesty, and the perversion of high moral standards.

Jeremiah challenged the people to seek a man "who does justice and seeks truth" (Jer. 5:1). He also asked, "Will you steal, murder, commit adultery, swear falsely, burn incense to Baal, and go after other gods that you have not known, and then come and stand before me in this house, which is called by my name, and say, 'We are delivered!'—only to go on doing all these abominations?" (7:9–10). Another time he shouted loudly, "I have seen your abominations, your adulteries and neighings, your lewd harlotries, on the hills in the field" (13:27).

Preaching to the exiles in Babylonia, Ezekiel told of a vision he had had of abominations in Jerusalem, and among the exiles too, of those who still worshiped idols and committed many other evils, of false prophets and prophetesses, idolators, unfaithful wives, wicked men, and harlots.

The prophets were not popular. They could not be, because they dared to denounce evil in the harshest terms. They had one objective. That was to make God more real to a generation that had forgotten him.

These three Major Prophets never accepted sorrow or defeat. Jeremiah remained hopeful and stalwart even when cast into a dungeon. Ezekiel preached on the day his wife died. Isaiah had these same indomitable qualities of the other two. So did the other twelve.

The prophets never lost hope in a hopeless situation, for they all were men who believed in the God who did indeed lay the foundations of the earth, who kept the stars on their courses, who saw man's spirit as his candle, whose power was beyond that of storm, earthquake, or fire. They never gave up in trying to make more real the message that God was intimately near to man, that his light pointed the right way to go, that he was all-compassionate, all-loving, all-merciful. Thanks to these great spokesmen for God, we too can trust and believe and live in the confident faith that God is ever present.

ISAIAH'S HOPE IN A MESSIAH

The youthful Isaiah began preaching in Jerusalem; here he ministered for more than forty years. His wife, by whom he had two sons, was a prophetess (Isa. 8:3). He was an orator, a statesman, a friend and counselor of kings, including King Hezekiah, and he aided in shaping national policies.

It is no wonder Isaiah had been called the most majestic of the prophets. One day as a youth when he went into the temple at Jerusalem he suddenly saw the Lord sitting upon a throne high and lifted up so that the whole earth was full of his glory. After Isaiah received this revelation of God's holiness, he was commissioned to preach.

With trust in God's promises and faithful action in the past, the young Isaiah poetically declared early,

> For the Lord of hosts has purposed,
> and who will annul it?

His hand is stretched out,
        and who will turn it back?
                    (Isa. 14:27)

Isaiah's thesis was that a nation can live by faith alone. When
it loses this faith, it relinquishes the possibilities of a future. His
chief indictment was against the ruling class, which reversed moral
standards and justified wrong as right. His chief hope was centered
on the religious remnant in Jerusalem. The seed of faith and hope
sustaining them is God's new construction, "a precious corner-
stone, of a sure foundation" (Isa. 28:16).

Isaiah, the most messianic of the prophets, has inspired music
for the great oratorios, including Handel's *Messiah*. This passage
is probably better known and more widely quoted than any in
Isaiah:

For to us a child is born,
        to us a son is given;
and the government will be upon his shoulder,
        and his name will be called
"Wonderful Counselor, Mighty God,
        Everlasting Father, Prince of Peace."
Of the increase of his government and of peace
        there will be no end,
upon the throne of David, and over his kingdom,
        to establish it, and to uphold it
with justice and with righteousness
        from this time forth and for evermore.
The zeal of the Lord of hosts will do this!
                    (Isa. 9:6–7)

Paterson, in *The Goodly Fellowship of the Prophets*, quoted
earlier, asserts that "a great God means a great hope, and here
[in the messianic message] we have the hope of a warless world
under the leadership of a king, who shall be a counsellor more
wonderful than Solomon, a friend and father more devoted than
David, a Prince of Peace who shall seek the good of his subjects
and inspire them to live in peace" (p. 75–76).

In the eleventh chapter, Isaiah soars on wings of faith. Here we
see something larger, what Paterson calls "the cosmic significance

of the divine redemption," in this Messiah who shall come from
the branch of Jesse, as Isaiah prophesies in 11:1–9. He says in part:

> There shall come forth a shoot from the stump of Jesse,
>   and a branch shall grow out of his roots.
> And the Spirit of the Lord shall rest upon him,
>   the spirit of wisdom and understanding,
>   the spirit of counsel and might,
>   the spirit of knowledge and fear of the Lord.
> And his delight shall be in the fear of the Lord.
>
> (Isa. 11:1–3)

Though a break occurs before the last chapters of Isaiah, as
mentioned, it is also prophesied in the latter part of the book that
a messenger of the Lord will come (Isa. 61:1–2). Speaking at the
synagogue in Nazareth, Jesus opened the Book of Isaiah at this
later passage and read,

> The Spirit of the Lord is upon me,
> because he has anointed me to preach good news to the poor.
> He has sent me to proclaim release to the captives
> and recovering of sight to the blind,
> to set at liberty those who are oppressed,
> to proclaim the acceptable year of the Lord.
>
> (Luke 4:18)

When Jesus closed the book he told his congregation, "Today
this scripture has been fulfilled in your hearing" (Luke 4:21).

The Book of Isaiah reveals the heartbeat of Israel's dreams for
the future. The remnant, who were certain that God ruled the
universe, did not give up hope for Jesus Christ, this deliverer, who
would appear in person.

The Second Isaiah not only saw his coming, but, like the writers
of the Books of Genesis, Job, and Psalms, saw the universe in its
cosmic wholeness when he asked,

> Who has measured the waters in the hollow of his hand
>   and marked off the heavens with a span,
> enclosed the dust of the earth in a measure
>   and weighed the mountains in scales
>   and the hills in a balance?
> Who has directed the Spirit of the Lord,
>   or as his counselor has instructed him? . . .

> All the nations are as nothing before him,
>> they are accounted by him as less than nothing and
>> emptiness.

(Isa. 40:12–13, 17)

Probably one of the most hopeful and beautiful passages of all Isaiah comes at the end of this same chapter when God's faithfulness and empowering grace come into their fullness thus:

> but they who wait for the Lord shall renew their strength,
>> they shall mount up with wings like eagles,
> they shall run and not be weary,
>> they shall walk and not faint.

(Isa. 40:31)

In his prophecy of the coming of the Messiah and in his knowledge of the infinite power, wisdom and faith of the Lord, Isaiah takes us to the sunlit heights where both God and his son, Jesus Christ, dwell.

JEREMIAH'S FAITH IN ISRAEL'S FUTURE

While the First Isaiah lived and wrote about seven centuries before Christ, Jeremiah (626–586 B.C.) appeared about a century later and was in Jerusalem during its subjection by the Chaldean-Babylonian armies in 609 B.C. Jeremiah has been called the most human of all the prophets and at the same time the most Christlike. He was truly a man of destiny, who learned to turn to God like a child to his father, so in God he lived and moved and had his being and called him "the hope of Israel" (Jer. 14:22, 17:13).

Jeremiah was born at Anathoth, within walking distance of Jerusalem, into an old priestly family with landed estates. Feeling that he was called to minister to the common men, early he walked their way. This he did for more than four decades. A poet as well as a prophet, he has been called the most sensitive and sympathetic of the prophets.

Assisted by the faithful Baruch, Jeremiah wrote under the stimulus of stirring political events, profound international changes, and great personal suffering. He was even beaten, imprisoned, and thrown into a dungeon.

The Northern Kingdom had already fallen; the Southern Kingdom was declining. Jeremiah prophesied that the latter kingdom would pass too. He lived on through the invasion and destruction of Jerusalem.

Although he spoke in a time of despair, he continued to proclaim his confidence in his country's future. Even when his fellow townsmen were plotting against his life, he prayed this ardent prayer to God for help:

> The Lord made it known to me and I knew;
>   then thou didst show me their evil deeds.
> But I was like a gentle lamb
>   led to the slaughter.
> I did not know it was against me
>   they devised schemes, saying,
> "Let us destroy the tree with its fruit,
>   let us cut him off from the land of the living,
>   that his name be remembered no more."
> But, O Lord of hosts, who judgest righteously,
>   who triest the heart and mind,
> Let me see thy vengeance upon them,
>   for to thee have I committed my cause.
>   (Jer. 11:18–20)

Jeremiah had many moments of doubt and fear, heartbreaking failures and frustrations, and yet a light seemed to guide him through the darkness of catastrophe and exile. In his personal relationship with God he was divinely protected. He even seemed to catch glimpses of the coming Redeemer in the person of Christ.

No prophet had a greater insight into the essence of religion than Jeremiah, one of the first to speak of it in universal terms. He saw that the religion of statute must give way to the religion of the spirit, for only as the spirit of man is lifted up can he hopefully rise above the little things that hedge him in. Jeremiah expressed this eloquently when he wrote, "Blessed is the man that trusteth in the Lord, and whose hope the Lord is" (Jer. 17:7, KJV).

Jeremiah's hope for his people did not diminish after the fall of Jerusalem. He spoke of them as lost sheep who had gone astray. He knew that their true habitation must be in the Lord, "the hope of their fathers" (50:7).

EZEKIEL: THE SPIRITUAL WATCHMAN OVER ISRAEL

Ezekiel, who was taken captive to Babylon when a young man, began his prophetic mission five years after he was taken captive. He was probably then about thirty years old. He lived with his wife at Telabib on the river Chebar. A contemporary of Jeremiah, he prophesied from 593–571 B.C.

In the years of his exile, hope for Israel's future was waning. This little country, like a lost ship, was without anchor. The exiles, already filled with despair, had news that life in Jerusalem was going from bad to worse.

It was at this time that the prophet Ezekiel had what he describes as "visions of God." The first two chapters of Ezekiel, which depict these visions in detail, are among the most remarkable passages of the Bible.

Ezekiel eloquently describes what we might call a space ship coming out of the north in a great cloud, with fire flashing forth, in the midst of which were four living creatures, which, like today's heavily clad astronauts, appeared strange to this ancient man, Ezekiel. Each of the four creatures, he said, had wings, under which were human hands. Their vehicle moved with lightning speed through glowing fire. It had four wheels, each seeming to be a wheel within a wheel. The remarkable thing was that each of the four creatures inside "went straight forward; wherever the spirit would go, they went, without turning as they went" (Ezek. 1:12).

Josef F. Blumrich, an Austrian aeronautical engineer, first trained in the German aircraft industry in the thirties, now best known as having helped to develop Skylab, space shuttle, and the Saturn 5 rocket, believes Ezekiel is describing an ancient space ship. Blumrich has studied Ezekiel's biblical record and has published his findings in a book titled *Da tat sich der Himmel auf*, which means "the heavens were opened," a phrase taken out of Ezekiel 1:1. The new American translation is called *The Space Ships of Ezekiel*. There follows Ezekiel's primitive description of what could have been a space ship in 592 B.C., and Blumrich has drawn a sketch of the space ship that Ezekiel describes, as it might be seen from a distance above of one hundred eighty feet, he says. He views Ezekiel's fiery chariot with wheels as a sort of cone-shaped central body with four landing vehicles that could be detached and flown independently as shuttle vehicles on earth, something like the command modules that circled the moon while astronauts explored the moon surface.

Ezekiel's lengthy description of this heavenly vehicle and its occupants presents a space ship, Blumrich says, more sophisticated than anything modern technology can construct now. It appears to have been an atomic-powered, atmospheric entry vehicle used for transportation on planets it visited in the time of Ezekiel's exile, some twenty-six hundred years ago.

There is no certainty from Ezekiel's description whether he rode in the space ship or not, but he was commissioned to go to the people of Israel (Ezek. 2:3), and he does say, "The Spirit lifted me up and took me away . . . and I came to the exiles at Telabib, who dwelt by the river Chebar. And I sat there overwhelmed among them seven days" (3:14–15). (It can only be assumed that Ezekiel rode in the ship, possibly from Israel to Babylonia, during the period of the exile there).

In the preceding verses, he says, "I heard behind me the sound of a great earthquake . . . the wings of the living creatures as they touched one another, and the sound of the wheels beside them, that sounded like a great earthquake" (Ezek. 3:12–13). Ezekiel could be describing his experience as he rode forth.

Before the journey he is overawed with what he calls "the likeness of a throne, in appearance like sapphire; and seated above the likeness of a throne was a likeness as it were of a human form . . . Like the appearance of the bow that is in the cloud on the day of rain . . . Such was the appearance of the likeness of the glory of the Lord. And when I saw it, I fell upon my face, and I heard the voice of one speaking" (Ezek. 1:26, 28–29).

The voice commissioned Ezekiel to communicate to Israel's rebellious, indifferent, and obstinate people that God's rule is supreme, that hope for Israel is secure on the promise and pledge of God, provided they obey his commandments.

So filled with wonder and awe was Ezekiel at coming into the presence of God's glory in the midst of Israel's frustration and hopelessness, that his experience holds out hope for our time, hope in the power of God to bring a nation, weakened by unrighteousness, back to justice and integrity, all through some miraculous power, such as Ezekiel discovered in his visions of God.

Another time, following the news of the fall of Jerusalem, Ezekiel speaks with hope and assurance of the restoration of the people of God. He reaches the heights in his parable of the lost shepherd, in which he tells of the sheep which were lost because there was no shepherd. It is with much pathos that Ezekiel says, "The word of the Lord came to me . . . 'My sheep were scattered, they wandered over all the mountains and on every high hill; my sheep were scattered over all the face of the earth, with none to search or seek for them'" (Ezek. 34:1, 6).

Then triumphantly God declares, "Thus says the Lord God: Behold, I, I myself . . . will seek them out . . . I will feed them with good pasture, and upon the mountain heights of Israel shall be their pasture; there they shall lie down in good grazing land, and on fat pasture they shall feed on the mountains of Israel. I myself will be the shepherd of my sheep, and I will make them lie down, says the Lord God. I will seek the lost, and I will bring back the strayed, and I will bind up the crippled, and I will strengthen the weak, and the fat and the strong I will watch over; I will feed them in justice" (Ezek. 34:11, 14–16).

What a hopeful message for a country then in exile! The people need not fear tomorrow. Jerusalem had fallen, but God had not fallen. The only times Ezekiel uses the word "hope" (Ezek. 19:5, 37:11) is when he looks back on seemingly hopeless situations.

Ezekiel was a prophet who had experienced and caught a vision of God's omnipotent and eternal power. He had an unshaken confidence in the morrow, when his people would return to the home of their fathers, and when their nation would be restored to a holy nation with a holy temple, with God at the center.

This spokesman for God, Ezekiel, was the one person who had sought to keep the exiled Hebrews confident that they were a distinct people, that they would return to Jerusalem, and that they had a divine destiny.

These three—Isaiah, Jeremiah, and Ezekiel—like the other twelve prophets who follow, are as relevant now as they were in their own time, for their ideas are universal and their principles valid and eternal.

CHAPTER 14

The Twelve Minor Prophets: Israel's Hopeful Redeemers

The prophecies of these twelve men provide a pertinent prelude to the New Testament. They and the three Major Prophets have left to the world a literature of the soul, a real spiritual phenomenon.

Like the three Major Prophets in the preceding chapter, the twelve included here have always stood together. St. Augustine, the fourth-century Latin father, first called them the "Minor Prophets," because of the brevity of their messages, and this connotation has been fastened to them ever since.

It is true that their messages encompass a narrower range of prophecies than that of the Major Prophets, often referred to as the "classic prophets." But what these Minor Prophets say is no less meaningful or spirited. They have had a direct influence on the ever-growing knowledge of God and his part in the history of their time from 750 B.C. until about five centuries later. This period took in the latter part of the Hebrew monarchy, the fall of Nineveh (612 B.C.), the fall of Jerusalem (586 B.C.), the fall of Babylon (538 B.C.), the first return of the exiles (537–536 B.C.), the completion of the temple at Jerusalem (516 B.C.), Ezra's return with a large band of exiles (458 or 398 B.C.?), and Nehemiah's homecoming (444 B.C.).

Amos, who prophesied during the reign of Jeroboam II (786–

746 B.C.), was the first chronologically. He actually was the first of all the prophets, the forerunner of Isaiah in the preceding chapter, but the Bible canonizers place him as the sixth of the fifteen. Chronologically, as a Minor Prophet, he is followed by Hosea (745–734 B.C.), Micah (701 B.C.), Zephaniah (628–626 B.C.), Nahum (614–612 B.C.), Habakkuk (605–600 B.C.), Haggai (520 B.C.), Zechariah (520–509 B.C.), Malachi (460 B.C.), Obadiah (after 597 B.C.?), Joel (350 B.C.?), and Jonah (about 400 B.C.). Although critics disagree on the date of these prophecies, either as a whole or in part, all of the prophets seem to be kindred spirits. And this is of first significance.

Like the three prophets in the preceding chapter, these twelve had a confident hope in a great future for Israel, if it obeyed God. This hope became an intrinsic element in their lives and a dynamic force that helped them drive on against tremendous odds. With fortitude and fearlessness they resisted the temptation to compromise hope and faith into irrational thinking or idle speculation.

Because of the leadership of these great men of God, we can easily understand why Israel, despite war, exile, and despair, survived as a nation. We see, too, why civilizations that were contemporary with Israel's crumbled and vanished into the sands of time.

The world has not yet caught up with the hopeful visions of these ancient prophets.

Their Personal Lives

Although all twelve prophets had one thing in common, a penetrating knowledge of God's part in history, in background and temperament they were entirely different. Amos, a rugged, stern, fearless man, who lived in Judah (the Southern Kingdom), ushered in the prophetic movement of the eighth century. He was a herdsman and tree pruner, who lived in the wild, rock-strewn Judean wilderness, near Bethlehem. Dressed in a sheepskin coat he made himself, he rode his donkey to the royal shrine at Bethel. There on the street corners, during the reign of Jeroboam II, he preached to expose the extravagant and callous ways of living among the lords and ladies of sophisticated Samaria (the Northern Kingdom).

Hosea was the first prophet to write of the covenant love between God and Israel, and this was based on his heart-rending experience of his own marriage. Other known facts on his life are discernible in his book, compiled in the eighth century.

Micah, a contemporary of Amos, Hosea, and Isaiah, lived near the coastal roads, only twenty miles from Jerusalem. Consequently, he seemed to be familiar with the traders, pilgrims, and soldiers who traveled between Egypt and Jerusalem.

Nahum, Zephaniah, and Habakkuk were contemporaries of Jeremiah. Zephaniah was of royal blood, a son of Cushi. Probably a third generation descendant of King Hezekiah, he was an old man when he wrote. Haggai, probably a prophet in Babylon during the Exile, is thought to have been an old man, too, when he became one of the prime movers of the restoration of the temple. His text implies that he had seen the temple before its destruction. Few definite facts are known of Haggai's personal life, or of either Nahum or Habukkuk.

About all that is recorded concerning Joel is that he was the son of the obscure Pethuel. But it is easy to assume that Joel was a country man, for he writes knowingly of the locust plague and droughts. Still less is known of Obadiah. Zechariah, Haggai's contemporary, was the grandson of Iddo, presumably a priest who returned from the Babylonian exile with Zerubbabel and the High Priest Joshua. Practically nothing is known about Malachi's personal life.

The writer of the Book of Jonah uses the name of Jonah, the main character, but Jonah was not thought to be the author.

These Minor Prophets are presented below, not according to the time they are thought to have spoken, but according to the way they are listed in the Bible.

1. Hosea: The Prophet of Love

While Amos thunders his prophesies loudly, his contemporary Hosea pleads tenderly. He conceives of God not as a power but as love itself. Because God is love, Hosea holds out hope that God will redeem his wayward people in Israel.

Hosea began his prophetic mission about a decade after Amos. He presents his message of God's love for his sinning people as a living parable centered around his marriage to Gomer, "a wife of harlotry." One can sense Hosea's poignant grief over the sin of this wife whom he loves, the mother of his three helpless children. Despite Gomer's past before her marriage, she sought other men after her marriage to Hosea. Although she proved faithless to her husband, he went on loving her.

Hosea began to understand that if he, a fallible human being, had tolerance toward an erring wife, surely God could be no less magnanimous toward a disobedient nation that he had loved.

Whether this was a real marriage no one knows. Probably it was. For Hosea developed revolutionary ideas in his thinking, in which were born his own concept of God and his love for all people. Hosea knew his little country was guilty of adultery too, and yet he did not give up hope for her.

Confident in this belief, Hosea expresses a trusting hope for Israel,

> But now listen,
> I will woo her, I will go with her into the wilderness
>   and comfort her:
> there I will restore her vineyards,
> turning the Vale of Trouble into the Gate of Hope
> (2:14–15, NEB)

Corrupt Israel was in trouble. But for both Israel and Gomer, this door of hope was yet open. With love ever present—love such as Hosea expressed for Gomer and love such as God has for all people—this door never closes.

Hosea was certain, too, that a God of love was a God of mercy, and so in one great sentence he revealed that he desired "steadfast love and not sacrifice, a knowledge of God, rather than burnt offerings" (6:6). Centuries later, inspired by Hosea's thought, "Go and learn what this means," Jesus said to the Pharisees, "'I desire mercy, and not sacrifice.' For I came not to call the righteous but sinners" (Matt. 9:13).

2. Joel: The Lord a Stronghold

In what is one of the finest poetical descriptions in the Old
Testament, Joel, like Amos before him, writes of a locust plague.
He sees the locusts swarming like an army for an attack on Israel.

Finally the locusts disappear, leaving behind a ravaged country,
but Joel, speaking in the name of the Lord, declares positively,
"I will restore to you the years which the swarming locust has
eaten" (2:25).

Here is hope at its best, with no place for despair or hopelessness, even in a desolate situation, amid the destruction of all vege-
tation by swarming insects. Here we understand that if God can
heal the ravages of nature, he also can redeem and regenerate the
soul of the Lord's people.

Joel concludes with prophecies of everlasting blessings for them,
a rebirth, a better understanding of man's spiritual nature, and
hope for the creation of a new social order.

3. Amos: The Champion of Justice and Righteousness

Amos did not stress religious rites, like some of the earlier religious leaders, but right itself. In doing so, he seemed to be paving the way for the coming of the greatest of all ethical teachers,
Jesus.

The thesis of the Book of Amos appears in 2:6–16, in which he
prophesies against the chosen people because they have not
obeyed the moral laws of God. He destroys the popular belief that
God will overthrow all the foes of his chosen people and usher in
a utopia for them. On the other hand, Amos predicts a day of
doom and holds out hope only for the spiritually minded and
morally upright. The literary gem and core of thought in the Book
of Amos is

> Let justice roll down like waters,
> and righteousness like an overflowing stream.
>   (5:24)

These are among the most widely quoted lines from these prophets. Amos makes it clear that righteousness and justice are not local or national but universal. The remarkable thing about these words is that they represent what scholars have called the first forceful call in antiquity to ethical religion, which Jesus reiterated in Matt. 23.

No age forgets the impact of these words, although people who try to practice righteousness and justice in every area of their lives, not just on Sunday but also in the market place every day, are oftentimes called eccentric.

Raymond Calkins, who has written one of the finest books on the Minor Prophets, titled *The Modern Message of the Minor Prophets*, comments,

> The one divine work—the one ordered sacrifice—is to do justice; and it is the last we are inclined to do. Thus the voice of Amos summoning men to an ethical religion needs to be heard today as truly as in the day in which he lived. Amos does not substitute morality for religion. On the contrary, he taught that all morality finds its roots, its spiritual source and its compelling power over the consciences of men in the character of God Himself, that is, in religion. Neither the reconstruction of society nor the reformation of human character can be achieved without the sanctions of a true religion. Both social and personal morality, if it is to be stable and adventurous, must be derived from a conscious relationship between God and men. But this religion must be rooted also in conscience. It must hate evil both in one's self and in the world wherever found. It must love justice and seek the good . . . Such is the message of Amos to our modern world.
>
> (p. 30)

Amos's words are filled with a hope that is enduring and sure, a hope that finds its way to the source of new, unknown possibilities for the future.

The Book of Amos is one of the most readable of the prophetic works. The literary style is superb, daring, direct, and easy to understand. With astonishing insight, Amos sees the corrupting evils in society then and now: the love of money and pleasure, the lust for power, and the oppression of the poor. All of these can sap a nation, as well as a person, of its God-given vitality.

Amos did not stand alone in his thinking, but he was the first in a golden age of prophecy. The three who followed, Hosea, Isaiah, and Micah, also taught that God demands righteousness of us. We see more clearly that those who love justice and seek good unconsciously move forward spiritually.

4. OBADIAH: HOPE IN VICTORY OVER EVIL

The time when Obadiah prophesied is uncertain, probably shortly after 597 B.C., according to most authorities. Israel then had to endure a perplexing problem, the constant menace of a long-time enemy, the Edomites, famous for secular wisdom but lacking in spiritual wisdom. These enemies gloated over Jerusalem's misfortunes, when barbarians passed through her gates and cast lots for her, when strangers carried off her riches.

Located in the mountainous region, south of the Dead Sea, that extended to the Gulf of Aqaba, Edom was close enough to Jerusalem to be a real threat. Petra, Edom's chief city, was in the rocky clefts and seemingly safe from Israel, but Obadiah was confident that Israel would ultimately triumph over Edom. He told the Edomites,

> Your pride of heart has led you astray,
> you whose home is in the holes in the rocks,
> who make the heights your dwelling,
> who say in your heart,
> "Who will bring me down to the ground?"
>
> Though you soared like the eagle,
> though you set your nest among the stars,
> I will still fling you down again—it is Yahweh who speaks.
>
> (1:3–4, JB)

Obadiah looked forward to the dawn of a new day for Israel. The Edomites might dwell in a high habitation, but the Lord was still higher. They might exalt themselves as the eagle. Their nests might be among the stars. But who made the eagle and the seven stars? Obadiah asked. God is his name.

Never admitting defeat of any kind, in the last verse of what

is the shortest book in the Bible, Obadiah hopefully declared that
victorious Israel will climb Mount Zion to judge Edom and that
the sovereignty shall belong to God.

5. JONAH: HOPE IN GOD'S MERCY AND LOVE

The Book of Jonah is an account of a prophet's experiences
rather than his prophecies. Jonah, the chief character in the book
which bears his name, is a self-centered, self-willed Hebrew who
despises foreigners.

When he was told to go and preach to Nineveh, a wicked city
long the incarnation of Israel's hatred of a barbarous foe, Jonah
did not head for Nineveh but for Joppa. There he took a ship for
Tarshish, a shipbuilding center in the south of Spain.

On his way he was in a violent storm at sea. The crew, fearful
that Jonah, this Hebrew, was the cause of the rough weather,
tossed him into the sea, where he was swallowed by a fish, in
whose belly he remained for three days and three nights. Inside
the fish, he prayed for deliverance. When he realized he had been
cast from the Lord's holy temple, he humbly vowed obedience to
him.

> When my soul fainted within me,
>   I remembered the Lord;
> and my prayer came to thee,
>   into thy holy temple.
> (2:7)

When Jonah was disgorged unhurt from the fish, he went on to
Nineveh, still filled with hate for the Ninevites. As he preached
to them, he thought they would be overthrown, because of their
wickedness. They were not. They repented instead. Even the king
removed his robe and donned sackcloth and ashes. The self-
righteous Jonah was distraught that God had spared Nineveh.
Then he made the marvelous discovery that all men are able to
embrace God's mercy, to repent and to dwell in his spirit.

Told in the form of a parable, like Jesus' parable of the Prodigal
Son and the Good Samaritan, the Book of Jonah is a timeless re-

buke to the contempt of people toward other races, creeds, and color. Redemption awaits all, even those who sin, for God is merciful to sinners.

Jonah is not only the self-righteous Hebrew, he is every man who lives entirely for his own interests and with nothing but hatred for those of a different color, race, and environment.

Jonah's narrow-minded attitude toward Nineveh is typical of the racial prejudice common today. Many of us, like Jonah, forget the essential equality of the human race and that a God of unlimited mercy loves all of his people. This truth lifts the Book of Jonah to the highest level of Old Testament prophecy, which later gave a new meaning in the Christian gospel.

Jonah's temporary entombment three days and three nights suggests Christ's three-day interment from which he arose. Long before Christ's ministry ended, he warned the scribes and Pharisees seeking signs that no sign would be given to their adulterous generation except the sign of Jonah.

"The men of Nineveh," Christ said to them, "will arise at the judgment with this generation and condemn it; for they repented at the preaching of Jonah, and behold, something greater than Jonah is here" (Matt. 12:41).

6. MICAH: THE PROPHET OF SOCIAL JUSTICE

Micah, another contemporary of Hosea, Amos, and Isaiah, lived on a coastal road near Isaiah. It is not surprising, then, that they depict the same social evils: greedy nobles who seize the lands of the peasants; corrupt courts where the poor man finds no justice; unethical merchants; brother murdering brother and other unhealthy relationships between families, such as sons who malign fathers and daughters who rebel against mothers.

Micah then prays fervently to God to shepherd his people with his staff (7:14).

In what is regarded as the finest poem in the Book of Micah (6:6, 8), a searching question throws light upon what is pure reverence in religion:

> With what shall I come before the Lord,
>   and bow myself before God on high?

In language that reaches a lofty height, Micah answers,

> He has showed you, O man, what is good;
>   and what does the Lord require of you
> but to do justice, and to love kindness,
>   and to walk humbly with your God?

Afterward, Micah accentuates man's hope of mercy when he seeks a humbler, closer walk with God.

One of the highest hopes expressed in the Book of Micah is the prediction of the coming Messiah and his reign (5:2-4). The prophecy was later fulfilled by the birth of Christ in Bethlehem.

7. Nahum: A Positive Faith in God's Rule

Nahum's prophecies, too often overlooked in Bible reading, reach a high spiritual peak in an exultant psalm of praise to the Lord's majesty (1:1-15). Here appears one of the most beautiful and buoyant verses in the Bible:

> The Lord is good,
>   a stronghold in the day of trouble;
>   he knows those who take refuge in him.
>   (1:7)

This was uttered in a dark hour, when the tyrants of the Assyrian empire were still in power. Because of its cruelty, barbarism, and ruthlessness, its capital, Nineveh, was much hated.

But Nahum hopefully prophesies that the wicked can not stand before a just and righteous God. And so he closes his prologue with the familiar words found also in Isaiah and Romans, based on the theme, "How beautiful are the feet of those who preach good news" (in this instance the coming destruction of Nineveh). This also implies the good news of hope for the oppressed.

The magnificent ode of Nahum, which takes in the siege, sacking, and destruction of Nineveh, ranks high in the poetic literature of the Old Testament. Nahum is outraged at a city that has so shocked the conscience of humanity. He calls it a "bloody city, all full of lies and booty" (3:1), a city of ruthless military power and dishonest merchants whose wealth has come at the expense of morality and honesty.

Nahum's words leap over the page with fire and beauty as he depicts Nineveh's sin and wickedness, which he is sure will yield a harvest of destruction. Finally Nineveh falls, never to rise again. In language of beauty and power, Nahum concludes with this poem of triumph:

> All who hear the news of you
>   clap their hands over you.
> For upon whom has not come
>   your unceasing evil?
>
>   (3:19)

8. Habakkuk: His Affirmations Like Luminous Stars

Habakkuk speaks out in this book, notable for its literary structure based on simple, majestic lines. Its three chapters stand like three august pillars, side by side, each complete in itself and unparalleled in power.

In the first chapter the prophet pours out the perplexing questions of his burdened soul. Why does evil go unpunished? Why will God use the more wicked to punish the less wicked? Then he is comforted because he knows "The reckless will be unsure of himself, while the righteous man will live by being faithful" (2:4, NEB).

In the second chapter, in which the prophet looks for answers from God, he prophesies that Israel's enemy Chaldea, an area independent of Assyria and dominating all of western Asia including Judea, will be punished. Why? Because of its greediness, covetousness, cruelty, and idolatry.

Some of the splendid affirmations about God in Habakkuk are as uplifting as any in the Bible. In the prayer for mercy, Chapter 3, the prophecy declares:

> His [God's] radiance overspreads the skies,
> and his splendor fills the earth.
>   He rises like the dawn
>   with twin rays starting forth at his side;
> the skies are the hiding-place of his majesty,
> and the everlasting ways are for his swift flight.
>
>   (3–4, NEB)

This entire psalm, sublime in poetic conception and majestic in diction, concludes in triumph, a marvelous affirmation of the victory of faith over every loss and disappointment:

> Yet I will exult in the Lord
> and rejoice in the God of my deliverance.
> The Lord God is my strength,
> who makes my feet nimble as a hind's
> and sets me to range the heights.
>
> (18–19, NEB)

In his comments on Habakkuk in *The Interpreter's Dictionary of the Bible* (Vol. 2, p. 505), E. A. Leslie says, "The little book is filled with truths which stand at the core of Hebrew religion. History has meaning if one takes the long view and judges events from the perspective of faith . . . Evil is found to fail in the end, even though it may seem victorious. There is no might but right."

In such beliefs, hope for a more righteous world comes alive again. And that is one of the basic joys of a prophet like Habakkuk.

9. ZEPHANIAH: AUTHOR OF THE HYMN OF HOPE

Zephaniah was a contemporary of Jeremiah. He prophesied shortly before King Amon's godly son Josiah found the lost Book of Deuteronomy in the temple at Jerusalem. In a period of religious disillusionment and general decay, Zephaniah, who was caught up in the pessimism of the time, compiled what has been called the saddest book in the Bible.

The first chapter is designated by scholars as the "Book of Doom." It is vastly important because it gives the Old Testament's best picture of the corruption of the Jewish religion during a period when the pagan beliefs dominated. Because the people had forsaken the pure worship of the Lord of their fathers, Zephaniah warns of the terrible judgment awaiting them.

His description of the day of wrath and mourning (1:1–18) inspired the "Dies Irae," chanted as a Christian requiem over a departed human soul since the thirteenth century. Its author was St. Francis' contemporary Thomas of Celano. The song later was associated with great Requiem Masses, Handel's, Mozart's, and others.

So pessimistic is Zephaniah that he predicts that invaders will drive the people away like drifting chaff. He calls the officials "roaring lions," the judges "evening wolves," the prophets "faithless men," and the priests "profane." He is certain their rebellious and defiled governments will be destroyed.

Zephaniah holds out hope for the people of God, however, but he envisions judgment on the surrounding nations. In one of his key passages, he begs:

> Seek the Lord, all you humble of the land,
>   who do his commands;
> seek righteousness, seek humility;
>   perhaps you may be hidden
>   on the day of the wrath of the Lord.
>
>   (2:3)

Like Hosea, Zephaniah knows that God is love and that the righteous find his love sovereign, everlasting, indissoluble, never failing.

At the end of the Book of Zephaniah is a beautiful Hymn of Hope (3:14–20), thought to be the work of a later hand. Whether it is or not, we shall not question. The blessing is there for all who suffer and for those who continually affirm that God is ever-present, victorious, and ever renewing us in his image. Among the most triumphant lines in this hymn are these:

> The Lord, your God, is in your midst,
>   a warrior who gives victory;
> he will rejoice over you with gladness,
>   he will renew you in his love.
>
>   (3:17)

10. HAGGAI: GO FORTH NOT IN FEAR BUT IN CONFIDENCE

Once in exile but now back in Jerusalem, Haggai made it known that Israel could not go forward in the religious heritage of its founders without a temple. He reminded them that they had expended time and money on building new houses for themselves but had not built a house of the Lord.

Solomon's great temple, which had served the people for more than four centuries, fell in 586 B.C. For about seventy years Jerusalem was without a house of worship. A new foundation was laid soon after the return of the exiles, but the building of the temple was delayed for about fifteen years. Finally, thanks to the preaching of Haggai and Zechariah, the work on the temple was resumed in 520 B.C. It was finished about five years later.

The task was completed largely through the comfort and hope of Haggai, who in the second chapter begs the people to take courage and go forward, not in fear but in confidence, for God's spirit dwells among them, making all things possible.

At the conclusion, Haggai named Zerubbabel, mentioned earlier, as the destined prince to preserve the messianic hope of the Jewish people. In the fullness of time, more than five centuries later, appeared Christ, a descendant of Zerubbabel.

11. Zechariah: Hope for the New Jerusalem

> Return to your stronghold, O prisoners of hope;
>   today I declare that I will restore to you double.
>   (9:12)

This is Zechariah's emphatic declaration to the people who still believed but were temporarily imprisoned by conditions over which they seemingly had no control. Zechariah writes of the coming restoration of Jerusalem, when the Lord "shall stand on the Mount of Olives" (14:4) and "living waters shall flow out from Jerusalem" (14:8) and "the Lord will become king over all the earth" (14:9).

Zechariah, a contemporary of Haggai, visualizes a city built "not by might, nor by power" (4:6), a city with a temple which becomes the center of worship, an anointed ruler, and a people worthy of both. Hope then will take the place of hopelessness because God's spirit is all-powerful, and obstacles seemingly in-

surmountable will vanish. Then will begin the messianic age, all
the gift of God.

Most of today's scholars believe that the last six chapters,
Chapters 9 through 14, were later appropriate additions to the
book but that the prophecies of the New Jerusalem are Zechariah's
own, for he is thought to have returned from Babylon to Jerusalem
with the first exiles in 537 B.C. Scholars call the message of Zechariah one of "the brightest, the clearest, the most hopeful" to be
found in prophetic literature. The apocalyptic nature of the book,
with the horsemen among the myrtles, the lampstand and the two
olive trees, and the flying scroll, indicates that while exiled in
Babylon, Zechariah learned to speak in Babylonian symbols. Yet
he was extremely practical and wrote of morality in perceptive
language like this: "Speak the truth to one another, render in
your gates judgments that are true and make for peace, do not
devise evil in your hearts against one another, and love no false
oath, for all these things I hate, says the Lord" (8:16–17).

12. MALACHI: NO ROOM FOR DESPAIR

Malachi prophesied a timeless message of God's love for his
people. This left no room for despair. He makes us know that
whenever we find ourselves baffled, bewildered, and disheartened,
we must remember there is a force at work in our lives that is
mightier than all the forces of evil.

To some, Malachi's message may seem outdated, but it is never
dead. Within it lies the spark of life that can not be extinguished,
for this prophet had mighty visions of the future where the nations
of power, like men of power, rise and fall. Malachi helps us to see
that both men and nations are saved if they seek to serve. If they
seek to destroy, they consume themselves.

Like some of his predecessors, Malachi saw that Israel's greatest
hope was the coming of one who would redeem Israel, and so he
prophesied: "Behold, I send my messenger to prepare the way
before me, and the Lord whom you seek will suddenly come to
his temple; the messenger of the covenant in whom you delight,
behold, he is coming, says the Lord of hosts. But who can endure

the day of his coming, and who can stand when he appears?" (3:1-2).

Finally, Jesus Christ, founder of the New Covenant of all Israel, appeared about four centuries later. It is fitting that Malachi's book of prophecy should end the Old Testament, although it is not the last book chronologically.

The messages of these Minor Prophets seem to be like guiding stars lighting the way for the Redeemer to come. In him was mankind's hope. Without him, the Major and Minor Prophets would have failed in their potential, but Christ fulfilled their every hope as the one whom God sent forth as the Savior promised long ago to reveal his light and truth.

SECTION FOUR

Jesus Christ
The Hope of the World

Some of the Old Testament men of hope in the preceding section either incarnated the Messianic hope or inaugurated the Messianic age.

These earlier studies help us to understand that the will of God is historically mediated. It came to humanity through Israel, whose people had one motivating purpose, to seek a closer relationship with God. In this, Israel holds the religious secret of the world and a unique place in the history of nations. And this religious consciousness is illuminated in Israel's history from the beginning.

In the Old Testament we see the human conception in the divine. In the New Testament we see the divine in the human, in the birth of Christ. And finally, too, in the New Testament dawns the grand conception of the kingdom of God in all its fullness, as revealed by Christ, thus bringing the New Testament into direct continuity with the Old Testament.

The idea of hope emerges confidently but slowly in the Old Testament. But in the New Testament God's covenant with Moses and his people is echoed and fulfilled in the new covenant initiated by Christ, who through his resurrection, is the hope of the world.

Hope in the Resurrection, in its full Christian context, reaches its highest point in the acts and writings of Paul, Christ's greatest apostle.

CHAPTER 15

John the Baptist: A Witness to the Light

John, the immediate forerunner of Christ, begins his ministry in the Judean wilderness and preaches and prophesies in the Jordan area, where he baptizes Jesus.

The connecting link between the Old and New Testament is one of the most unique figures in the Bible, John the Baptist. As the advance guard of Christ, his own cousin, and born three months before Christ, John came with a special mission. The Gospel of John explains this in all its wonder: "There was a man sent from God, whose name was John [the Baptist]. He came for testimony, to bear witness to the light, that all might believe through him. He was not the light, but came to bear witness to the light" (John 1:6–8).

All four Gospels state that John was not the Christ as the priests and Levites first thought. When John was baptizing at Bethany beyond the Jordan, he was asked who he was, and his answer was "I am the voice of one crying in the wilderness, 'Make straight the way of the Lord,' as the prophet Isaiah said" (John 1:23).

As the contemporary and relative of the one of whom he spoke, John's place as a prophet is also unique. That which had been spoken by other prophets in parables several centuries earlier, John the Baptist declared in plain words. His declarations immortalize him as one of the greatest of all the prophets—the last of the prophets under the old covenant and the forerunner of the prophet of Nazareth, Jesus Christ.

It is no wonder that John the Baptist could state so positively that "he [Christ] must increase, but I must decrease" (John 3:30). He had such hope in Christ and his mission that he stood meekly by, not to perpetuate himself but to glorify this one greater than he.

Because John lived in a realm of hope, he was the first to perceive Christ's glory, veiled from others, typified in his pure divinity, his humanity, and his example of love and sacrifice, qualities certain to inaugurate a new era in the life of mankind.

John's testimony brought hope to believers and calmed unbelievers. Because of his witness, the long-slumbering faith in the Messianic expectancy was aroused in all the people of Judea. This was not a wild hope based on a far-off kingdom but the inspiring hope of an approaching reality. Inspired by John's prophecy and faith, others learned to live in this realm of hope.

His Supernatural Birth

John's birth, like Christ's, was encompassed by signs and wonders. Malachi, the last of the Old Testament prophets, predicted the coming of Elijah (the personification of the first Elijah delineated in an earlier chapter). The angel Gabriel explained that "he [John the Baptist] will go before him [the Lord] in the spirit and power of Elijah . . . to make ready for the Lord a people prepared" (Luke 1:17–18).

While the priest Zechariah, John's father, burned incense in the temple, the angel Gabriel predicted that he and his wife, Elizabeth, would have a son. The angel announced,

> And you will have joy and gladness,
>   and many will rejoice at his birth;
> for he will be great before the Lord . . .
>   (Luke 1:14–15)

Zechariah was so awe-stricken that he lost his voice and did not regain it until after his son's birth. Both Zechariah and his wife, described as "righteous before God," were advanced in years. When Elizabeth was six months with child, her young cousin Mary, three months with child, came to visit her in what is thought to be the village of Ain Karem, where Zechariah was a priest. The humble Elizabeth, filled with the Holy Spirit, exclaimed to Mary on her arrival:

> Blessed are you among women, and blessed is the fruit of your womb! And why is this granted me, that the mother of my Lord should come to me? For behold, when the voice of your greeting came to my ears, the babe in my womb leaped for joy. And blessed is she who believed that there would be a fulfillment of what was spoken to her from the Lord.
>
> (Luke 1:42–45)

These confident words prompted Mary's "Magnificat" (vs. 46–56).

While others doubted, Elizabeth bestowed a further blessing on Mary when she confirmed there would be a fulfillment of what was spoken to Mary in the Annunciation. Mary was filled with new wonder as she remained with Elizabeth for about three months. Only Luke relates the details of John's conception and Mary's visit, all a link in Jesus' miraculous birth. Matthew, Mark, and John also point to John's birth as of historic significance to Christ.

Zechariah was so filled with the miracle surrounding his son's birth that, after he regained his voice, he praised God in the Benedictus (Luke 1:67–80). In this short canticle Zechariah says of his son,

And you, child, will be called the prophet of the Most High;
for you will go before the Lord to prepare his ways . . .

(v. 76)

John was reared in a home where his parents tenderly cared for him, all the while supporting him with their own unswerving belief in the coming Messiah. It is no wonder that it could be written that their "child grew and became strong in spirit, and he was in the wilderness till the day of his manifestation to Israel" (Luke 1:80).

His Ascetic Appearance

Like Elijah, John chose to live an austere life similar to that of the Essenes. When he sought refuge in the dreary, scorching wilderness that lies between Sinai, the center of religious hope, and the southern frontier of Palestine, he followed the example of other spiritual giants like Moses and Elijah.

John's principles were strengthened in his asceticism. His tall, gaunt figure, his long hair, his dark skin tanned by the sun, his homemade garment of camel's hair with a girdle of lambskin, his ascetic demeanor, all must have created the image of the sanctified recluse he was.

He not only was austere in his dress but also in his eating habits. In the wilderness he lived on wild honey formed in hives of bees in the crevices of rocks or in the rotting trunks of trees, and dried locusts that had hopped through the rocks and trees. His whole demeanor seemed to be a protest against an affluence that tended to smother inspiration and the abundance of personal possessions that clouded out everything else, especially the things of the spirit.

The suddenness of John's prophecy, after the silence of some four hundred years from the time of Malachi, his fearlessness, humility, integrity, all mark John as a distinctive character, almost a saint. Add to these the horror of his beheading, and he stands alone among the servants of God.

Like Elijah when he went to the wilderness to prepare himself for the great challenges that awaited him, John too sought a tranquil way of life for a time, in order to seek divine guidance for his ministry. This preparation became the prelude to his high destiny to proclaim Christ as the Messiah, and to baptize him.

The Preacher and Prophet

With the Holy Spirit working within him, with the knowledge that the hand of the Lord was upon him, and with a deep intuitive sense of the events happening all about him, John the Baptist was ready for his authoritative command.

In the fifteenth year of the reign of Tiberius Caesar, when Pilate was governor of Judea and Herod was the tetrarch of Galilee, the word of God came to John in the wilderness, summoning him to begin his prophetic mission in order that "all flesh shall see the salvation of God" (Luke 3:6).

John now set forth to preach as well as to prophesy. Mark says that the scene of his preaching was the wilderness, while Luke includes the country around the Jordan. Probably the wilderness of Judea, stretching westward from the Dead Sea and the Jordan to the edge of the central plateau of Palestine, continued to be his home. When he preached he doubtless went to villages on the edge of the desert. Since his preaching and his water baptism were interrelated, he probably also moved about a great deal in the area of the Jordan.

Repentance was the theme of John's sermons. His central thought was that the kingdom of heaven is at hand. His summons was that those called to participate in this new day must turn to righteousness. If Israel as a whole was to receive the full blessings of Christ's presence, John declared, its people must also join together as one faith. John's trumpet-voiced proclamation drew Pharisees and publicans, Jews and Gentiles from Jerusalem and Galilee.

John also taught his followers to pray, to fast, and to meditate on the scriptures. In such a rigid self-discipline, some of John's followers became austere ascetics, and some were Christ's most loyal supporters. Andrew and Peter, his first disciples, are thought to have been among them.

THE BAPTIZER

John's baptism of Jesus ushered in that moment in time when Jesus was filled with the spirit of God for his divine mission. Prophet that John was, he could see that sublime spiritual cleansing would come through the Messiah himself: "I baptize you with water for repentance," John told those he baptized before Jesus, "but he who is coming after me is mightier than I, whose sandals I am not worthy to carry; he will baptize you with the Holy Spirit and with fire" (Matt. 3:11).

To declare that the Messianic calling would receive its fulfillment in Christ was John's mission, so John's baptism became a baptism of promise and preparation.

When Jesus first appeared to John the Baptist for baptism, the Gospel of John reports, the baptizer said, "I myself did not know him . . ." (John 1:33), probably not as the Messiah until "the Spirit [descended] as a dove from heaven" upon him (v. 32). This was John's sign that Jesus was the expected Messiah.

Jesus came to John for baptism because he recognized John's baptism as a symbolic way of dedicating oneself to the ideals and demands of a new life of righteousness. John, because of his own unworthiness, first hesitated to baptize Jesus.

John's stress on baptism with water reverted to the ceremonial rites of early Jews. From Levitical times, large stone jars filled with water were set aside for ceremonial cleansing. (From such jars of water Jesus turned the water into wine at the wedding at Cana.) John's baptism finds its historical roots in these ceremonial rites, but his cleansing by water was essentially an ethical rite, with demands for the moral and spiritual dedication.

CHRIST'S APPRAISAL OF JOHN

Many tributes were paid to John by Christ. He recognized his limitations, but he saw them not as weaknesses but as pioneering efforts making straight the path for him and his church.

When Jesus discoursed with Nicodemus on the necessity of man's being born "of water and the spirit" (John 3:5), he indicated the deep religious values of John's water baptism, while at the same time stressing the spiritual birth that comes only from God.

When John was in prison, he sent disciples with his last message to Christ, asking, "Are you he who is to come, or shall we look for another?" (Matt. 11:3). Christ sent word, "Go and tell John what you hear and see: the blind receive their sight and the dead are raised up, and the poor have good news preached to them. And blessed is he who takes no offense at me" (vs. 4–6).

When the messengers left, Jesus spoke to the crowds in praise of John. His greatest tribute was, "I solemnly assure you, history has not known a man born of woman greater than John the Baptizer. Yet the least born into the kingdom of God is greater than he. From John the Baptizer's time until now the kingdom of God has suffered violence, and the violent take it by force. All the prophets as well as the law spoke prophetically until John. If you are prepared to accept it, he is Elijah, the one who was certain to come. Heed carefully what you hear!" (Matt. 11:11–15, NAB).

At his own resurrection, Jesus justified John by inaugurating the rite of baptism as the distinctive symbol of his reforming activity. But Jesus went further. He transformed baptism into a sacrament of the Christian Church, a symbol of the gospel of forgiveness, the sign and seal of true discipleship.

John's Last Tragic Days

Early in his career John opposed the marriage of Herod Antipas and Herodias, the divorced wife of Herod's brother and a member of the Herod family herself. As the rulers of Galilee and Perea, Herod and Herodias were highly angered at John when he declared to Herod, "It is not lawful for you to have your brother's wife" (Mark 6:18). Herodias was so furious at John the Baptist that she wanted to kill him, but she could not. Why? Her husband feared John, this righteous and holy man with many followers, and Herodias dared not touch him.

Finally, Herod cut short his protection of John the Baptist when his popularity began to draw crowds. Not only did Herod fear him but the Roman authorities were uneasy about him too. And so Herod had John the Baptist imprisoned. Josephus confirms that the castle of Machaerus, on the east shore of the Dead Sea, was the scene of John's imprisonment and death.

Here he was when the time arrived for Herodias to give a large birthday celebration to honor Herod. To this party came courtiers, officers, and the leading citizens of Galilee. After the guests were wined and dined, Herod asked his stepdaughter to dance for them. To please him she did. Then he asked her what she wanted most. She appealed to her mother for the answer. Her immediate reply was, "The head of John the Baptist." Rushing to Herod, the stepdaughter demanded, "Give me the head of John the Baptist here on a platter" (Matt. 14:8).

The king regretted the request, but with so many distinguished guests looking on, he would not break his word, even if it meant the beheading of so noble a man as John the Baptist.

So Herod ordered the soldiers of his guard to go and behead John the Baptist where he was imprisoned. And they did, bringing his head back on a platter. Herod presented John the Baptist's head to his stepdaughter, and she in turn gave it to her mother.

After John's disciples learned of the martyrdom of their beloved leader, they came and took his headless body and laid it in a tomb.

Amid poignant suffering and shocking tragedy, such as that of John the Baptist, others searching for spiritual renewal oftentimes find in him new images of hope, hope in the indestructibility of the lasting values, hope in true repentance, such as John taught, and hope in the immortality of man's living soul. Herod could destroy John's body but not his spiritual being.

The radiant light around John the Baptist from the time he was born could not be extinguished even by so tragic a death, and that light he came to witness glows even now, nearly two thousand years later.

CHAPTER 16

The Risen Christ: The Living Hope

Jesus Christ—the Messiah—brought the revelation of God to man. Following his miraculous ministry of less than three years, he is transfigured in the presence of three of his disciples. Later his enemies crucify him. Three days later he arises from the grave and forty days later he ascends.

Jesus Christ, possessing all the qualities of the divine nature of God, assumed a human body and human attributes for the purpose of man's restoration and redemption. This God-man, both human and divine, embraces three radiant principles.

1. A New Being, who represents the Righteousness of God in all things, and for all believers he is the focus of an all-embracing hope, now no longer a prophecy but a reality.

2. The Lordship of the Crucified One, as signified in his spiritual exaltation, which transcended his physical suffering.

3. The Promise of a new life after death as a result of his resurrection.

These principles fulfill every worthy hope in the Old Testament promised to or prophesied by its great spiritual giants, beginning with Abraham and extending through the prophets.

Not any of these promises end in Christ's appearance after the Transfiguration, Crucifixion, Resurrection, and Ascension, but in him these miracles are liberated and validated. Early believers, many of them eye witnesses, knew what it was to experience "the blessed hope, the appearing of the Glory of our great God and Saviour Jesus Christ" (Tit. 2:13).

In his book *The New Being*, Paul Tillich, the eminent theologian, writes that if he were asked to sum up the Christian message in two words, he would say, with Paul, it is a message of a "New Creation." Then Tillich adds, "Let me repeat one of his sentences in the words of an exact translation: 'If anyone is in union with Christ he is a new being; the old state of things has passed away; there is a new state of things.' Christianity is the message of the New Creation, the New Being, the New Reality" (p. 15).

With Christ's resurrection and ascension as the very ground of the Christian hope, the Church was born. The early Church was positive that the Resurrection was the hope of its calling (Eph. 4:4), the hope of the Gospel (Col. 1:23), and that it would wait for the hope of righteousness (Gal. 5:5).

Christ's perpetual presence, accentuating moral and spiritual renewal, permeates the twenty-seven books of the New Testament with a divine influence that never ceases to bring into the lives of Christian believers a hope that expands into infinity, for in Jesus, who endured such terrible suffering and tribulation, we gain patience in our own hopes.

In a remarkable passage, the writer of Hebrews says that we must learn to live in the assurance of God's unchanging covenant promise and "seize the hope set before us. We have this as a sure and steadfast anchor of the soul, a hope that enters into the inner shrine, behind the curtain, where Jesus has gone as a forerunner in our behalf" (Heb. 6:18–20).

Worthy ideals and faith radiate our pathway, forming a collective hope, a part of our religious heritage as faithful believers.

In spite of all that might have driven Christ from God—persecution, betrayal, unbelief on the part of his followers, even crucifixion—he never lost his union with God. Before our very eyes he raises the curtain on a new dimension of the Eternal where God dwells, and where hopelessness and despair cannot exist. This new vision of hope upholds faith and keeps it moving forward and enables us to journey toward new horizons, boundless and glowing with promise.

THE MYSTIC POWER OF HIS BIRTH

The Annunciation, the Nativity, and the visit of Mary and Joseph to the temple in Jerusalem were marked by signs and wonders: angels who made several appearances; wise men who studied the heavens and followed a wondrous star in the east, lighting the sky over the manger in Bethlehem; shepherds watching in the fields; and songs such as "Glory to God in the Highest." These have inspired Christians with reverent hope these almost two thousand years since his birth.

The first wonder appeared when the angel Gabriel "was sent from God to a city of Galilee named Nazareth, to a virgin betrothed to a man whose name was Joseph, of the house of David; and the virgin's name was Mary. And he came to her and said, 'Hail, O favored one, the Lord is with you'" (Luke 1:26–28). The angel told Mary that she would conceive and bear a son and that his name would be Jesus. Then the angel spoke the most inspiring words of the entire annunciation:

> He will be great, and will be called the Son of the Most High;
> and the Lord God will give to him the throne of his father David,
> and he will reign over the house of Jacob for ever;
> and of his kingdom there will be no end . . .
> The Holy Spirit will come upon you,
> and the power of the Most High will overshadow you,
> therefore the child to be born will be called holy,
> the Son of God.
>
> (1:32–33, 35)

After this Mary went to a nearby town to visit her cousin Elizabeth, mother-to-be of John the Baptist, as related in the preceding chapter, and Elizabeth addressed Mary as "the mother of my Lord." This inspired her famous "Magnificat," or "Song of Mary" (Luke 1:45–56), in which she magnified God for regarding "the low estate of his handmaiden and continuing in the promise to Abraham and his posterity."

Matthew's Gospel opens with an account of the Savior's humanity and his descent as a man. Mark takes us back to the age of prophecy, from the times of Isaiah and Malachi, whose words are no longer a promise but a reality. Luke places his Gospel in the framework of the Levitical priesthood and the services of an earthly sanctuary, a shadow of good things to come. John soars above all three. He refers to the birth of nature in the beginning and shows how the word of God in the fullness of time was made flesh and dwelt among us.

Christ's miraculous birth, most dramatically depicted in Luke, demonstrates that God in his creativity can bring forth great wonders, some of which can neither be comprehended nor explained. Sheathed in an indescribable light, they never cease to inspire our faith.

On the night Christ was born in Bethlehem of Judea, his parents went their way unnoticed after arriving in Bethlehem from their home in Nazareth, Mary probably riding a donkey and Joseph walking at her side. They had come to be listed in the census, according to an order sent out to all citizens of the Roman empire by the Emperor Caesar Augustus.

When they arrived in Bethlehem, the town was filled with other enrollees, so many that there was no room for them in the inn. They finally found sanctuary in a stable inside a cave, traditionally located underneath what is now the Church of the Nativity, thought to be Christ's birthplace. No door or curtain covered the opening of the cave. There was no crib for the child, only a feeding trough used by animals, probably a hollowed-out stone, covered with hay.

But at Christ's birth wondrous events began to take place, all to announce to a slumbering world that the long awaited King of Kings had been born. Little did the majority of the people realize that the greatest of all of God's creations had come forth, that in this child was not only a new life but a new creation named Jesus, meaning "God saves," as the angel had said in the Annunciation. ("Christ" is the Greek equivalent of the Hebrew "Messiah," meaning "the anointed one.")

The last to comprehend the meaning of his birth were the powerful rulers of the time: Emperor Caesar Augustus; Herod the Great, Rome's ruler of Palestine and the neighboring world; Pontius Pilate; the Roman governor of Judea; and others of earthly rank.

But those nearest to the birth of this child, the patient, uncomplaining, trusting folk, live on as faithful witnesses to the wonder of his birth.

When his parents took him to the temple at Jerusalem forty days after he was born, Anna, the aged prophetess in the temple, had the perception to speak the first words of Messianic hope to those looking for redemption in Jerusalem when she saw his parents enter the temple with him. She was the first to acclaim him as the Christ. Anna, this spiritually sensitive woman, was in tune with wonders in heaven above, and signs in the earth, as promised by Joel, the prophet of old.

The venerable Simeon, the priest in the temple, immediately sang praise to God for having seen his salvation when Mary and Joseph brought their child to the altar. Who but his mother could know that her son would increase in wisdom and stature and in favor with God and man? Who but she could keep all these things in her heart? Why? Because they were too filled with promise to spread abroad among strangers who would not understand. She and all these about her, who were intimate with revelations of the promises of the prophets, now saw God more than events and God in these events.

Those nearest the young Jesus realized that power no longer resided in an earthly emperor in Rome but in this new-born Savior and Lord, who would declare his allegiance not to an earthly kingdom but to the unseen Kingdom of God. And so great miracles now began to surround his birth, and these grew in wonder as the centuries passed.

The Spirit of Christmas

In the sixth century, Dionysius, the monk and scholar of scripture and astronomy, proposed that the entire course of history be reckoned from Christ's birth. All events before his birth were to be dated as "B.C." (before Christ). All after that were to be classified as A.D. (Anno Domini, the year of our Lord). Dionysius introduced the annunciation of the birth of Christ as the starting point of modern chronology and December 25 as Christmas. The entire calendar, first adopted in Europe and now used all over the world, remains a testimony to the spiritual riches that Christ brought with him. Ernest Renan, the nineteenth-century French historian, expressed it so well when he wrote, "All history is incomprehensible without Christ."

Many centuries have come and gone since time was turned around to honor Christ and since the world began to celebrate his birth.

How could this one solitary life become so real at Christmas? The explanation of the miracle is hidden in the Holy Spirit representing God as present and active in the spiritual experience of all people. It represents a presence that has neither shape nor form, as invisible but as real as a fresh breath of air.

The miracle of Christmas lies in Christ's own spirit as God's own Son. This miracle is surrounded by a mystic power that produces a harvest of love when a subtle force, a new thoughtfulness, animates the coldest person, even a Scrooge. This spirit of Christmas goes beyond that which pervades the earth at other times of the year. It goes deeper than the giving of gifts, the decorating with poinsettias, Christmas trees, wreaths of holly, and glimmering candles. A jolly Santa Claus and these other symbols of Christ are all a source of much joy, but only the outside wrappings.

Wondrous and unexplainable miracles abound. Suddenly every child is holy. Every kind word is a hymn. Every star shines brighter. The little town of Bethlehem seems to cry out the words of Phillips Brooks's carol,

> O holy child of Bethlehem!
>   Descend to us, we pray;
> Cast out our sin and enter in,
>   Be born in us today.
> We hear the Christmas angels
>   The great glad tidings tell;
> O come to us, abide with us,
>   Our Lord Emmanuel!

Another miracle is that we better comprehend the mystery of the word made flesh. A new radiance from Christ enlightens us, so that as we come to know God in visible form, we are caught up through him to the love of things invisible. And the sun on earth beneath turns in space like a gold wreath, for suddenly Christ is with us as we begin to experience the kind of love that is willing to forget self for others. We now know better the meaning of the word, "No man is all of himself. Those whom he loves and who love him are the rest of him."

We can not possess this oneness with the Messiah at Christmas or any other time unless we remember that his image signifies the greatest spiritual love imaginable, a new concept of self-giving based upon the life of Jesus, this man from Galilee, who dealt gently with the weak and discouraged, who discharged his high mission as a Son of God, who maintained his hope in God even when his labors were misunderstood by those he came to serve.

We celebrate best his humble spirit in the words of the nineteenth-century English poet Christina Rossetti,

> What can I give Him
> Poor as I am?
> If I were a shepherd,
> I would bring a lamb,
> If I were a Wise Man,
> I would do my part,—
> Yet what I can I give Him,
> Give my heart.

These words suggest so well the humble way of life of the child Jesus, who so soon after his birth at Bethlehem was to return to Nazareth with his parents, Mary and Joseph.

His Miraculous First Years

Evil schemers became jealous of this holy child, but Joseph was warned to flee to Egypt when it became known Herod was about to search for the child to destroy him.

After Herod's death, an angel appeared again in a dream to Joseph, telling him to take the mother and child and go into Israel, so he withdrew to the district of Galilee. And they dwelt in Nazareth, fulfilling what the prophet had spoken, "He shall be called a Nazarene" (Matt. 2:23), and each year of Christ's childhood, his parents journeyed with him from Nazareth to the Feast of the Passover at Jerusalem.

"When he was twelve years old, it is recorded that after they had left the Temple and had started on the homeward journey, they missed him. First thinking that he was journeying with another group of pilgrims on the dusty road behind, they were not concerned that their son was not at their side. The road was thronged with people, some on foot, some on donkeys, and some on fine riding camels. But at nightfall Mary and Joseph became anxious and turned back to find him. After a three-day search they discovered him in the Temple, sitting among the doctors at law" (*All of the Women of the Bible*, p. 165).

Until this time Jesus had been the silent, sweet, obedient child, but when his mother asked him why he had remained absent so long, he answered, "Do you not know that I must be about my Father's business?" Not even his parents discerned that he was wiser than his teachers and transcendentally greater. Although he was confident of his own mission, he remained obedient to his parents and went up for a time with them to Nazareth and was subject to them.

A greater change came over him after he was baptized by his cousin John the Baptist. As Jesus was praying, "the Holy Spirit descended upon him in bodily form, as a dove, and a voice came from heaven, 'Thou art my beloved son: and with thee I am well pleased'" (Luke 3:22).

A new sense of wonder filled Christ's being and others saw a radiance illuminate his face. Believers no longer doubted his messiahship.

For him the God of Israel began to reveal himself as the Lord and Savior of mankind, and John wrote, "He came to dwell among us, and we saw his glory, such glory as befits the Father's only son, full of grace and truth" (John 1:14, NEB).

THE PERSON OF JESUS CHRIST

God's love for man as revealed in the person of Jesus Christ is the central theme of his life. Slowly he emerged as a man who lived in the world but was not of it, who accomplished wonders spiritually but none of the things usually associated with material greatness.

Born in the likeness of man, he knew hunger and weariness, temptation and perplexity, uncertainty and disappointment, hard work and discouragement, and poignant human suffering. He was unlike other men in only one respect. He led a sinless life but never lost compassion for a sinning world, for he saw all human beings as children of God struggling toward the light.

He participated in all activities of other believing Jews. He read the books of the Old Testament. He took part in worship services. He observed the great festivals like the Passover. He fished with his disciples, tarried by the wayside to talk with strangers, sought sanctuary in the home of friends, Martha and Mary and others. He taught, preached, and knelt to pray.

Through his work we come to know that God is involved in the human situation. He does not hide himself from the ignorant and humble. He reveals himself to all men as an inviting God, a forgiving God, a seeking God, a God who is personal, selfless, a true Father who needs us as we need him.

Amid the wonders that unfolded around Christ, he warned his followers against unbelief when he declared, "I am not of this world, I am from above."

What he looked like no one really knows. All of the paintings of him are conceived from the artists' imagination. Only one ancient description exists, whether authentic or not no one knows. It was written in the year A.D. 32 by Publius Lentus, a resident of Judea in the reign of Tiberius Caesar. It says:

> There lives at this time in Judea a man of singular virtue —whose name is Jesus Christ. He is a tall man. His forehead is high, large, and imposing. His cheeks are without spot or

wrinkle, his nose and mouth are formed with exquisite symmetry. His beard is most suitable to his hair. In body proportion, he is most perfect.

Of his human appearance we probably will never be positive. But we are certain he was righteous, compassionate, concerned for all humanity, kind, never arrogant or proud but meek and lowly. He served as an itinerant preacher for less than three years, and yet in that service he turned the world upside down.

As one anonymous writer expressed it:

He never wrote a book. He never held an office. He never had a family or owned a house. He never went to a famous school. He never visited a city. He never traveled two hundred miles from the place where he was born. He had no credentials but himself.

Centuries have come and gone, and today he is the central figure of the human race, and the leader of mankind's progress. All the armies that ever marched, all the navies that ever sailed, all the parliaments that ever sat, all the kings that ever reigned, put together, have not affected the life of man on earth as much as that one solitary life.

And he lives on as the faithful and true servant of God who has gone forth as a forerunner in our behalf. Books in countless numbers continue to flow from the presses about him, but none describes him better than he described himself, "I am the way, the truth, and the life."

THE RADIANT PROPHET AND MINISTER

After Jesus was baptized by John the Baptist, as related in the preceding chapter, he was tempted in the wilderness:

The devil took him up to a high mountain and showed him all the kingdoms of the world and the glory of them; and he said to him [Jesus], "All these I will give you, if you will fall down and worship me." Then Jesus said to him, "Begone Satan! for it is written, 'You shall worship the Lord your God and him only shall you serve.' Then the devil left him, and behold, angels came and ministered to him."

(Matt. 4:8–10)

After Christ's denial of this and other temptations, he began his ministry with a proclamation of hope in a new way of life, a new relationship to God, a new form of consciousness. "The time is fulfilled," he said, "and the kingdom of God is at hand" (Mark 1:15). And now believers saw in him a new light.

Prophet that he was, when he went to minister in the synagogue at Nazareth on the Sabbath, as he had always done as a young boy, he stood up and read the scroll of the prophet Isaiah (Isa. 61:1–2). In his own words, Christ said,

> "The spirit of the Lord is upon me because he has anointed me;
> he has sent me to announce good news to the poor,
> to proclaim release for prisoners and recovery of sight for the blind;
> to let the broken victims go free,
> to proclaim the year of the Lord's favour."
> He rolled up the scroll, gave it back to the attendant, and sat down; and all eyes in the synagogue were fixed on him.
>   (Luke 4:18–20, NEB)

He went on to say that "in your hearing this text has come true."

What Christ began to accomplish in his far-reaching ministry is best expressed by Matthew (12:18–21): He it was who "shall lead justice on to victory"; he it was upon whom "the nations shall place their hope" (vs. 20–21, NEB).

One of Christ's first ministerial duties was to call his first four apostles, Peter and Andrew his brother and James the son of Zebedee and John his brother. Later, when he began preaching on the kingdom of God, he called his other eight apostles, Philip and Bartholomew, Thomas and Matthew, James the son of Alphaeus, Thaddaeus, Simon, and Judas Iscariot, who would betray him.

As he taught and preached, his messages took on many forms, some in conversations with friends, some in the presence of witnesses to his miracles, some to his disciples alone, some to crowds, some as parables, some through his own personal example. His messages were delivered in many places, some in Bethany and Jerusalem and others in Tyre and Sidon. Every word he spoke helps us to know better what God is and what the kingdom of Heaven is like.

"God is spirit, and those who worship him must worship in spirit and truth" (John 4:24), he told the woman of Samaria he met by the side of the well, a woman who had had five husbands and was now living with a man who was not her husband.

This is the Bible's best definition of what God is. It is remarkable that it came to the woman of Samaria, who had lived for carnal pleasures but who was now spiritually famished. This is also one of the best examples of Christ's everyday ministry to others, and this encounter, strangely enough, came about unexpectedly at a well.

The woman gave Christ water from the well but he gave her the eternal gift, living water for the soul. Having glimpsed this and the spirituality of all worship from Christ, the woman of Samaria went forth on winged feet to share with others in Samaria what she had learned from him.

This definition of God is the foundation stone of all of Christ's preaching and teaching. He had experienced the spirit of God from childhood. Then he had been baptized with the power of the spirit of God, as related in the preceding chapter. He had been led by the spirit and he had cast out demons by the spirit.

The inseparable three, God the father, Christ the son, and the Holy Spirit, were later unified in the doctrine of the Trinity. As Christ's disciples set forth to preach and to minister to others, this concept came into greater fullness. They proved to others how the spirit of God can purify and illuminate lives.

What then is Christ's concept of the Kingdom of God? "It is that condition of human life in which the will of God as revealed in Jesus Christ is in complete control" (*Harper's Bible Dictionary*, p. 367).

Christ enlarged upon this when he said the Kingdom of God is within each of us, if we but seek to dwell in God's invisible presence, but to do so, he further said, we must be born again. Then we become children of God set apart to do his will.

THE SERMON ON THE MOUNT

Many of Christ's basic teachings during his ministry appear in the Sermon on the Mount, recorded by Matthew in Chapters

5–7. Here Christ sets forth his unswerving devotion to God's will. The discourse in Luke is shorter but corresponds.

The master painters have portrayed Jesus as the visible bearer of the divine majesty. Truly he is this in the Sermon on the Mount, for here, as he upholds the highest essence of God, he explains the Christian life style of the true disciple.

Christ opens with the Beatitudes, in which he stresses the timeless rules for the good life. They describe the qualities of the true believer; the poor in spirit; those who mourn—not just those who are bereaved but also those who "bewail the ways of the world and long for the establishment of God's kingdom"; the meek, for they shall inherit the earth; those who hunger and thirst for righteousness; those who are merciful and pure in heart; those who are the peacemakers, for only these can come into God's presence. He also praises those who are persecuted for righteousness sake, because for these a reward is already laid up in heaven. Finally, he holds out great hope for those who are reviled and persecuted, against whom all kinds of false accusations are made. He reminds these that the prophets suffered the same kind of persecution.

In the Sermon on the Mount, Jesus also describes what the believer is like—"both the Salt of the Earth and the Light of the World."

Then he gives an exposition of several of the Ten Commandments, not according to the old law of Moses but according to the new laws of the kingdom of heaven. The greatest of these is the law of love. In essence, it means to love your enemies and to pray for those who persecute you.

Christ also explains the difference between the old righteousness and the new, that the test of a man's character is based upon his highest aspirations.

He tells how to pray, not on the street corners but in the quiet of one's own room, not with empty phrases but with a pure heart seeking to reach out:

Our Father who art in heaven,
    Hallowed be thy name.
Thy kingdom come,
Thy will be done,
    On earth as it is in heaven.
Give us this day our daily bread;

> And forgive us our debts,
> > As we also have forgiven our debtors;
> And lead us not into temptation,
> > But deliver us from evil.
> > > (Matt. 6:9–13)

He defines true riches, light and darkness, God and Mammon, trust and anxiety, censure and reproof, and in a few words sums up the Golden Rule: "Whatever you wish that men would do to you, do so to them" (Matt. 7:12).

An exhaustive study of the Sermon on the Mount provides the spiritual key to unlock the nature of God as revealed in the mystery of the Gospels, which are the "good news about Christ." Provided largely as teachings for his disciples, this sermon opened for them, and it opens for us, a vista upon a life that can be transformed by God.

The conclusion of this great sermon is a call to decision and a portrayal of Jesus as prophet and teacher.

THE MASTER TEACHER

In his book *The Mind of Jesus*, William Barclay says Christ was "one of the world's masters of the technique of teaching" (p. 89). Fifty times in the short space of the Gospels he is called "the teacher."

His teachings take in a wide scope of subjects, such as directions for Christian behavior, already mentioned, and instructions to his apostles. His teachings also encompass many human problems: anger, adultery, divorce, revenge, charity, fasting, riches in heaven, the payment of taxes, God and possessions, and judging others.

Christ's emphasis, always on the ethical, based on God's moral nature, includes everything from the blessedness of discipleship to the necessity of absolute obedience to the kingdom of heaven's demands. In all, he is the energizing, integrating force in the life of the believer.

Although the word "hope" is not used often by Jesus, it is implied in all his teachings. It does appear in Jesus' words in Luke

6:34 and John 5:45 of the Revised Standard Version, but it is not enlarged upon.

We find him teaching in the temple at Jerusalem, by the seashore, on a fishing boat, in the city streets to crowds, and along village roads in discussions with the foremost scholars and again to little children and the lowly. Some of his greatest teachings were in the intimate circles of his own apostles.

Christ taught in parables which reflect the contemporary scene, the good Samaritan, the sower, the hired laborers in the vineyard, the hidden treasure, the wedding garment, the wise and foolish virgins. He taught in word pictures too, none more colorful than that of the story of the demons that went from the men into a herd of swine, which disappeared in the sea. Living in a time with no means of printing, Christ had to teach in word pictures in order for his lessons to be remembered.

He also used the paradox, such as "unless you turn and become like children you will never enter the kingdom of heaven" (Matt. 18:3), and the hyperbole, such as "if your right hand causes you to sin, cut it off and throw it away; it is better that you lose one of your members than that your whole body go into hell" (Matt. 5:30). Dramatically he applied the unforgettable epigram, such as "whoever exalts himself will be humbled, and whoever humbles himself will be exalted" (Matt. 23:12). His messages were ethical, both timeless and universal. As Barclay concludes, "Jesus had something to say and he knew how to say it, and the teacher still will find in him the perfect model" (p. 97).

Most of all, Christ's messages hold forth hope in the good and belief in the invisible. In them there is a complete denial of hopelessness and despair, for such conditions can not exist in the Kingdom of God.

THE DIVINE HEALER

As compared to the moral and spiritual revelations of God, Christ's miracles were not his greatest works. And yet if we remove them, his Gospel loses much of its inspiration. Most of his miracles give action to his words and represent signs of another and higher order, leading on to a sphere of higher being and diviner possibilities for humanity.

Before Christ went up on the mountain to preach, "they [the people of Galilee] brought him all the sick, those afflicted with various diseases and pain, demoniacs, epileptics, and paralytics, and he healed them" (Matt. 4:24). His fame by now had spread as far away as Syria. He did what the prophet Isaiah had spoken, "he took our infirmities and bore our diseases" (Matt. 8:17).

He made the lame to walk, the blind to see, the deaf to hear. He cleansed lepers and he restored a withered hand to usefulness. He cast demons (devils, or malignant spirits) out of many. He stilled the waters of the sea, and he walked on the sea as if it were dry land. He also turned water into wine, and he miraculously fed the masses with little that was visible.

He raised three from the dead—Lazarus, the brother of Martha and Mary; the only son of the widow of Nain; and Jairus' daughter. To Martha, when he raised Lazarus, he said, "I am the resurrection and the life." To Jairus' daughter he confidently spoke, "Be not afraid, only believe." Absolute belief on the part of the petitioner or recipient was one of the secrets of his miracles. Matthew reports that Jesus "did not do many mighty works there [at Nazareth] because of their unbelief."

Jesus performed his miracles with a heart thankful to God. When he raised Lazarus from the dead, thanking God he said, "I knew that thou hearest me always, but I have said this on account of the people standing by, that they may believe that thou didst send me" (John 11:42). Among his believers present were Martha and Mary, as well as other witnesses, who saw Lazarus walk from the grave. Earlier Jesus "wept" when he saw Mary weeping over Lazarus, for he was deeply moved by her sorrow.

In all his healings he proved the power of the mind over matter, of the spirit over the body. He called them "works," a part of the day's labor for human beings sick and sorrowful.

Christ reached forth also to aid the rich and poor alike. Sometimes it might be a nobleman's son or a centurion's servant, or a poor woman with a crooked body or a forgotten woman with an issue of blood. He went about his miracles with a positive approach, a sense of dignity, and helpfulness. He might be beside the one ill, who was cured at his mere touch, or he might be far away and yet that one felt his touch.

Christ's healings were not confined to his time. He taught all believers how to do the same: "Therefore I tell you, whatever you ask in prayer, believe that you receive it and you will" (Mark 11:24).

As the great physician who teaches us that nothing is impossible, he gives us the hope to enter into triumphant spiritual experiences when we too can sense his oneness and feel his nearness to comfort and to heal.

THE LIGHT OF THE WORLD

Christ is "the true light that enlightens every man" (John 1:9). It is impossible to convey this true likeness in pictures, on canvas, in stained glass, tapestry, or marble, or in words on the printed page.

The Old Masters have brought us Christ in a panorama of magnificent and varied portrayals that have become the classics of the ages. He is the sad one in Leonardo's *Last Supper*, painted on the wall of what was a convent dining room in Milan. He is the inspired one in Raphael's *Transfiguration*, the man of miracles in Murillo's portrayal of his feeding of five thousand, the thoughtful guest in Veronese's painting of the wedding at Cana when he turns the water into wine. He is the wise one in Van Dyck's *Christ and the Tribute Money*.

These and other paintings by the Old Masters help us to see Christ as the true light of the world, who taught that we never need walk in darkness. Even at the Cross, he placed himself in the light. Several of the master artists have caught this halo of light around him at the Cross, as well as at other illuminating moments of his career. These pictures and others present him in many other aspects, as the suffering servant, the man of sorrow, the man of prayer, the friend of publicans and sinners, the good shepherd, the high priest, and the humble Nazarene.

He also was a man of sorrow when Judas betrayed him, when Thomas doubted him, when Peter denied him, when he foresaw that Jerusalem had not recognized that he had come to bring peace and he wept for them over what was to come.

We also know him as a man of joy, who went out among the lilies of the field, visited the busy little lake port of Capernaum, as one who prayed on the Mount of Olives and who walked up a high, unidentified mount with Peter, James, and John, where he was transfigured. Wherever Christ was, his heart and mind were filled with beauty, a beauty born of God.

He was the distressed one because he saw so much evil in Jerusalem. He was the positive one, running the money changers out of the temple. He was the forgiving one, even of the woman taken in adultery.

Christ could look deep into the faces of children, yellow, black, brown and white, knowing that children never resent one another, regardless of race. All children he saw as the hope of the world.

Appreciative of those who toiled with their hands, he became the master workman, busy in his father's carpenter shop. He was the inspirer who taught others how to pray, the consoler of the grieved as they stood over the grave of loved ones.

He was the exemplary one as he humbly washed the feet of Peter. He was the confident one who made his followers believe they could accomplish even greater works than he.

THE MAN OF PRAYER

In prayer Jesus lived, moved, and had his being. Through prayer he met every problem, conquered every foe, healed every disease.

He went up into the mountain to pray. He went into the wilderness to pray, into the synagogue, into the homes of friends. Prayer was his way of intimate communion with the Father.

Since he knew that God is a spirit, he sought to dwell in this spirit while in prayer and afterward was led by the spirit. This gift of the spirit was one of the threefold revelations of Christ, along with the Resurrection and the Church. He showed others that when believers seek to live in the spirit of prayer, life changes for them.

Often Christ prayed all night. He prayed for a right attitude toward others, for faith in God, for submission to God's will. He prayed when God had blessed him as in the feeding of the five thousand. He was praying when he was transfigured and again when he was in agony in Gethsemane, knowing he was on the way to the Cross. And he died on the Cross with a prayer.

His prayers seldom were for himself but for others, the mentally and physically ill, the needy, the sinners, and others with all manner of human needs. And always the purpose of his prayers was that others might behold his own manifestation of the glory of God, a gift that only God can give.

His private prayers were long, and something wondrous always took place afterward. He prayed long before he named his disciples, through whom the church came into being. In his high priestly prayer (John 17) before his betrayal and arrest, he again prayed for his disciples, asking God to keep them in his name and to sanctify them in the truth. He also prayed for the Church, asking that its members "may become perfectly one . . . that the love with which thou hast loved me may be in them, and I in them."

In this same prayer, even though his last hours had come, he asked nothing for himself, only that he be glorified "with the glory which I had with thee before the world was made."

His public prayers are much shorter than his private prayers, most of them less than a minute, some from only three to five seconds. The Lord's Prayer, in all its rhythmic cadence and harmonious transition from beginning to end, takes only forty-five seconds. His invocations at meals are terse, too; so are his blessings upon little children.

These are in keeping with Christ's advice to his disciples—"when you pray, go into your room and shut the door and pray to your father who is in secret; and your father who sees in secret will reward you. And in praying do not heap up empty phrases as the Gentiles do; for they think they will be heard for their many words" (Matt. 6:6–7).

Alone in his agony in the Garden of Gethsemane on the Mount of Olives, we see him as the humble Christ, the sorrowful

Christ, the Christ in conflict, but praying on persistently, sincerely, and obediently, positive that God heard him. Never was he more alone than here, for the disciples who had gone with him had fallen asleep.

Even during his crucifixion he never gave up hope in God's will, showing us that prayerful men of hope mature under the most difficult situations.

No matter what the circumstances, Christ persevered, "faithful over God's house as a son," showing us "we are his house if we hold fast our confidence and pride in our hope" (Heb. 3:6).

THE SUFFERING SERVANT TO THE END

At the end, only the few closest to Christ knew what bitter agony and excruciating pain awaited him. He already had prophesied that he would have to go to Jerusalem and suffer many things, death finally, but that he would rise on the third day. Isaiah's prophecy of old in his servant song (Isa. 53) had come to pass. Christ knew he was "despised and rejected by men, a man of sorrows, and acquainted with grief." He knew his life was a tragic failure to men but a glorious success to God.

He now promised his disciples that "If any man would come after me, let him deny himself and take up his cross and follow me."

Eight days later he was transfigured on a mountain in the presence of Peter and the brothers James and John, the only disciples to witness that moment when "his face shone like the sun, and his garments became white as light" (Matt. 17:2).

Even though he still had much to suffer, he was the activist to the end, not just the praying saint. Shortly after his transfiguration, not far from the garden tomb from which he would arise, he came down from the Mount of Olives to cure an epileptic boy, to restore sight to two blind men: then he discoursed on humility, presented new laws on church discipline, answered questions on marriage, and blessed little children.

After this he entered the region of Judea beyond the Jordan and large crowds followed him, many of whom he healed. He also answered the question from the ambitious mother of James and John, who asked that James might sit on one side of him in his kingdom and John on the other. But he told her this was not his to give.

Soon after this he made his triumphal entry into Jerusalem, "a king mounted on a colt, the foal of an ass." He paused to enter the temple at Jerusalem where he drove out the money-changers. His authority to speak out against evil was now challenged.

One of his last laments was over Jerusalem, which had killed the prophets and stoned others sent to help them.

The plot to kill Jesus was reaching such proportions that Mary of Bethany lovingly anointed him in preparation for his suffering at the Crucifixion. At the Last Supper he told his disciples, "My time is at hand." He also prophesied that one of the twelve disciples would betray him.

As his agony was about to begin, he went again to Gethsemane to pray, "My Father, if it be possible, let this cup pass from me: nevertheless, not as I will, but as thou wilt." Right after this, Judas betrayed him and his arrest followed. He was taken before Caiaphas, the high priest, and afterward delivered to Pontius Pilate by the Sanhedrin.

Then he took up the heavy weight of his cross and carried it along the Via Dolorosa, "the Way of Sorrow," amid scoffing crowds. In the distance were a few of his faithful followers, who stayed with him to the end, among whom were "many women, looking on from afar, who had followed Jesus from Galilee, ministering to him."

Jesus suffered every indignity possible. The local police arrested and bound him. Judas, the betrayer, kissed him, and then the crowds with Judas came out as against a robber with swords and clubs and seized him.

Caiaphas, the high priest, tore Christ's robe and accused him of blasphemy. The soldiers of the governor's battalion stripped him in the praetorium and put a scarlet robe upon him, plaited a crown of thorns, and put it on his head. They then spat on him, mocked him, slapped him in the face, and struck him in the head.

During Christ's earlier hour of agony in Gethsemane his sleeping disciples finally forsook him and fled. After this Peter thrice denied that he ever knew him.

For showing the world what the kingdom of God is like, Christ received a cross. For his denial of self, he was crucified between two thieves. While he was dying, his executioners gambled for his clothing, the only property he had on earth. When he was dead he was laid in a borrowed tomb.

Amid all of these afflictions which he bore, all to show us the way to God, he looked up and asked, "Father, forgive them, for they know not what they do."

Never has this tragedy at Calvary been more poignantly presented than in the Negro spiritual by an anonymous writer. These questions begin each of the six verses:

> Were you there when they crucified my Lord?
> Were you there when they pierced him in the side?
> Were you there when the sun refused to shine?
> Were you there when they laid him in the tomb?
> Were you there when he rose from the dead?
> Were you there when he ascended on high?

After each of these verses the spiritual rings out, "It causes us to shudder and tremble, tremble, tremble." Even in the last two verses when Christ has arisen and ascended on high, there are these same significant words, "it causes me to tremble, tremble, tremble."

THE HOPE OF EASTER

Christ sanctified the grave as a bed of hope, signifying to all believers that they are not to die as men without hope.

In the joy of Easter comes a song out of the darkness. It is heard in the trill of a mockingbird. It is seen in the first blossoms of spring, in the mighty oak that has burst forth from a tiny acorn, in the joyful faces of little children, in the power that releases us from the entrapping forces that waste life.

In such hope is the conviction that although death comes to all, in the end not death but life is triumphant, that although life often seems filled with hopelessness and despair, these will never completely foreclose on man's hopes or dreams.

Before these miracles there is uncertainty, but as life unfolds in all its fullness, assurance of new life finally asserts itself and will not let doubt have the last word.

With Easter, too, comes the promise that another day will bring a new chance. And out of this mysterious center comes a symphony of sound, the birth of a beautiful child, the miraculous unfolding of a rose from a dormant plant.

So it is in Christ's resurrection. In the same manner that he had raised Lazarus from the tomb, he too arose. His only witness was the faithful Mary Magdalene, who hurried to the apostles, who had left at the Crucifixion, to tell them what Jesus had said as his body changed from a material to a celestial form: "Do not hold me, for I have not yet ascended to the Father; but go to my brethren and say to them, I am ascending to my Father and your Father, to my God and your God" (John 20:17).

Even the apostles were not prepared for this evidence of his resurrection. It was such a change from the despair of the Crucifixion that it could only be explained as a rebirth.

In such an experience the soul is no longer housed in a material body, as if it were still a part of the womb of earth, but is now born into a new dimension beyond the material scope. The new man is no longer an heir of his material parents but an heir of God and an inheritor of new spiritual legacies, among which are salvation, the grace of God, and a new being immune to the contamination of the world.

When Christ ascended forty days after the Resurrection, his followers were not yet beyond the reach of death, but they were now able to participate in the life of the Resurrection. When two of the apostles, not having heard of the Resurrection, were walking to Emmaus, they still were sorrowing for their crucified Lord. Jesus himself drew near them. Not recognizing him, they answered him as if he were a stranger, and said, "We had hoped that he [this Jesus of Nazareth] was the one to redeem Israel" (Luke 24:21). But they had been to the tomb and did not find his body.

He said to them, "O foolish men, and slow of heart to believe all that the prophets have spoken! Was it not necessary that Christ

should suffer these things and enter into his glory?" (Luke 24:25).
Later Christ and these two disciples joined the other ten disciples
in Jerusalem and he showed them the holes in his hands and
feet.

The Ascension into the unknown did not signify that the same
body had been raised in the Resurrection but that a new celestial
body had been born and that it was ready for a new mode of existence and a new set of relationships on another plane of
existence.

He had passed this way only thirty-three short years. But
through the aeons of time, his life stands out as the perfect one in
history. The exemplary life he led shows us how to draw nearer to
God himself and to live according to a pattern of righteousness.

Christ is still the center of the evolving universe. His resurrection, the living hope of the world, is the greatest of all of his miracles and the proof of his deity. It places him at the center of
the universe and as the fountainhead of the Christian faith. His
example makes all things possible, even our own resurrection. This
is positively expressed in these words: ". . . if the Spirit of him
who raised Jesus from the dead dwells within you, then the God
who raised Christ Jesus from the dead will also give new life to
your mortal bodies through his indwelling Spirit" (Rom. 8:11,
NEB).

Finally, in the First Letter of Peter is this, the most hopeful
message on hope in the New Testament:

> Praise be to the God and Father of our Lord Jesus Christ,
> who in his great mercy gave us new birth into a living hope
> by the resurrection of Jesus Christ from the dead! The in-
> heritance to which we are born is one that nothing can de-
> stroy or spoil or wither. It is kept for you in heaven, and you,
> because you put your faith in God, are under the protection
> of his power until salvation comes—the salvation which is
> even now in readiness and will be revealed at the end of time.
> (I. Pet. 1:3-5, NEB)

The ensuing lines in this chapter, including the one saying,
"Fix your hopes on the gift of grace" (v. 13), assure you, that even
though trials beset you, they purify your faith and fill you with
greater love for the Risen Christ, the living hope of the world.

CHAPTER 17

*The Twelve Disciples: Communicators of Hope
in Christ*

*According to Mark, the twelve disciples were Simon (Peter),
James, John, Andrew, Philip, Bartholomew, Matthew, Thomas,
James the son of Alphaeus, Thaddaeus, Simon the Canaanean
and Judas Iscariot. Matthias (not to be confused with Matthew),
the thirteenth disciple, was named after Judas' betrayal.*

What an unexpected hope for greatness was fulfilled in these
humble men of Galilee! Unsophisticated, unlettered, unfamiliar
with the material destinies of mankind as governed by the affluent,
the powerful, and the tricky, these disciples (afterward to become
fishers of men) achieved eminence despite their own guilelessness.

How could these ordinary men become such extraordinary men?
Through faith in Jesus Christ, who came to reveal humanity at
its highest and best, and through preparation for their disciple-
ships from the Savior himself, in whom they were "one in hope."
Thus armed, these twelve, named collectively above and individually below, set forth to teach and to preach the highest ethics
ever set for mankind.

The number "twelve" had a mystic meaning. The coming of
Christ, the head of a divine government and a universal religion,
represented a spiritual culmination of many hopeful promises
of old. In explaining to the twelve the meaning of their mission,
he said, "You who have followed me will also sit on twelve
thrones, judging the twelve tribes of Israel" (Matt. 19:28).

The time was right for the twelve disciples to communicate hope in Christ, for Christian believers were now sustained by the inexhaustible resources of a believing hope, fulfilled in both the resurrection and ascension of Jesus Christ.

Those convictions, worthy of hope, salvation, eternal life, and the glory of God as revealed through his son, all are integrated in Christ himself. And the disciples helped to perpetuate them, as they courageously went forward, confident that if hope in the Gospel was to be realized, they must embrace its message and transform the thoughts and actions of unbelievers.

THEIR EXPECTANT MISSION

Although their place in the Gospels and the Book of Acts is lofty, they are never magnified as persons. Jesus alone is magnified, as the Son of God. Before he chose the disciples, he went into the hills and prayed all night. Then he announced their names and explained to them their mission, which was to go forth and preach that the kingdom of God (the rule of God) was at hand, to heal the sick and to cast out demons, to raise the dead, to cleanse lepers, to seek out widows and orphans, the infirm, and the afflicted, and to free debtors persecuted by creditors.

He also gave the disciples instruction on the nature of the divine kingdom, on prayer and true holiness, on his own person and claims, on the doctrine of the Cross and his coming death, on humility and other virtues, and on the doctrine of self-sacrifice. These services undergirded Christ's universal religion, inspired with a love large enough to embrace all mankind.

Jesus also instructed his disciples to live simply, neither to carry extra money in their belts nor a staff to lean on, nor extra tunics or sandals.

As they trudged from village to village, they were guests in homes of believers. When others were not receptive to the Christian message, they moved on, as he advised. They also sought, as he admonished them, to be wise as serpents and harmless as doves among unbelievers. As they went about spreading the Good News, the disciples often were hated, maligned, persecuted, and flogged, but no matter what they suffered, they continued on their mission, that of nurturing in its cradle the infant Church that was to come.

And so it was these unmoneyed men of humble birth, no education, and lowly occupations took up his cross and became servants in his work. Often they faltered in what Christ would have them become, but because they consecrated their lives to his mission, all except Judas Iscariot grew in nobility.

Uplifted by Jesus' words, "In the world you have tribulation, but be of good cheer, I have overcome the world" (John 16:33), they willingly accepted their role calling for change, bringing not material but heavenly rewards. Inspired with renewed zeal in their sacrificial service, they remembered also that Jesus had said: those who kill the body cannot kill the soul. Willing to forsake family, friends, and comforts, they ministered to many, strengthening Christ daily, because they were willing to forsake all and follow him.

In his definitive work, *The Training of the Twelve*, first published more than one hundred years ago, A. B. Bruce points out that the faith of the disciples was what one would expect in beginners, but it was valuable in that it brought them into close fellowship with Christ, in whose company they were to see greater things than when they first believed. This truth, growing constantly, Bruce declared, was "like the stars appearing in the evening sky as daylight fades" (p. 10).

What kind of men were these twelve disciples as listed in Matthew 10:2–4, Mark 3:16–19, Luke 6:14–16, and Acts 1:13? Much discussion centers around their names as listed in the Gospels and Acts. And these vary in different gospels, but this chapter follows the listing of Mark, the oldest of the Gospel writers.

1. PETER (ALSO SIMON BAR-JONA, SIMEON, CEPHAS): "THOU ART THE CHRIST"

Peter's name appears first on all the Gospel lists of the disciples. Because of his leadership in the establishment of the New Testament Church, he is often called the "Pillar Apostle."

He was a son of Jona, the head of a hospitable family at Beth-

saida, a fishing village on the north shore of the Sea of Galilee.
Like his older brother Andrew, Peter was a fisherman. Because
of his size he is often referred to as the "Big Fisherman."

The two brothers, Andrew and Peter, were fishing partners of
two other brothers, James and John, the sons of Zebedee. All four
were called into service by Jesus as they were mending their nets.

Peter made a home for his wife, his mother-in-law, whom Jesus
healed, and Andrew, who took Peter to Jesus. At that time there
was some doubt and confusion in the minds of other disciples
about Christ's Messiahship, but Peter blurted out, "You are the
Christ, the Son of the living God" (Matt. 16:16). Recognizing
that Peter had planted his feet on the rock of eternal truth, Christ
praised Peter for his faith, saying, "Blessed are you, Simon Bar-
Jona! For flesh and blood has not revealed this to you, but my
Father who is in heaven. And I tell you, you are Peter, and on this
rock I will build my church, and the powers of death shall not prevail against it" (vs. 17–18).

Was Peter born great? Or was greatness forced upon him? His
pre-eminence seemed predestined when he declared Jesus was the
Messiah, a fact confirmed later when Jesus went with Peter, James,
and John on a high mountain, where he was transfigured. They
heard God speak, "This is my beloved son with whom I am well
pleased; listen to him" (Matt. 17:5).

Peter not only walked with Jesus as a witness to some of his
greatest triumphs, but he possessed many qualities of greatness
that placed him in the forefront of the disciples. He was a born
leader, courageous, immovable, valiant, fearless. What's more, he
was a seeker after truth and sought information from Christ himself on the parable of the good steward, the laws of forgiveness
and defilement, and the prophecy concerning Jesus' second
coming.

Peter also performed many miracles, until people longed to be
in his shadow. He walked on the Sea of Galilee. He cured Aeneas
of palsy. He raised Dorcas (Tabitha), the charitable woman at
Joppa, from the dead. Having been present when Jesus healed
his (Peter's) mother-in-law and when he raised Jairus' daughter
from the dead, Peter learned at firsthand what it was to serve
others in their sorrows and afflictions.

But with all of his admirable qualities and spiritual powers, Peter was full of contradictions. He was hopelessly unstable at times. He could not deny himself easily. He found it difficult to do as he was bidden, preferring first to look around to see what others were doing. He was naturally impulsive, presumptuous at times, cowardly at times, and slow to apprehend deeper truths. While he made two great confessions of faith in Christ, he also thrice denied Christ after his betrayal and arrest at a time when Christ most needed Peter. Peter suffered grievously over this sin. Afterward, remembering Christ's loving but pained look, Peter went out and wept bitterly.

He also lost faith when Christ was crucified and he went home, leaving Christ all alone. However, Peter took the lead afterward in investigating Mary Magdalene's account of the open tomb and Jesus' words, "I ascend unto my Father." Peter was the first of the disciples to enter the open tomb after Christ arose on the third day. This time he appeared first to Peter (Cephas) and then to the others (I Cor. 15:5).

Following the Resurrection, when Jesus appeared to his disciples at the Sea of Galilee, Peter swam out to meet Christ, who conferred on him the office of chief shepherd of his flock. Peter's service to the Church, as recounted in the first twelve chapters of Acts, were manifold. These are further delineated in the last section of this chapter on the onward march of the Church.

Although the First and Second Letters of Peter open with a salutation from him and include many of his experiences and thoughts, there is some question among scholars about whether he wrote them. But the Gospel story highlights Peter more than any other disciple. He is their leader and spokesman. Peter, the Big Fisherman, the Evangelist, the Church Administrator, the Man of Prayer—in these and other roles Peter stands tall in the history of the New Testament Church, right next to Paul, the greatest of the apostles.

The great dome of St. Peter's in Rome bears these words in Latin in golden letters, thought to have been spoken by Christ, "Peter lived and died for the church that it might not perish from the earth."

2. Andrew: First Disciple to See Christ

While John the Baptist was baptizing at Bethany beyond the Jordan, Andrew and his younger brother Peter became his disciples. Andrew was the first who heard John speak, and he followed him. Then he found Simon Peter and said to him, " 'We have found the Messiah' . . . He brought him to Jesus. Jesus looked at him, and said, 'So you are Simon the son of John? You shall be called Cephas' (which means Peter)" (John 1:41–42).

In this act "Andrew may have done more thereby for the cause of Christ than did any of the other disciples," says Emil G. Kraeling, author of *The Disciples*, who also calls Andrew the first confessor of Jesus' Messiahship as well as "a sort of secretary in charge of appointments to interview the Master" (pp. 28–29).

A fisherman by trade, Andrew, like Peter, might be called "the first fisher of men," for Jesus said to him, "Come with me, and I will make you a fisher of men." He and Peter were casting their nets in their father's boat when Jesus called them, and they threw down their nets and went with him.

Andrew might also be called the first missionary of the disciples. Before his last public discourse, Andrew told Jesus that the Greeks wished to see him. This showed Jesus the growing interest of the Gentiles in his message. Philip had the same opportunity but he was hesitant to make the report. Again, unlike the perplexed Philip, Andrew reported the lad's five loaves and fishes, which Jesus multiplied to feed the five thousand.

Loyal to the end, Andrew went with Peter and James and John to the Mount of Olives and conversed with Jesus about things to come: when Jerusalem would be destroyed, what would be the signs of Christ's coming again, and the time of the end of the world. But Jesus did not fix a time for any of these. He did say that many kingdoms would rise and fall and there would be wars and rumors of wars, famines, earthquakes, pestilences, violence, sorrow, falsehood.

This loyal disciple Andrew was not as eloquent as his brother Peter but he was faithful to the cause of Jesus to the end. He did not seek a big role but he lived a big one. No great cathedral like St. Peter's in Rome is named for Andrew but thousands of smaller churches are named "St. Andrew's."

3, 4. JAMES AND JOHN: THE SONS OF ZEBEDEE

While mending their nets in a boat with their father, Zebedee, James and John, without hesitation, left their fishing nets with the hired servants and went with Jesus when he called them to be his disciples. And they became one in their service to their master, who surnamed them "Boanerges" (sons of thunder), meaning they possessed fiery eloquence.

They were at the synagogue when Jesus healed the man with the unclean spirit, at Simon Peter's house when Jesus healed his mother-in-law, and on the mountaintop as witnesses to the Transfiguration, as already cited.

Probably because he was the older, James asked to sit at the right hand of Jesus. Joining in the request, John asked to sit at the left. Their mother, Salome, made the same request for her two sons. Jesus' answer to all was, "To sit on my right hand, and on my left, is not mine to give, but it shall be given to them for whom it is prepared of my Father."

These two brothers no doubt met the needed qualifications of true discipleship, for at the Last Supper they were sitting at the places they had requested. Both also were at the trial of Jesus and at the Sea of Galilee when Jesus revealed himself after the Resurrection.

James, it is thought, preached in Palestine and Egypt. John became the more active in the Church after James was killed by Herod Antipas with a sword. However, both are mentioned along with Peter as pillars of the early Church (Gal. 2:9). Some scholars have asked, "Could this be another James?" This is not thought to be likely, for throughout their early lives together, James and John walked side by side and usually with Jesus and Peter and Andrew.

It is quite probable that this John was the disciple Jesus loved and to whom he entrusted his mother at the last. This John also figured more prominently at the Resurrection. He also was with Peter when he gave his second sermon in Jerusalem and when he healed the lame man. He is also thought by some to be the John who labored among the churches of Asia Minor, especially at Ephesus.

The Letters of John and the Book of Revelation may have been written by this John, but the Letter of James may have been the work of James, the brother of Jesus. One thing is certain about these two brothers: they were true servants of the Lord.

5. Philip: First to Call Jesus a Prophet

Philip, along with Andrew, heard Jesus make the solemn announcement, "The hour is come that the Son of Man should be glorified." The day after that, Jesus was baptized by John the Baptist at the Jordan and was about to leave from there for Galilee when he came upon the unassuming Philip, who asked to be one of his disciples.

Now guided by Christ, Philip zealously went forth from his home at Bethsaida, on the Sea of Galilee, to aid Jesus in his work. He clearly recognized him now as the one of whom Moses and the prophets spoke, the one whom God had raised up as a prophet for his people as proclaimed in Deut. 18:15, and also the one who would "bring forth justice to the nations" (Isa. 42:1).

Philip, no doubt a friend of Andrew and Peter, was the disciple who gathered provisions for Jesus and his company. Andrew was the first to be the medium of communication between the Gentile world and Jesus. Andrew in turn took Philip into his counsel.

Philip appears in one of Jesus' major discourses on the way, the truth, and the life (John 14:1–11). Here Philip shows his slowness to understand Christ's relationship to the Father when he asked, "Lord, show us the Father, and we shall be satisfied." And Jesus asked Philip, "Do you not believe that I am in the Father and the Father in me?" (vs. 8, 10).

Then Philip heard Jesus speak of the promises of greater works to come, the Holy Spirit, and peace to come, and all the disciples who heard were filled with new hope.

Philip was the one, too, who introduced his friend Bartholomew to Jesus. Philip, along with Andrew, was present when Jesus said, "The hour has come for the Son of man to be glorified" (John 12:23). Philip also was with the faithful who prayed in the upper room after Christ's ascension.

This Philip, the disciple, is not to be confused with another, later, Philip, the evangelist and father of the four daughters who prophesied.

6. BARTHOLOMEW (NATHANAEL): A MEDITATIVE MAN

Bartholomew, listed in Matthew, Mark, Luke, and Acts, is usually identified with Nathanael of John 1:43–51. Bartholomew appears after Philip in the first three Gospels and Nathanael is in the same position in the fourth gospel, so "Bartholomew" may not be this disciple's full name. If we can equate Bartholomew with Nathanael, then we have some insight into this disciple's mystic nature.

Everything about him shows that he was a man of moral excellence, spiritual depth, open-mindedness, honesty, and frankness.

John records that Nathanael hesitated about accepting Jesus of Nazareth as the Messiah, not because he doubted him but because he could not believe one so great could come from a village adjacent to his own rural Cana. Because of his own prompt declaration of faith in Jesus, when he finally conversed with Jesus, we see this disciple filled with hope and faith in Jesus as the Son of God and the King of Israel.

In his confession of faith, Nathanael gave Jesus for the first time the title "Son of God" (John 1:49). Alluding to Jacob's experience at Bethel, Jesus answered Nathanael, "Truly, truly, I say to you, you will see heaven opened, and the angels of God ascending and descending upon man" (v. 51). This declaration from the Master himself gave Nathanael and the other disciples new hope in their destiny, but more than that, a wondrous concept of the glory of life in Christ. They were now willing to give all for his cause.

Nathanael is listed again after the Crucifixion with that faithful group when Jesus appeared to them at the Sea of Galilee. Whether this Nathanael and Bartholomew are one or two persons, there is no certainty, but, again, dedication, faith, and sincerity are common to both men, and, after all, the character of a man is of more significance than his first or his last name.

7. MATTHEW (LEVI): THE TAX COLLECTOR

No greater command could have come to a disciple than Jesus' words to Matthew, "Follow me." Matthew was then sitting in his tax-collecting booth on the overland customs route at Capernaum, between Damascus and the Mediterranean, when Jesus came walking along the road by the shore of the Sea of Galilee. Matthew left his booth and followed Jesus, who had chosen Matthew not for what he was but for what he could become.

The names of "Levi" and "Matthew" are thought to be the same, says Kraeling. "In the narrative of Mark, we read of a publican or tax collector called Levi, son of Alphaeus (Mark 2:14). In the first Gospel's account (though not in Luke's) his name is altered to Matthew (Matt. 9:9). Rather strangely there is no Levi son of Alphaeus in the lists of the Twelve; a Matthew appears in them, instead, and in that of the first Gospel the designation 'the publican' is added to the name. Since there was a James son of Alphaeus among the Twelve, one may suppose that he and Levi were brothers. Whether Levi changed his name to Matthew, or whether Levi and Matthew were different persons who have become fused in retrospect are questions that cannot be answered with certainty" (*The Disciples*, p. 157).

The early Church believed that Matthew was the author of the Gospel According to Matthew, recognized early as the most comprehensive record of the life of Jesus. Many Renaissance paintings accentuate this. Eusebius, one of the early historians, says Matthew and John were the only disciples of Jesus to leave writings.

As a tax collector who kept accounts, Matthew was qualified to write a Gospel record. If he did, he performed a great service in explaining the Old Testament's hopeful prophecies fulfilled in Christ and in his genealogy going back to Abraham and David.

8. THOMAS: "THE DOUBTING ONE"

Thomas was both great and small. He also possessed a steadfast loyalty that made him stand by Jesus in spite of danger. Thomas, a quiet reflective type, also insisted on finding the truth out for himself, rather than accepting the testimony of friends.

Although he appears in all four lists of the disciples, he is more prominently featured in the Gospel of John, particularly in the conversation with Jesus after the Last Supper when he asked, "Lord, we do not know where you are going; how can we know the way?" Jesus replied, "I am the way, and the truth, and the life; no one comes to the Father, but by me. If you had known me, you would have known my Father also" (John 14:5–7). The doubting Thomas could not grasp Jesus' thoughts on eternal life until Jesus explained it to him.

It is to Thomas' credit that he understood earlier, before the other disciples, that Jesus would be on the way to his death. When Christ said, "'Lazarus is dead . . . let us go to him,' Thomas, called the Twin, said to his fellow disciples, 'Let us also go, that we may die with him'" (John 11:14–16).

After Christ's resurrection and appearance to the ten in Jerusalem, Thomas, inclined to be pessimistic, had to be shown the nail wounds in his hand. He had to place his finger in the mark of the nails and his hand on Christ's side before he would believe that he was the risen Christ. Eight days later, when Jesus appeared to Thomas and the ten, Thomas declared, "My Lord and my God!" (John 20:28). Jesus then asked Thomas, "Have you believed because you have seen me? Blessed are those who have not seen and yet believe" (v. 29).

Thomas of Galilee is also called by his surname of Didymus (the Greek for "twin"). He is thought to have carried the Gospel to India and is claimed by Syrian Christians to be the founder of their Church.

9. The Other James: The Son of Alphaeus

James, the brother of Jesus, is not to be confused with this James, the son of Alphaeus, mentioned earlier. James, the son of Alphaeus, is sometimes called James the Less (meaning of small stature), or James the Younger, or James the Just, but he refers to himself as "a servant of God and of the Lord Jesus Christ."

Ecclesiastical differences have arisen around this James since the time of the first-century historians, Josephus and Origen, and the fourth-century Church fathers, Jerome and St. Augustine. If the latter two were right, this James might be the author of the Letter of James and resident head of the mother church in Jerusalem and next to Peter in authority in the early Church.

Probably the most inspiring connection of this James with Christ is that Christ appeared to him in the Resurrection, then to all the apostles (I Cor. 15:7). This James embodied the living spirit of Jesus' teaching and was a man who labored hard in the Church for the cause of Christ, both before his resurrection and afterward.

10. Simon the Canaanean (Judas, Son of James?): The Least Known One

Each of the four lists of the disciples has a second Simon who is not Simon Peter. These second Simons have caused confusion among scholars for centuries. The oldest translation of Matthew and Mark from the Latin Vulgate refer to "the Canaanean," probably the correct designation.

In the other two lists, Luke 6:14–16 and Acts 1:13, there is no Canaanean mentioned. The name in his place is Judas the son of James. Since the Revised Standard Version is the basic text for this book and Kraeling is the most quoted authority on the disciples, this book follows Kraeling's listing on page 15 of *The Disciples.*

There is no positive identification for any of the activities of this disciple. What his name was, what his background was—these are not that important. That he was trained by Jesus himself as a disciple, that he must have lived to become an apostle, and that he was with the apostles when "all these with one accord devoted themselves to prayer" places this disciple among the never-forgotten Christians of New Testament history.

11. THADDAEUS (SIMON THE ZEALOT?): ONE OF THE LESSER LIGHTS

Thaddaeus, like the preceding disciple, has been the subject of much controversy. Some have identified him with Simon the Zealot (Zelotes, in Acts).

The King James Version of Matthew 10:3 reads "Lebbaeus, whose surname was Thaddaeus." Again, this disciple has been called "Jude" or "Judas." The Revised Standard Version and other versions list these readings in footnotes.

This wide variation in names has been explained in different ways, one being that a few deceased members of the twelve were supplanted by new disciples, whose names were used in later texts.

In this book, keyed to the theme of hope, we only know that this disciple was one of the original twelve. Although one of the lesser lights, he was there when Jesus told the disciples what their mission would be, when he gave them his farewell address before his ascension, and finally when the apostles participated in the founding of the Church at Jerusalem. He also took part in many other miracles recounted in Acts, the Bible book that highlights the most important acts of these apostles, personally appointed by Jesus.

12. JUDAS ISCARIOT: THE HOPELESS TRAITOR

Jesus knew from the moment of his selection of his disciples that there was one who would betray him. "Did I not choose you, the twelve, and one of you is a devil?" (John 6:70).

Judas is thought to have been the one who asked why Mary of Bethany wasted the ointment on the anointing of the feet of Jesus when it might have been sold for three hundred denarii, which could then be given to the poor. Judas was the only one who voiced such criticism. After this anointing, the money-loving Judas went to the chief priest with the offer to betray Jesus. Matthew clarifies the point as to the amount: thirty pieces of silver. Luke sees Satan as entering into Judas at this moment.

During the Last Supper, Jesus further declared, "One will betray me, one who is eating with me" (Mark 14:18). When Judas asked, "Is it I, Master?" Jesus answered "You have said so" (Matt. 26:25).

When the hour for his betrayal was at hand, Jesus awakened Peter, James, and John, saying, "The hour has come, the Son of Man is betrayed into the hands of sinners. Rise, let us be going; see, my betrayer is at hand" (Mark 14:41–42). Judas arrived with a crowd carrying swords and clubs, and, in kissing Jesus on the cheek, he led the chief priests, scribes, and elders right to him. Christ's arrest followed. The remorseful betrayer later admitted, "I have sinned in betraying innocent blood" (Matt. 27:3).

What became of Judas and his money? He tried to cast it into the treasury in the house of the Lord. But this was blood money and it was not accepted.

It is finally concluded in Matthew 27:5 that Judas hanged himself. There is also this other version: Peter declares "Now this man [Judas] bought a field with the reward of his wickedness; and falling headlong he burst open in the middle and all his bowels gushed out. And it became known to all the inhabitants of Jerusalem, so that the field was called . . . Field of Blood" (Acts 1:18–19).

THE APOSTOLIC COMMAND: AN ANCHOR FOR HOPE

Ready to assume the robe of divine majesty, as typified in the Ascension, Christ now summoned the eleven disciples and presented this, his apostolic mission, to them.

> Full authority has been given
>   to me
> both in heaven and on earth;
> go, therefore, and make disciples
>   of all nations.
> Baptize them in the name
> "of the Father,
> and of the Son,
> and of the Holy Spirit."
> Teach them to carry out
>   everything I have commanded you.
> And know that I am with you
>   always, until the end of the world!
>   (Matt. 28:18-20, NAB)

With Christ yet among them, the disciples realized they were still learners, as the word disciple implies. As witnesses to his person and his ministry, empowered by him to go forward in his work, soon they would become apostles. Though they no doubt felt their own weaknesses and feared their ability to follow out this his last command, at the same time they had a strong anchor in the immutable promises of God and in the knowledge of the eternal presence of Christ.

He not only had shown them a life with God but a life from God and had made them realize that God had a loving purpose for all men and that they as apostles must now go forth and teach others what Christ had taught them—a right relationship with men and God. Without this there could be no hope for them or for mankind.

This apostolic mission was worthy of Jesus, but how could these poor Galilean fishermen be worthy to receive it? By themselves they could do nothing, but he had promised them there would come a power from on high. This would be their spiritual legacy and their inspiration, and when it would manifest itself in a spirit of love, they would no longer be weak men but strong men, taught by Jesus himself in the mysteries and promises of the kingdom. Soon they would know he had left them more than eloquence or money or material power.

A noble and challenging responsibility now lay ahead of the apostles. They must not be frustrated or hopeless but ready to carry forward in a great undertaking, the establishment of a spiritual and universal religion, with Christ as the head.

As they prepared for their mission, they no doubt understood better Christ's intercessory prayer (John 17:6–19), one of unparalleled sublimity. It is in three divisions: his own glorification as the Son of God; the sanctification of the disciples, and the prayer for the Church.

The apostles were beginning to know what it was to be a part of a communion of believers combining an organic unity of those who belong to the mystical body of Christ. While his struggles had ended, theirs would just begin, in a world-wide mission for which he had prepared them.

THEIR ONWARD MARCH FOR THE CHURCH

While they waited for a power from on high, the disciples assembled together and prayed in an upper room in Jerusalem. Like the moth arising from the chrysalis stage into the winged state of a butterfly, suddenly the miracle of Pentecost came, a sound from heaven "like the rush of a mighty wind and it filled the house where they were sitting . . . and they were all filled with the Holy Spirit" (Acts 2:2,4). Now they spoke with a new boldness.

After this miracle of Pentecost, the disciples, one in the body of Christ, developed into an inspired apostolate with one concern, the triumph of Christ's Church. They were even more inspired after Peter's great Pentecostal sermon (Acts 2:14–36), after which about three thousand converts were added to the Church. Peter, now "born anew to a living hope," would lead the disciples forth to bear their testimony to the resurrection of the Lord Jesus.

Soon the Sanhedrin began to wonder at the power of these uneducated, common men like Peter and the other ten, who were bringing new converts to Christ. At Peter's suggestion the twelfth, Matthias, was elected in the place left vacant after Judas Iscariot betrayed Jesus.

As converts multiplied, persecutions increased, and all of the apostles were put in a common prison. But the Bible tells us that "an angel of the Lord opened the prison doors and brought them out" (Acts 5:19).

After this, Peter, the leader in the infant Church, and the others continued in the ministry of witnessing, preaching, and healing. He went before the Sanhedrin and defended the Church. He participated in the first Jerusalem conference, called to establish rules for the growing Church. He took the responsibility of investigating conditions in Samaria. He converted the Gentile centurion Cornelius and afterward baptized him and his household. When Church stewardship was violated, as in the case of Ananias and Sapphira, Peter acted as judge.

The more Peter and the other apostles accomplished, the greater their persecution. Once, when the inspired Peter was bound in two chains, an angel appeared again and said to him, "Get up quickly." And the chains fell off his hands. Regardless of the suffering of Peter and the others, "the word of God grew and multiplied" (Acts 12:24).

Those who had been hopeless men at the Crucifixion, now were transformed into stalwart men, willing to attack the impossible. They were paving the way for the coming of the greater apostle Paul, who would go forward on "the right hand of fellowship" (Gal. 1:9), extended to him by Peter, James, and John. The Church could not perish, for these earliest apostles had triumphed valiantly as the successful communicators of hope in Christ.

But they, like Christ before them, not only had borne many crosses, but they were to bear others. Tradition has it that four, Simon Peter, Andrew, James the younger, and Thaddaeus were crucified, that James the son of Zebedee, was beheaded by Herod at Jerusalem, that Bartholomew was flayed to death, that Simon the Canaanean, Matthew, and Thomas died as martyrs. Judas Iscariot had already taken his own life. Only two, John and Philip, died natural deaths.

Had they not been willing to die as martyrs, Christianity would have suffered, because it is the cause and not merely the death that makes the martyr. By the mere act of suffering, the disciples proved their own faith. It is no wonder that St. Jerome could say several centuries later, "the blood of the martyrs is the seed of the Church."

CHAPTER 18

Paul: His Steadfast Hope in Jesus Christ

Christ's greatest apostle, Paul, was founder of churches, author or inspirer of many of the New Testament letters, and a missionary who played a vital part in shaping the history of the Western world.

Paul, the mastermind of the apostolic age, is the most towering figure after Jesus in the New Testament. He wrote probably a third of it and had more to say about hope than any writer in the Bible. In Col. 1:23, he calls himself the minister of the gospel of hope.

A religious genius, he lived in two worlds: the visible, transitory world of death, corruption, heartache, and persecution and the invisible, imperishable world of the spirit, where there is neither hopelessness nor despair.

Although born in an area filled with evil, slavery, sexual immorality, cruelty, and callousness to human suffering, as well as countless physical barriers, illiteracy, paganism, poor communications, and difficult travel conditions, he labored on tirelessly to glorify Christ as the long-awaited Messiah, the light of the gospel, and the basis of the Christian hope. The validity of the promise to the patriarchs and the prophecies to the prophets were confirmed in the resurrection of Jesus Christ; and it was Paul who went forth as its chief spokesman.

In times when we are inclined to view our own world negatively and fearfully, it is heartening to remember that the Christian faith, with Paul as its first evangelist, took root and flourished amazingly amid conditions that would have suddenly killed anything less vital. To churches springing up all over this ancient world, Paul took his doctrine of faith in Christ. To Rome, the capital of the Roman empire. To Corinth, capital of the Roman province of Achaia. To Philippi, the Macedonian city on the great Egnatian highway between Rome and Asia, and to other important cities of Macedonia. In Paul's time the latter extended from the Adriatic to the Aegean. To this broad area, Paul set forth confidently, armed with the good news that what God promises he has fulfilled in Jesus' resurrection.

One can hear the echo down the centuries of Paul's prayer (in the epigraph to this book), "May the God of Hope fill you with joy and peace in your faith, that by the power of the Holy Spirit, your whole life and outlook may be radiant with hope" (Rom. 15:13, Phillips trans.). In this and many other positive declarations, we see hope as the heart of Paul's existence.

His Early Years

The Book of Acts (more than half of it) and Paul's letters give us our only well-founded account of his life and career as an authentic messenger for Christ.

The approximate date of his birth in Tarsus in Cilicia is about A.D. 11, two decades before the crucifixion of Christ. His family, members of the tribe of Benjamin, named him for the tribe's early hero Saul, first king of Israel. Because he was a Roman citizen, his Roman name was Paul.

Little is known about his parents, except that they were Pharisees, who had a knowledge of the law and the prophets as well as of the Aramaic and Hebrew languages. Jesus spoke Galilean Aramaic, which Paul learned when he was sent to Jerusalem to study under the celebrated Rabbi Gamaliel. Paul was highly educated for his time, far ahead of the other apostles. Familiar with Greek, his later quotations from the Old Testament reflect the

Greek affiliation of his Judaism and his knowledge of the God of his ancient fathers.

Paul, a Jew, not only was fortunate in his educational and religious heritage, but also in his birthplace. Tarsus had a thriving maritime trade, a university supported by the Roman empire, and a high state of civic consciousness, thanks to which roads, bridges, arcades, and aqueducts were built.

Located as it was on the banks of the swift Cydnus River, (silted up centuries ago) and a flourishing harbor of ancient Cilicia, Tarsus was near the Mediterranean and thirty miles from mountains veined with lead and silver. The melting snow of these mountains cascaded to the plain where Tarsus sprawled seventy feet above sea level.

Although Paul was educated in the law, he had a trade too. In Tarsus he learned to make *cilicium*, a goat's-hair cloth used for tents, sails, awnings, and cloaks. In later years, as Paul traveled from church to church, he used his trade as a livelihood and became well known as a tentmaker.

In its way of life Tarsus reflected the Oriental attitude. This had a long-time influence on Paul's ideas which sometimes diverged from those of others in Judea. In Tarsus, too, Paul had the opportunity to observe those aspects of Christ's Gospel acceptable to Jews and Greek alike.

Paul was never married. No one in his immediate family, except a sister's son, is mentioned. This nephew gave information to the chief captain of a plot to kill Paul while he was under trial before the Sanhedrin at Jerusalem.

HIS DENIAL AND CONVERSION

When Stephen, one of the first church deacons, was appointed to distribute food and other necessities to the poor in Jerusalem, there grew up around him those who "could not withstand the wisdom and the spirit with which he spoke" (Acts 6:10). Because Stephen was a man of zeal and power, a group of reactionaries called "Freedmen" stirred up the elders and scribes against him.

They took Stephen before the council and brought false wit-

nesses against him. In this group was the young Saul, then study-
ing in Jerusalem, who had succumbed to student fanaticism. Soon
Saul was known as an ardent persecutor of the Christians, among
whom were this holy man, Stephen. When he was arrested,
brought to trial, and finally stoned to death, the witnesses laid
down their garments at the feet of Saul. This happened while
Stephen was praying and in his death throes and while Saul stood
by, consenting to his death.

As he witnessed Stephen's dying agony, never once did Saul
come to his defense. Consequently, after this, Saul was more popular with the agitators. The high priest made him leader of the radical group that had killed Stephen. And Saul still breathed threats
and murder against the disciples of the Lord. He went to the
high priest for letters to the synagogues at Damascus, so that if
he found any disciples there he might bring them bound to Jerusalem.

But something happened to Saul on the sun-baked road on the
way to Damascus. As he approached there, he saw a flash of light
from heaven and he "fell to the ground and heard a voice say,
'Saul, Saul, why do you persecute me . . . I am Jesus, whom you
are persecuting'" (Acts 9:4–5). Although those around Saul could
hear the voice, they could see no one. When Saul arose, his companions brought him to Damascus. For three days he was blind
and neither ate nor drank. But when Saul came in touch with Ananias, who probably was the leader in the small Christian community of Damascus, a miracle occurred. "Something like scales
fell from his [Saul's] eyes and he regained his sight. Then he arose
and was baptized, and took food and was strengthened" (vs. 18–
19). Such a vast change came over him that he was no longer Saul
the persecutor, but Paul the converted, and so filled with the Holy
Spirit that all who saw him could not believe that he had once
been the star dissenter.

After his conversion, according to his own record, Paul went
into Arabia (Gal. 1:17). Arabia is represented in scripture as a
lonely desert conducive to great spiritual revelations, like those
that came to Moses, Jacob, Elijah, and finally to Paul, while there.
Arabians were in Jerusalem at Pentecost (Acts 2:11). It could be
that Paul had two reasons for going there. One was to see if it

were a good area to evangelize. Another was to meditate on his own remarkable conversion. Here, in these so-called "hidden years," he had time to ponder God in all his power and wisdom, time to think through his own problems, time to gain peace and to learn the true meaning of righteousness. And when he came away, after what was thought to have been eight to thirteen years of solitude, he was willing to endure any suffering for Christ.

When Paul finally set forth on his inspiring ministry for Christ, he "confounded the Jews who lived in Damascus by proving that Jesus was the Christ" (Acts 9:22). They even plotted to kill him, but his new disciples "took him by night and let him down over the Damascus wall, lowering him in a basket" (v. 25).

When Paul arrived at Jerusalem, the new Christians were afraid of him, but Barnabas, who was to become his close associate in his first missionary journey, assured them that Paul, who had seen the Lord on the road to Damascus, was a new man. He was. And he continued to preach boldly about Christ in Jerusalem.

His First Missionary Journey

Finally Paul set forth on the first of his three missionary tours, all of which were to take him throughout the Roman empire from about A.D. 45 to 60. His responsibilities would be many. He would organize churches. He would counsel new members. He would preach the Gospel. He would raise funds. He would comfort the sick and the needy, all the while carrying on his trade as a tentmaker in order to provide for his own needs and those of others.

Although the journey would be filled with a variety of uplifting spiritual experiences, Paul would also endure many trials. He enumerates some of the latter: his tremendous labor, his imprisonments, and his countless beatings, which often brought him near death:

> Five times I have received at the hands of the Jews the forty lashes less one. Three times I have been beaten with rods; once I was stoned. Three times I have been shipwrecked; a night and a day I have been adrift at sea; on frequent journeys, in danger from rivers, danger from robbers, danger from

my own people, danger from Gentiles, danger in the city, danger in the wilderness, danger at sea, danger from false brethren; in toil and hardship, through many a sleepless night, in hunger and thirst, often without food, in cold and exposure. And, apart from other things, there is the daily pressure upon me of my anxiety for all the churches.

(II Cor. 11:24–28)

There was also that "thorn" in Paul's flesh to keep him "from being too elated by the abundance of revelations." What the thorn was no one knows. Could it have been caused from injuries in serious beatings? Or was it a physical infirmity from malaria contracted in his trials? Or was it epilepsy?

Paul's first missionary journey, related in Acts 13–14, started from Seleucia, the port of Syrian Antioch and one of the most important commercial harbors of the ancient Mediterranean world. This journey was actually under the leadership of Barnabas, with Paul as the second member. The young John Mark, who was related to Barnabas, accompanied them part of the way.

They went forth, as Paul said, "not like so many, peddlers of God's word; but as men of sincerity, as commissioned by God, in the sight of God we speak in Christ" (II Cor. 2:17).

The first stop was Cyprus, the island home of Barnabas. They landed at Salamis, then crossed Cyprus to Paphos. The second portion of the journey took them into the Asia Minor mainland to the districts of Pamphylia, Pisidia, and Lyconia. The last two were in the part of the Roman province of Galatia. Among the cities they evangelized were Pisidian Antioch, Iconium, Lystra and Derbe. Then they retraced their course back to Pamphylia and returned to Syrian Antioch.

One of the highlights of this first journey occurred at Paphos, an ancient Phoenician city at the southwest tip of Cyprus and a seat of the Roman government. Here, one of Paul's first converts was Sergius Paulus, an influential Roman proconsul. Elymas (also called Bar-Jesus), a false prophet, sought to turn the proconsul away from God. Then Paul, looking at him intently, rebuked him saying, "You son of the devil, you enemy of righteousness, full of all deceit and villainy, will you not stop making crooked the straight paths of the Lord?" (Acts 13:10). This false prophet, it is recorded, was stricken blind for a time, and the people were astonished at Paul's teaching of the Lord.

Afterward, at Lystra, in Galatia, Paul and Barnabas were hailed at the entrance of the city as "Jupiter and Mercury." Here Paul healed a lame man crippled from birth, and those around saw the man stand upright on his feet and walk again after he came into Paul's presence.

On finishing this first missionary tour, Paul and Barnabas went to Jerusalem for the Apostolic Assembly, to discuss circumcision and other controversial subjects that were unsettling to the converts, largely Gentiles.

The Jews demanded the circumcision of the new Gentile converts, but the council, led by Peter, Paul, and James, made the decision that unchastity, idolatry, and other evils were more threatening to Christian liberty than the old Mosaic law demanding circumcision. Paul explained, "For through the Spirit, by faith, we wait for the hope of righteousness. For in Christ Jesus neither circumcision nor uncircumcision is of any avail, but faith working through love" (Gal. 5:5–6). Galatians has been called the "Magna Charta" of Christian liberty.

THE SECOND MISSIONARY JOURNEY

Paul's second missionary tour (Acts 15:36–18:22) took him into Macedonia. This time he was accompanied by Silas and afterward joined by Timothy and Luke. They traveled by land through Syria and Cilicia and revisited the Galatian churches organized on the first tour. Then they went to Philippi, the first city in Europe to be evangelized. Here they stayed at the house of Lydia, "a worshiper of God" and faithful helper in the establishment of the new Church.

Soon after their arrival in Philippi, Paul and his fellow travelers were dragged into the market place, beaten with many rods, and finally imprisoned. This abuse was administered by owners of a slave girl soothsayer, who had brought her owners gain. When she was converted by Paul as a Christian believer, they were without the income she had brought them.

Paul and the others with him, now miraculously released from prison at Philippi, proceeded from there to Thessalonica, where there was a Jewish synagogue. Here Paul went first to his own Jewish people to proclaim Jesus as the Messiah. "But the Jews in their jealousy recruited some low fellows from the dregs of the populace, roused the rabble, and had the city in an uproar" (Acts 17:5, NEB), a scene not unlike some that occur today.

When night came, members of the Thessalonian congregation sent Paul and Silas to Beroea, where many were converted. When some of the Thessalonian Jews learned of Paul's success in Beroea, they came there to stir up trouble.

The congregation sent Paul on to Athens, but Silas and Timothy remained behind. In this city filled with idols, Paul gave his first sermon in the court of the Areopagus on Mars Hill, where he told his pagan listeners, "The God who created the world . . . does not live in shrines made by men . . . he [God] is not far from each one of us, for in him we live and move, in him we exist . . . As God's offspring, then, we ought not to suppose that the deity is like an image in gold or silver or stone shaped by human craftsmanship and design" (Acts 17:24, 27–29, NEB).

From Athens Paul journeyed to Corinth where he lived in the home of Priscilla and Aquila, tentmakers like himself, and they worked and worshiped together. Again Paul affirmed before the Jews there that the Messiah was Jesus, but again they resorted to abuse, and he "shook out the skirts of his cloak and said, 'Your blood is on your own heads! My conscience is clear; now I shall go to the Gentiles'" (Acts 18:6, NEB). Paul was so well received by the Gentiles that he stayed at Corinth for eighteen months.

During the early part of his stay at Corinth, Paul received disquieting news brought by Silas and Timothy, who came from Macedonia. Because of the unsettled conditions there, he sat down and wrote his first letter to the Christians at Thessalonica. This was I Thessalonians, the oldest book in the New Testament. It was in this letter that Paul thanked the Thessalonians for their "labor of love and steadfastness of hope in our Lord Jesus Christ."

THE THIRD MISSIONARY JOURNEY AND LAST TRAVELS

When Paul finally left Corinth he sailed to Ephesus and then journeyed once more to Syrian Antioch. From there he started on his third missionary tour (Acts 18:23, 21:19), this time accompanied by Timothy, Titus, Erastus, and Sosthenes. At the end of this journey he was joined by Luke and several others.

After revisiting the church at Galatia, he went once more to Ephesus. Here he found a small remnant of followers of John the Baptist, along with Jewish exorcists, magicians, members of an emperor cult, and believers in the goddess Artemis (Diana).

Paul's preaching on Christ's Gospel cut into the business of many of the false believers, such as that of the silversmiths, who made the Artemis shrines. A tense situation arose around Paul, and some of the disbelievers acted like "fierce wolves."

From Ephesus Paul wrote I and II Corinthians. He expressed to the people there the hope that as their faith increased, their field of work might be enlarged, and the Gospel might be preached in lands beyond them.

After his third missionary journey, Paul spent some time in Jerusalem, visiting the churches there. Because he spoke out for the cause he believed in, the authorities denounced him and he was removed to Caesarea as a captive, where probably about two years later, his trial before Felix took place.

Before visiting in Malta, Paul, it is thought, went into Spain and possibly farther, but as little is known about this journey as about his hidden years in Arabia. His last trip was as a captive to Rome, with a shipwreck off Malta en route. The miraculous account of this incident (Acts 27:27–44) is one of the best sea tales in antiquity.

When Paul arrived at Rome he called the local leaders of the Jews together and told them that he was delivered a prisoner from Jerusalem into the hands of the Romans: "When they had examined me, they wished to set me at liberty, because there was no reason for the death penalty in my case. But when the Jews objected, I was compelled to appeal to Caesar—though I had no

charge to bring against my nation. For this reason therefore I have
asked to see you and speak with you, since it is because of the hope
of Israel that I am bound with this chain" (Acts 28:18–20).

Some of his own people were convinced, but others still pro-
tested. As the end of his life drew near, Paul lived for two years
at Rome, preaching and teaching.

His Letters to Young Churches

Paul's letters written before the Gospels, between A.D. 45 and
60, are the oldest part of the New Testament. They were read
in the first churches along with the oldest Old Testament manuscripts then in existence, but today lost in the mold of the ages.
For many years they remained as letters on papyrus, probably
kept in wooden chests. How easily they could have been lost! But
in time, due to the work of dedicated translators, they were combined with the Gospels as the sacred scriptures of the New Testament, and finally they became a vital part of the Bible record.

Of the twenty-seven letters to young churches no fewer than
thirteen bear Paul's name. Scholars are of the opinion that several
of these were written by Paul's co-workers and credited to him in
order to maintain his apostolic legacy. Some of these are the two
letters to Timothy, the one to Titus, the letter to the Colossians,
the letter to the Ephesians, and the second letter to the Thessalonians. Some of the others, whether written by Paul or not,
put us in direct communication with Paul's thoughts and ideas.

Paul's letters still speak to the minds and hearts of Christians
more vividly than books involved with his theology. They are distinctive in that one hears the voice and feels the breath, as it were,
of this man who either wrote or inspired most of these letters.

In them Paul achieves a living quality by using a variety of
forms: salutations, sermons, arguments, confessions, prayers,
hymns, blessings, and warmhearted greetings to the Church
friends to whom they are written.

Like the writers of most letters, Paul no doubt saw his as make-
shifts in which he attempted to express his dreams, aspirations,
faith, and hope; because he did, we become eye witnesses to his

innermost thoughts. Even if we read them again and again, we never catch up completely with the thought of this great man.

Paul was not consciously writing Holy Scripture. He was writing to those first Christians, and many times he wrote against tremendous odds. And yet these letters have a vigorous style, and Paul's preaching eloquence at times leaps like a flame.

There are four points common to all of them, says J. B. Phillips in his preface to his translation of Paul's writings, *Letters to Young Churches*. First, he says, there is a tremendous sense of the overwhelming moral perfection of God. Next, there is a continuing condemnation of false teachers. Third, they describe man's present life as if it were only an incident in his development as a spiritual being. Finally, Christianity becomes a real experience in each one of the letters.

They also provide, says Phillips, "that spiritual vitamin, without which human life is at best sickly and at worst dead. While scarcely touching on any modern problem, they yet manage to give pointers of principles which show the way, and the spirit in which the problems of even a highly complex age such as ours may be tackled successfully" (*Letters to Young Churches*, preface, p. xii).

His Basic Message

It is impossible to pinpoint Paul's basic message to the world in a few words. Paul himself could not do it, and millions of words have been written to try to explain and amplify what he said. His own words, still our best explanation of his life and work, center around several fundamental principles. One is the power and righteousness of God. Paul sees God as the source, not the object, of the righteousness of God. He speaks often of the grace of God, the love of God, and the fatherhood of God.

Paul sees Christ as the divine being that he was, and his cross and resurrection as inseparable. Paul no doubt saw in Christ's voluntary acceptance of his cross the true meaning of the "suffering servant" of Isaiah 53, that his own daily cross of hardship and service was easier to accept, and that Christ's cross was a necessary prelude to his resurrection. Those who hear and heed the word of God and the example of Christ are the saints. Their love of God and their reverence for the example of his Son, Jesus Christ, point the way to sainthood.

Paul describes the Church as "the body of Christ" and therefore divinely constituted. Its believers are called "a Colony of Heaven" and its members, "Children of Promise."

Even in times of despair Paul could find great hope in the little churches struggling against mighty Rome. His vision was right. The Church still survives. The Roman empire vanished centuries ago.

The fruits of the spirit—love, joy, peace, patience, gentleness, kindness, goodness, faithfulness, and self-control—express Paul's highest sense of morality. Good deeds, according to Paul, are the natural expression of a God-filled life. These divine graces of God in Christ make possible a morality higher and more natural than that of mere law, for they are a part of one's inner being.

Salvation, best defined as deliverance from sin and its consequences, achieved only in a right relationship with God through Christ, is an important theme with Paul. It is the gateway to faith, which also signifies obedience, receptivity, and surrender.

Only in faith and love does one become God's own: "For God knew his own before ever they were, and also ordained that they should be shaped to the likeness of his Son, that he might be the eldest among a large family of brothers . . . And those whom he called he has justified, and to those whom he justified he has also given his splendour" (Rom. 8:28–30, NEB).

His Many-sided Character

Paul never would have called himself a saint. He seemed to realize that God exhibited him and his helpers as apostles last of all, "but more like men sentenced to death, because we have become a spectacle to the world, to angels and to men" (I Cor. 4:9).

He could arouse passionate defense and equally passionate opposition. Whatever his trials, he never failed to acknowledge human frailty, both in himself and others. He was always under pressure because he was always slaving for others. A man of inward peace and overpowering opposition against evil, he was both loved and revered, feared and hated.

He had not even a little charisma and sometimes turned people against him by his very appearance. In the Acts of Paul, the second-century legend, he is described as "small in stature, bald-headed, bow-legged, of vigorous physique, with meeting eyebrows, and a slightly hooked nose." And then we can imagine that he limped as he walked because of that thorn in the flesh, already mentioned.

Influenced by several cultures—Jew, Gentile, Christian, and Hellenistic—Paul was always in the midst of controversy, with the Jews because he insisted that Christ was the long awaited Messiah; with the Gentiles, to whom he came as an apostle to preach the unsearchable riches of Christ; and with the new Christians, who, though believers, were not always his loyal supporters.

Naturally, Paul's Near Eastern background shaped his opinions, some of which caused him to be narrow, regarding, for example, public worship by women. And yet he recognized, as he stated to the Galatians, "There is neither Jew nor Greek, there is neither slave nor free, there is neither male nor female; for you are all one in Christ Jesus" (Gal. 3:28).

His decisions were usually resolute and seldom subject to change. In his letters he could express great love; then, he could fight evil with fire. Despite his limitations, his greatness looms larger with time.

In a sense, Paul was as much a statesman as a missionary. He had great vision and the intuitive sense to choose strategic centers for his work.

Whatever his varied experiences he could be both optimistic and depressed. In his spiritual conflicts he could regretfully say, "O wretched man that I am; who will deliver me from the body of this death?" Then he would make a fuller surrender to the life of Christ.

Paul also had the capacity for genuine friendship. In a short passage in Romans 16, he lists the names of sixteen friends to whom he sends greeting. In phrases here and there, Paul shows eloquent concern for each of these friends.

Amid all of his own complexities of character and the controversy that surrounded him, Paul could still write one of the Bible's
most beautiful gems, I Cor. 13, on the course of love. In this passage he defines a love that is patient and kind, not jealous or boast-
ful, not arrogant or rude, does not insist on its way, is not irritable
or resentful, does not rejoice at wrong, but rejoices in the right.
Love that bears all things, hopes all things, endures all things.

In this treatise on a love that is imperishable, Paul concludes,
"So faith, hope, love abide, these three; but the greatest of these
is love."

HIS MANY PERSECUTIONS AND DEATH

As Christ's most ardent disciple, willing to suffer and die for
him, Paul faced even greater persecution than he had brought
upon Stephen and endured suffering almost as unbearable as
that of Christ. Patiently, Paul accepted one desperate situation
after another: treachery, ingratitude, affliction, distress, flogging,
stoning, imprisonment, shipwreck, hunger, thirst, cold, nakedness,
reproaches.

But for the cause of Jesus, Paul could still say, "We are troubled
on every side, yet not distressed; we are perplexed, but not in despair; persecuted, but not forsaken; cast down, but not destroyed"
(II Cor. 4:8–9, KJV).

His early persecutions as the great apostle to the Gentiles came
largely from his own people. They called him "a pestilent fellow,"
an agitator among all the Jews throughout the world, and a ring-
leader of the sect of the Nazarenes. They said he even tried to
profane the temple, "but we seized him." And so they beat him,
tied him up with thongs, and brought him into the barracks, crying out, "Away with such a fellow from the earth."

Afterward, dissension against Paul became so violent that the
tribunal was afraid Paul would be torn to pieces. Later forty con-
spirators plotted to kill him. He was brought into trial before the
Sanhedrin, and the Jerusalem high priest Ananias commanded
those who stood by to strike him on the mouth. But he cried out,

"Brothers, I am a Pharisee. I find myself on trial now because of my hope in the resurrection of the dead" (Acts 23:6, NAB).

Nowhere did he enjoy complete freedom from oppression and hardship. At Antioch hostile Jews attempted to stone him, then dragged him out of the city, but he regained consciousness, arose and walked into the city again.

The next Sunday, however, the multitudes came out to hear Paul speak, but those who had scoffed and beaten him were now so jealous that they reviled him. But again he went forward with his preaching, prayers, and fasting, assuring others that it is through many tribulations that we must enter the kingdom of God.

One of the most dramatic moments in Paul's life was toward the end of his life when he came before King Agrippa II, manacled with chains, and testified, "I stand here on trial for hope in the promise made by God to our fathers, to which our twelve tribes hope to attain, as they earnestly worship night and day. And for this hope I am accused by Jews, O king! Why is it thought incredible by any of you that God raises the dead?" (Acts 26:6–8).

King Agrippa almost became a Christian on hearing Paul's testimony before military tribunes and prominent men of the city that day in the judgment hall at Caesarea. Accused unjustly of sedition and profanation of the temple and tried before Agrippa, one of the most wicked men of the time, Paul became the central figure in one of the most unfair court scenes in ancient history. Although Paul had done nothing worthy of death or of bonds, he was released from neither sentence. He would go back to prison manacled in his chains. He would continue writing his letters until, in a short time, he would die a martyr's death at Rome. But in these and other moments of suffering for Christ, Paul knew real spiritual triumph.

The Book of Acts, which takes Paul's life right up to the end, does not relate his final death after his arrival at Rome for the last time, but there is a tradition, and early historians confirm it, that Paul died a martyr's death in Rome in the gladiator's ring and that he was stalwart and unafraid to the end.

There, about A.D. 67, he was imprisoned with Peter in the Mamertine prison, near the Roman Forum. Here criminals and captives awaited execution or death in the gladiator's ring. The second-century Tertullian of Carthage says Paul was beheaded. Gaius of Rome wrote in the third century that Paul suffered martyrdom on the Ostian Way. The third-century Christian theologian Origen recorded that Paul suffered martyrdom under Nero. The fourth-century Christian historian Eusebius made a similar statement.

There stands near the Ostian Way in Rome the magnificent basilica of St. Paul-Without-the-Walls, a monument to the fact that Paul was buried in this area.

Whatever the period and manner of his death, the voice of Paul rings out, "I have fought the good fight, I have finished the race, I have kept the faith" (II Tim. 4:7).

The Mystery of the Resurrection

In his explanation of death and resurrection, Paul saw beyond his lifetime into the eternal, where he and other great souls are conformed to the body of Christ's glory.

In one of Paul's grandest spiritual revelations (I Cor. 15), he analyzes the Resurrection, its assurance and logic, a fact that gave birth to the Christian faith. He maintains confidence in the incredible mystery of Christ's resurrection. "If for this life only we have hoped in Christ," Paul declares, "we are of all men most to be pitied" (v. 19). First, Paul repeats the historical evidence of the Resurrection (vs. 1–11) and after that he shows that the denial of the resurrection of the dead signifies a denial of Christ's resurrection (vs. 12–19). He eloquently explains the consequences of Christ's resurrection (vs. 20–28) and enlarges upon the importance of the hope of resurrection in Christian life (vs. 29–34).

The so-called "mystery moment" of resurrection comes at that point in time when the earthly body is laid to rest. Paul draws the analogy of the bare kernel, seemingly brown and dead when sown in the ground, but afterward springing into a beautiful flower or tree. "What you sow," he says, "does not come to life unless it dies" (I Cor. 15:36). So it is with the body laid in the grave. In the same manner, a celestial body arises into another dimension we can not see and is ready for a new mode of existence and a new set of relationships we can not yet comprehend.

Like the sun, moon, and stars born out of darkness but finally evolving into varying degrees of brightness, so will man's resurrected body be far brighter and more glorious than his material body. Christ's resurrected body was so wondrous that it could be transported from place to place. A perfect abode for the spirit and free from the limitations and imperfections of the material body, it could even pass through closed doors and finally ascend.

As one becomes a new creature in God, one's mortality disappears. Says Paul: "Lo! I tell you a mystery. We shall not all sleep, but we shall all be changed . . . For this perishable nature must put on the imperishable, and this mortal nature must put on immortality. When the perishable puts on the imperishable, and the mortal puts on immortality, then shall come to pass the saying that is written, 'Death is swallowed up in victory'" (I Cor. 15:51, 53–54).

Paul's triumphant explanation of the Resurrection helps us to know that his own tragic death, like that of Christ's, was "swallowed up in victory." The Christian world does not dwell on the tragedy of Paul's last days but on his whole life and outlook, so radiant with hope. The kind of hope that rose above every material affliction: chains, imprisonment, beatings, hunger, illness, and finally a martyr's death, probably in the arena at Rome, where the last thing he saw was either a raging lion or a soldier's uplifted sword flashing in the morning sun. Then he lost consciousness of the material world and its sorrows; and the immortality he had written about was now his to experience.

He, whose life had been radiant with hope, he who knew the true meaning of the Resurrection, he who had uplifted so many, could not be hopeless in the new state he was about to enter. He had prepared his immortal soul for its ascent into eternity.

SECTION FIVE

Other Men of Hope in the Bible

These other Bible men of hope, alphabetically presented, though oftentimes in the background in the Bible narrative, strengthen the theme of hope. Many of us can more easily identify with them since nearly all were humble folk, pursuing less conspicuous tasks for the great men they inspired and were inspired by, and served.

The names from the Old Testament include every one from Aaron, who strengthened his younger brother Moses in all of his great tasks, to Zerubbabel, who brought hope out of hopelessness for the exiles returning to Jerusalem from Babylon. The New Testament list runs from Apollos, the eloquent Jew from Alexandria who learned more about the Christian faith from Aquila and his wife Priscilla, to Trophimus and Tychicus, Paul's Asian Gentile friends who were with him on his last missionary journey.

Included also are two unnamed groups healed by Jesus, Peter, and Paul.

Other Men of Note in the Bible

Other Men of Hope in the Bible

AARON: THE FIRST HIGH PRIEST OF ISRAEL

More than three hundred listings of Aaron appear in the Old Testament alone, in Exodus, Leviticus, Numbers, Deuteronomy, Joshua, Judges, I Samuel, I and II Chronicles, Ezra, Nehemiah, Psalms, and Micah. These affirm his importance as the prophet and spokesman for his younger brother Moses, as well as Israel's first high priest. Aaron's name also appears in Luke, Acts, and Hebrews in the New Testament.

Zealous for the national honor and religion of his people, Aaron sustained Israel's priestly ideals long after his death, at age one hundred twenty-three, on Mount Hor. His name also typified Israel's religious hope for the generations after Israel's exodus from Egypt.

Because Aaron was an excellent speaker, Moses had him go with him to confer with Pharaoh, ruler of the Egyptians, and Aaron spoke eloquently against Egypt's cruelties to the children of Israel during their last years' sojourn there.

Although Moses was founder of the priesthood, Aaron initiated its first function and served as its head for forty years. He was a descendant of Levites through his mother and father, Jochebed and Amram. The Levite priesthood performed the subordinate tasks of the tabernacle service, but Aaron's priestly descendants

were known as Aaronites, a higher order. This line continued into
New Testament times. John the Baptist had full priestly descent
through his father, Zechariah, of the division of Abijah, and
through his mother, Elizabeth, one of the "daughters of Aaron"
(Luke 1:5).

Aaron was made the first priest of the desert tabernacle in a
significant anointing ceremony in which he wore sacred garments.
No such pageantry existed earlier and no priest had dressed in
priestly attire.

Of the four sons of Aaron and his wife, Elisheba, the first two,
Nadab and Abihu, died early. Eleazar was his father's worthy successor. Aaron's other son, Ithamar, assisted his father on special
occasions.

This Aaronic blessing, in continual use in temples, synagogues,
and churches, stems from the first tabernacle service of Aaron and
his sons,

> The Lord bless you and keep you:
> The Lord make his face to shine upon you
>   and be gracious to you:
> The Lord lift up his countenance upon you,
>   and give you peace.
>   (Num. 6:24–26)

In this blessing, one senses joy, peace, and hope for Israel and
all other believers in God.

Aaron was Moses' mouthpiece from the time of the last years
in Egypt and the Exodus, through the years of wilderness wandering. Although Aaron remained in the shadow of his distinguished
brother all of his life, Moses was greater because of Aaron's
support.

When Moses fled to Midian, Aaron remained behind to share
the hardships of his people. In leading the people out of Egypt,
Aaron was second only to Moses. When Moses went into battle
with the Amalekites, Aaron and Hur were there to aid in Israel's
victory. When Joshua and Moses first went up on Mount Sinai,
Aaron, along with Hur, served faithfully as a judge over the people. When Moses went up to the mountain of God again, Aaron
and his two priestly sons and seventy elders of Israel went with

him and saw the glory of God from afar as Moses experienced God in all his fullness (Ex. 24:1, 9–10). In later centuries the Psalmist wrote, "Thou didst lead thy people like a flock, by the hand of Moses and Aaron" (Ps. 77:20).

Despite his strength, Aaron had his weaknesses. He passively yielded to the peoples' demands to build a golden calf while Moses was on Mount Sinai. After the departure from Sinai, Aaron took the part of his sister Miriam in a protest against the authority of Moses. They complained of Moses' later marriage to a foreign woman, probably following the death of Moses' first wife, Zipporah, the mother of his sons.

God, however, continued to be the creative center of Aaron's life. He sought to remain true to the priestly ideals, and the people held him in such reverence that when he spoke, they believed and bowed their heads and worshiped.

Like his brother Moses, he was not permitted to journey into Canaan. When the land was not assigned to him, he did not whimper, for God assured him, "I am your portion and your inheritance among the people of Israel" (Num. 18:20). And Aaron, "the holy one of the Lord" (Ps. 106:16), believed in the power of his true inheritance from God.

The author of Hebrews, who calls Christ "God's appointed high priest," adds, "he is called by God, just as Aaron was" (Heb. 5:4).

ABEL: THE FIRST HERO OF FAITH

(Gen. 4:2, 4, 8, 9, 25; Matt. 23:25; Luke 11:51; Heb. 11:4, 12:24)

The second son of Adam and Eve, Abel, was a shepherd who looked after the family flock.

Genesis, a primitive study of great spiritual truths about God, relates this story of the offerings of Cain and Abel: "Now Adam knew Eve his wife, and she conceived and bore Cain . . . And again, she bore his brother Abel. Now Abel was a keeper of sheep, and Cain a tiller of the ground. In the course of time Cain brought to the Lord an offering of the fruit of the ground, and Abel brought of the firstlings of his flock and of their fat portions.

And the Lord had regard for Abel and his offering, but for Cain and his offering he had no regard. So Cain was very angry" (Gen. 4:1–5).

It was Abel's faith that first brought him in touch with God, and his gift was the more commendable because of his inner motive. God saw Abel the giver and not the gift. Jesus understood this well when he later declared, "You will know them by their fruits" (Matt. 7:16). The Book of Hebrews honors Abel because by faith he "offered to God a more acceptable sacrifice than Cain, through which he received approval as righteous" (Heb. 11:4).

Because God was so pleased with Abel, Cain was jealous and hated his brother passionately. Unable to master his anger, Cain invited Abel out into the field and murdered him.

Jesus, too, was murdered by those who hated him, but there is a difference. He is called "the mediator of the New Covenant" (Heb. 12:24). His gift of himself to mankind on the Cross speaks more graciously than the blood of Abel.

When God afterward asked Cain, "Where is Abel your brother?" he answered, "I do not know; am I my brother's keeper?" (Gen. 4:9).

Cain the murderer lived on in the body, but he died spiritually when he took the life of his brother Abel. "Then Cain went away from the presence of the Lord, and dwelt in the land of Nod, east of Eden" (Gen. 4:16).

But Abel, this first martyr, "through faith . . . is still speaking" (Heb. 11:4). What a glorious tribute to Abel, who aspired to the best, a lofty objective achieved through faith and hope.

ACHAICUS: A HOPEFUL CHRISTIAN MESSENGER

(I Cor. 16:17)

Along with Stephanas and Fortunatus, leaders in the Corinthian Church, Achaicus went to visit Paul at Philippi, where a new church had been established in an open enclosure on the banks of the Gangites River.

Their presence greatly relieved Paul's anxiety for the Corinthian Church. Paul afterward wrote that the messengers refreshed his spirit (I Cor. 16:18).

Paul, who suffered in order that the cross of Christ not be emptied of its power and who experienced every emotion from hopeless despair to ecstatic joy, must have found an indescribable comfort in the visit of Achaicus and his companions.

It is thought that Achaicus and the other two took a letter to Paul from the Corinthian Christians regarding low marriage standards (I Cor. 5:1–5) in their church. In answer to these and other questions Paul wrote I Corinthians, in which he deals with such matters as sexual morality, Christian liberty, public worship, church unity, and the Resurrection.

ANANIAS: THE RESTORER OF SAUL'S SIGHT

(Acts 9:10, 12, 13, 17, 22:12)

A Christian disciple living in Damascus, Ananias found Saul (Paul) praying after "breathing threats and murder against the disciples of the Lord."

In a vision Ananias was led to the street called Straight and to the house of Judas, a prominent Jerusalem Christian (Acts 9:11). There Ananias came upon the blind Saul, in deep meditation, after having recently been converted on the Damascus road. As Ananias laid his hands on the praying Saul, Saul was healed of his blindness.

It was with great hesitancy at first that Ananias went to visit Saul, for he knew how much evil he had done to the saints in Jerusalem. But, following the Lord's command, when he came into Saul's presence, he said, "Brother Saul, the Lord Jesus who appeared to you on the road by which you came, has sent me that you may regain your sight and be filled with the Holy Spirit" (Acts 9:17).

The miracle happened. "Something like scales fell from Saul's eyes and he regained his sight" (Acts 9:18). Then he arose, was baptized by Ananias, took food, gained strength, and went forward in his ministry for Christ.

After his experience on the Damascus Road, Paul was told by Ananias that he must go forth as a witness to all men and be willing to suffer much for Christ's sake.

Ananias is called "a devout man according to the law, highly respected by all Jews," one who brought Saul out of a mood of hopelessness.

APOLLOS: POWERFUL IN THE USE OF THE SCRIPTURES

(Acts 18:24, 19:1; I Cor. 1:12, 3:4–6, 22, 4:6, 16:12; Tit. 3:13)

An eloquent Jew from Alexandria, Apollos came to Ephesus during Paul's absence. There he was taught in Christian doctrine by Aquila and Priscilla.

He is described as an "eloquent man . . . full of spiritual fervor . . . [who] taught accurately the facts about Jesus, though he knew only John's baptism. He now began to speak boldly in the synagogue, where Priscilla and Aquila heard him; they took him in hand and expounded the new way to him in greater detail" (Acts 18:25–26, NEB).

In Alexandria, a remarkable meeting place of East and West, Apollos had been instructed only in the Messianic hope of John the Baptist, not about the living hope of the Risen Christ. When he arrived at Ephesus, the metropolis of the Roman province of Asia and one of the great cities of the eastern Mediterranean, along with Alexandria and Syrian Antioch, he grew in knowledge under the teaching of this husband and wife team, Aquila and Priscilla. Probably at this time Paul was in Galatia and Phrygia, and their home was the Ephesus rendezvous for those desiring to know more about the new faith; and so they baptized Apollos in the name of Jesus.

Afterward Apollos went in to Achaia to teach the brethren there, making it known to them through the scriptures that Christ was Jesus.

Apollos was so effective as a teacher and preacher at Corinth that his supporters credited him with starting the Church at Corinth. Some of these supporters created rivalry for Paul, but Apollos had no desire to set himself up as a rival of this greatest of apostles.

Later, Paul had the opportunity to preach on Christ united (I Cor. 1:10–17), not Christ divided into several factions. His mission, he said, was "to preach the gospel . . . lest the cross of Christ be emptied of its power" (1:17). Paul compared himself to one who planted, Apollos to one who watered, the new converts to a garden, and God as the one who made it grow.

Apollos and Paul devotedly helped each other. Almost Paul's last words written from Macedonia to Titus at the church on the island of Crete, were, "Do your best to speed Zenas the lawyer and Apollos on their way; see that they lack nothing" (Tit. 3:13).

Aquila: A Believer in the Mission of the New Church

(Acts 18:2, 18, 26; Rom. 16:3; I Cor. 16:19; II Tim. 4:19)

A Jew whom Paul found at Corinth when he arrived there from Athens, Aquila and his wife, Priscilla, had such hope for the new Church that they set up their own church for the household at Ephesus and at Rome. Here they and their friends met for fellowship, worship, and a common meal commemorating the Last Supper. Like other early Christians, Aquila had his "hope set on the living God, who is Saviour of all men, especially of those who believe" (I Tim. 4:10).

Aquila, a widely traveled Jew, was a native of the Asiatic province of Pontus, an ancient country in northeast Asia Minor, bordering on the Black Sea. He migrated to Italy, where he and his wife, it seems, were later expelled by the Emperor Claudius because of disputes in the synagogues over the new teaching about the Messiah.

Like Paul, Aquila and his wife were tentmakers. On Paul's first visit to Corinth he lived in their house, and the three of them wove cilician cloth for tents together and talked of Christ as they sewed.

When Paul left Corinth, Aquila and Priscilla accompanied him to Ephesus, remaining there after Paul went to Jerusalem. At Ephesus they taught the Alexandrian Apollos about Jesus.

Writing to the Romans, either from Ephesus or Philippi, Paul sent salutations to Aquila and Priscilla, describing them as "my fellow workers in Christ Jesus, who risked their necks for my life" (Rom. 16:4). This may have been during a riot over pagan gods in Ephesus when Paul first went there to preach.

Later, it seems, Aquila and his wife were living in Rome again. Paul continued to commend them and "the church in their house."

Although there is no biblical source for their return to Rome, apparently they did return. A church on the Aventine in Rome was called the "Titulus Aquila et Prisca." Paul's last greeting to them appears in II Tim. 4:19.

Paul's work at Corinth and Ephesus was more effective because of Aquila, this zealous advocate of the good news about Christ, this helper in his trade, this amiable host who, with his wife, opened his home to him.

ARISTARCHUS: PAUL'S HUMBLE AND LOYAL FRIEND

(Acts 19:29, 20:4, 27:2; Col. 4:10; Philem. 24)

Aristarchus was with Paul on his third missionary journey through Asia Minor.

Aristarchus is little more than a name in the five times he is mentioned, but he is always a helper in a variety of instances— when enraged pagans at Ephesus threatened Paul and him during a riot, in tempestuous winds sailing along the shores of Crete, in a wreck as Paul's sailing vessel drifted across the Sea of Adria en route to Rome, in prison in Rome when Paul wrote to the Colossians and to Philemon.

Nothing is recorded of what Aristarchus said or did, what he looked like, whether he was young or old, but in his loyalty and service to Paul, he stands out as a sincere man of faith with hope in the gospel of Christ.

Few other facts are known about Aristarchus, except that he was a Gentile from Thessalonica and seems to have been with Paul until the end of his work in Macedonia. These facts are incidental. What is more significant is that when Paul, the great apostle, was in the foreground, the unpretentious Aristarchus was in the background, modestly standing by but ever ready to render menial service to this faithful minister of Christ.

BARAK: ONE OF THE EARLY HEROES OF FAITH

(Judg. 4:6, 8, 9–10, 12–14, 22, 5:1, 12, 15; Heb. 11:32)

Honored as one who through faith became mighty in war and put foreign armies to flight, Barak shared with Deborah in the leadership of the North Israelite militia during a victorious campaign against Sisera, commander of the powerful Canaanite forces of Jabin, king of Hazor. This was in the period of the tribal heroes who judged, about thirteen centuries before Christ.

Deborah, who assumed command of the army of Israel at a time when so many of the men were afraid, summoned Barak to aid her in the fight against the oppression by the Canaanites.

Hopefully she spoke to the fainthearted Barak, "The Lord, the God of Israel, commands you, 'Go, gather your men at Mount Tabor, taking ten thousand from the tribe of Naphtali [Barak's own tribe] and the tribe of Zebulun,'" (Judg. 4:6). Then she told Barak she would draw forth Sisera, the general of Jabin's army, to meet him by the river Kishon with chariots and troops.

Barak answered Deborah, "'If you will go with me, I will go; but if you will not go with me, I will not go.' And she said, 'I will surely go with you'" (Judg. 4:8–9). The rains came, and the enemy's chariots and troops bogged down, but Barak, with Deborah's support, defeated the Canaanites. Barak and Deborah then joined in the song of victory, one of the earliest martial songs in history (5:1–31).

BARNABAS: "SON OF ENCOURAGEMENT"

(Acts 4:36, 9:27, 11:22, 25, 30, 12:25, also chapters 13, 14, and 15; I Cor. 9:6; Gal. 2:1, 13, 19; Col. 4:10)

A Levite and companion of Paul on several of his journeys, Barnabas' willingness to suffer for Christ encouraged others to believe in him. And he and Paul suffered much together. On their first missionary journey, he and Paul made new converts to Christ, first at Antioch in Syria, then at Antioch in Pisidia, and finally at Lystra and Iconium in Galatia.

Barnabas, one of the first converts at Jerusalem and the first to be sent by the apostles there to evangelize at Syrian Antioch, had a magnetic and robust appearance. When he was later ministering with Paul at Lystra, the people there thought he and Paul were gods, and they called Barnabas "Zeus" (Acts 14:12) after the chief deity of the ancient Greeks. It is no wonder Barnabas was so successful as both an apostle and a preacher.

Barnabas is described as "a good man, full of the Holy Spirit and of faith" (Acts 11:24). He was not only good in the common acceptance of the term but good in the divine sense. And he rejoiced when he found goodness in others.

He also was a generous man. After the miracle at Pentecost, he was the first to sell a field which belonged to him, and he "brought the money and laid it at the apostles' feet." In this act he fulfilled the binding agreement made by members of the early Christian community that all share with one another.

In his compassion for the needs of others, his giving had no end. Before he and Paul joined together on the first missionary tour, they each had carried a contribution from the Church at Antioch to the poor in famine-stricken Jerusalem. Fourteen years later they were commended by the church council there as "men who have risked their lives for the sake of our Lord Jesus Christ" (Acts 15:26). This same council commissioned Barnabas, Paul, and John Mark to undertake their arduous missionary journey to Gentile lands.

Like Paul, Barnabas willingly accepted self-denial and cross-bearing. Wherever they journeyed together, they carried a message of hope in the midst of tribulation, hope in "a living God who made the heaven and the earth and the sea and all that is in them" (Acts 14:15), as well as "the good news that what God promised to the fathers, this he has fulfilled to us their children by raising Jesus" (Acts 13:32–33).

Barnabas was a native of Cyprus and probably knew Paul before his conversion when he lived at nearby Tarsus. After Barnabas first added a large group of converts at Antioch, he went to Tarsus to look for Saul (Paul) "and when he had found him he brought him to Antioch. For a whole year they met with the church, and taught a large company of people; and in Antioch the disciples were for the first time called Christians" (Acts 11:26).

Right after Paul's conversion on the Damascus road, Barnabas defended him when some of the other apostles in Jerusalem were skeptical about the genuineness of Paul's spiritual regeneration. "But Barnabas took him [Paul], and brought him to the apostles, and declared to them how on the road he had seen the Lord, who spoke to him, and how at Damascus he had preached boldly in the name of Jesus" (Acts 9:27). Both Paul and Barnabas were Jews who worked with Gentiles, and together they encouraged believers to "remain faithful to the Lord with steadfast purpose" (Acts 11:23).

Barnabas was older than Paul, and in the first records of their fellowship, the name of Barnabas comes first, but beginning with their first missionary journey together, Paul's name is first.

Paul had great confidence in his faithful partner, Barnabas. When Paul spoke to the church at Jerusalem he thanked the leaders there for giving to him and Barnabas "the right hand of fellowship" (Gal. 2:9). Their spiritual and cultural kinship seemed to bind the two of them together wherever they went.

Only once did Paul and Barnabas disagree. That was over the young John Mark, Barnabas's nephew, when he left them on their first missionary journey and returned to his home in Jerusalem. A sharp contention arose over John Mark, so Barnabas and Paul separated. Barnabas took Mark with him and sailed to Cyprus. Paul afterward chose Silas.

In standing by the young Mark in a moment of weakness, Barnabas no doubt helped to encourage Mark in his monumental literary career, the writing of the Gospel of Mark and the Book of Acts.

One thing stands out about Barnabas in the biblical record. His references are the best and his companions the noblest. He did not reach the spiritual heights of Paul, but he helped Paul in his climb to greatness.

BARUCH: JEREMIAH'S CLOSE FRIEND AND SECRETARY

(Jer. 32:12–13, 16, 36:4–5, 8, 10, 13–19, 26–27, 32, 43:3, 6, 45:1–2)

Baruch was the faithful helper to the prophet Jeremiah in the reigns of Jehoiakim (609–598 B.C.) and Zedekiah (598–587 B.C.).

Baruch took dictation from Jeremiah, spoke for him, acted as his business manager in the purchase of property, and preserved the deed of purchase in an earthen vessel.

When Jeremiah first received visions of the coming destruction of Jerusalem, he summoned Baruch to come to his prison, with scrolls and ink, and take dictation. As a spokesman for God, Jeremiah prophesied to the people of Judah that because of their evil ways, they would be taken captive by the enemy, but if they would turn from their iniquities, God would forgive their sins.

When the scroll was finished, the imprisoned Jeremiah was debarred from going to the house of the Lord to read it, so he sent Baruch there to present from the scroll the words he had dictated, a part of what is probably the Book of Jeremiah.

The scroll was afterward taken to King Jehoiakim and read aloud to him at his winter house. On hearing it, the angry king cut the scrolls one by one with his penknife and threw them into the fire of a brazier. He ordered that Baruch and Jeremiah, then in hiding, be seized, beaten, and imprisoned again.

But the message was not lost. Jeremiah dictated it again to Baruch and probably added to it before the two of them went into exile in Babylon, where Baruch is said to have died about 574 B.C.

He is thought to have been of a noble family, as the name of his father, Neriah, is repeated several times in the narrative. He doubtless was a skilled writer too. The Book of Baruch, one of the short Apocryphal books and attributed to him, is a compilation of the religious thought and practices of the Jews living outside Palestine, their prayers, their faithful reading of the sacred book, their resistance to idolatry, and their worship of the law. Scholars give abundant evidence that the Book of Baruch was accepted by the Christian Church from A.D. 175 up to the Reformation, though it was never canonized.

BOAZ: THE NOBLE HUSBAND OF THE WORTHY RUTH

(Ruth; I Chron. 2:11–12; Matt. 1:5; Luke 3:32)

Boaz immediately recognized worthy qualities in Ruth, the widow of his kinsman Mahlon when she came to glean in his grain fields at Bethlehem.

In his later marriage to the admirable Ruth, Boaz became the father of Obed, the grandfather of Jesse and the great-grandfather of David. The genealogy of Jesus includes Boaz as an ancestor.

Boaz's story is told in the Book of Ruth, named for its central figure, a Moabitess, who embodied all that was fine in a young widow. With her aged mother-in-law, Naomi, who, like Boaz, was a member of the tribe of Judah, she left Moab for Bethlehem.

Boaz noticed Ruth first as she performed one of the lowliest of tasks, the gathering of fragments of grain left behind for the poor. She did not reveal to Boaz that her first husband was his kinsman, but when Boaz, this wealthy landowner, later came into his field and saw the pretty, modest, young Ruth, he was attracted to her. Promptly he offered her his protection. First he asked her not to glean in any field but his own. Next he ordered his young men to not touch her.

Their romance began to take form when he invited her to break bread with him and when he told his reapers to give her some extra stalks from their bundles. He also passed parched grain to her.

Finally, she threw herself upon Boaz's protection, after which he honored her confidence in him by redeeming a portion of land belonging to her husband's next of kin, according to the levirate marriage law of these ancient times. His confidence in Ruth and her trust in him culminated in a marriage which still inspires faith, hope, and love. It resulted in a line "famous in Israel" (Ruth 4:14), the line of David, the greatest king of Israel.

The left entrance pillar of Solomon's temple was named after

Boaz (I Kings 7:21), this man of integrity and strength of purpose, qualities Christ typified at their best.

CALEB: AN OPTIMIST IN TIME OF DESPAIR

(Num. 13, 14, 26, 32, 34; Deut. 1:36; Joshua 14, 15, 21; Judg. 1; I Sam. 25:3, 30:14; I Chron. 2, 4, 6, etc.)

A man who dreamed dreams and saw visions, Caleb faithfully looked forward, not backward, even when hopelessness seized the majority. Honest, stalwart, confident, and fearless, he instilled confidence in others.

Caleb, a prince of Judah who came with Moses out of Egypt, stepped into the foreground at a time when the Israelites should have been filled with gratitude and hope, but they grumbled and complained though they had experienced many miracles. Among the miracles were the release from Egyptian domination after the parting of the waters of the Red Sea; an abundance of manna and quail when they were hungry; the face-to-face experience of Moses with God on Mount Sinai; the emergence of a well-organized and formidable nation, with the Ten Commandments the central core of its laws.

Although Caleb's faith had stimulated Moses in his leadership, he had remained somewhat in the background nationally. Then the time came when the Israelites had to make a decision about whether they should claim the Promised Land.

Caleb and Joshua were chosen along with ten other spies from the tribes of Israel to make a comprehensive study of Canaan before the children of Israel would later journey there. While ten of the spies gave in to cowardly despair, Caleb and Joshua hopefully went forward.

Forty days later Caleb, Joshua, and the others came back with the report that the land was flowing with milk and honey but that the people were strong and that their cities were well fortified. These outward appearances filled the ten fearful spies with apprehension about claiming the Promised Land. "But Caleb quieted the people before Moses, and said, 'Let us go up at once, and occupy it; for we are well able to overcome it' " (Num. 13:30).

The ten doubters said, "We are not able to go up against the Canaanites for they are stronger than we . . . all the people that we saw in it are men of great stature . . . We seemed ourselves like grasshoppers, and so we seemed to them" (Num. 13:31–33).

The children of Israel then cried and wept and murmured against Moses and Aaron, saying, "Would that we had died in the land of Egypt! Or would that we had died in this wilderness! Why does the Lord bring us into this land, to fall by the sword?" (Num. 14:2–3).

Caleb, this man with a different spirit, who had followed God fully, became the motivating force in releasing the people from their mood of hopelessness.

Patiently Caleb waited for Moses to announce the time to advance. It must have been a good many years later, about thirty-nine. Finally, Moses took the children of Israel up to the heights of the hill country, to look into the Promised Land. It was then decided that they should go forward across the Jordan into Canaan, under the leadership of Joshua. The ten spies were punished for their disbelief in God's promise and were not allowed to enter Canaan.

Joshua gave Caleb Hebron, one of the choice areas, as an inheritance for himself and his descendants. A man ahead of his time, Caleb shared with Achsah, his daughter, even better land —land with an abundance of spring water—than he had shared with his three sons. He was a fair man, too. His daughter married Othniel, who had recaptured Debir, a fortress city of Hebron. Othniel's reward for victory was Caleb's much prized daughter and the land with springs.

The next that we know of Caleb he is eighty-five years old, and he has never been in better health. He, who "wholly followed the Lord, the God of Israel" (Josh. 14:4), rejoices that God had kept him alive through forty-five difficult years of wandering: "I am still as strong to this day, as I was in the day that Moses sent me; my strength now is as my strength was then, for war, and for going and coming. So now give me this hill country of which the Lord spoke on that day" (Josh. 14:11–12).

CORNELIUS: THE FIRST GENTILE CONVERT

(Acts 10)

Cornelius was converted and baptized at Caesarea, in a bringing together of Jews and Gentiles that marked the emergence of Christ's Church in its larger aspect.

"Well spoken of by the whole Jewish nation" (Acts 10:22), Cornelius was ideally suited to bridge the gap between Jews and Gentiles. A centurion of the Italian cohort at Caesarea, he also bore the name of one of the noblest Roman families. Not only was he an eminent man but he was also a devout one, "who feared God with all his household" (v. 2). He was also a generous benefactor to the Jews, who had a high regard for him, but he remained an outsider because he was an uncircumcised Gentile.

The conversion of Cornelius came about through simultaneous visions, which first came to Cornelius at Caesarea and three days later to Peter at Joppa, thirty miles away. This led Peter to call at the house of Cornelius. As Peter approached the outer gate, Cornelius, hastening to meet him, fell down at his feet and worshiped him. Afterward Cornelius assured Peter that his entire household anxiously awaited his message.

Peter's sermon to Cornelius and his household, a succinct summary of the Christian proclamation (Acts 10:34–43), concerns the history of Jesus Christ, who is described as being clothed with miraculous power and filled with tender compassion, "the one ordained by God to be judge of the living and dead" (v. 42).

When Peter and others in the Church saw that the gift of the Holy Spirit had been poured out even on Gentiles, they were amazed. After this, Cornelius and his household were baptized in the name of Jesus Christ.

Cornelius' conversion had great significance for the Church in that it provided one of the motives for the Jerusalem conference (Acts 15). The legalistic problem regarding the circumcised and the uncircumcised, as vexing as some of today's unanswered social problems, was now resolved. Cornelius' conversion also made easier Paul's work in establishing a church for all men of faith. Furthermore, it brought forth the realization of Jesus' hopes for the ideals of the church universal, as opposed to the narrow views of the cult of the Pharisees.

CRISPUS: SYNAGOGUE RULER WHO BELIEVED IN CHRIST

(Acts 18:8; I Cor. 1:14)

Crispus, who was in charge of the synagogue at Corinth, accepted Christ as the Messiah.

Although Paul baptized Crispus, along with Gaius and the household of Stephanas, Paul wrote afterward, "Christ did not send me to baptize but to preach the gospel, and not with eloquent wisdom, lest the cross of Christ be emptied of its power" (I Cor. 1:17). The few words written about Crispus indicate several important facts. Though a Jew and the chief figure in the synagogue, he was a believer in Christ. So was his entire household. Lastly, he was humble, willing to take up the cross of Christ.

DANIEL: ONE OF THE FIRST TO WRITE OF RESURRECTION

(Ezra 14:14, 20, 28:30; Dan.; Matt. 24:15; Mark 13:14)

The Resurrection becomes a confident hope in Daniel's prophecies.

"And many of those who sleep in the dust of the earth shall awake, some to everlasting life," Daniel says (Dan. 12:2–3). The only other Old Testament prophecy on the Resurrection appears in Isaiah, who, about three centuries earlier, foretells, "Thy dead shall live; their bodies shall rise . . . awake and sing for joy!" (Isa. 26:19). This belief in the resurrection of a new, celestial body took on new dimension when Christ arose three days after the Crucifixion.

The Book of Daniel, bearing the name of its chief character, was written to give comfort to the persecuted. The narratives in the first six chapters and the visions of Daniel in the last six are harmoniously bound together by an anonymous author, who embodied his own and his nation's ideals in this heroic character, Daniel, an exiled Jew in Babylon, who rose to a high place in the government of Nebuchadnezzar II, ruler of the new Babylonian empire. The writer, who seems to be indifferent to the details of history, is thought to have written the book during the Maccabean rebellion when the Syrian king, Antiochus Epiphanes, added to the sufferings of the Jews in Palestine by trying to wipe out all signs of Judaism.

In the early part of the book, Daniel is depicted as a youth of superior moral and physical strength. He and his three companions, Shadrach, Meshach, and Abednego, were deported to Babylon from Jerusalem before its fall. King Nebuchadnezzar specified that the youths selected for special education at the royal court were to be those "without blemish, handsome and skilful in all wisdom, endowed with knowledge, understanding, learning, and competent to serve in the king's palace, and to [be taught] the letters and language of the Chaldeans" (Dan. 1:4). Daniel and his three friends lived up to these requirements.

During their three years of instruction in the Chaldean language, the youths were offered meat, wine, and delicacies from the king's table. But Daniel resolved that he would not defile himself with the king's rich offerings.

Because Daniel and his three companions also refused to worship Nebuchadnezzar's golden calf, they were thrown into a fiery furnace, but divine help came and they emerged unharmed. Although Daniel's Hebrew religion was declared illegal, he continued to worship in the faith of his fathers. When his enemies found him praying to God, they threw him into a den of lions. Again he escaped uninjured.

When the handwriting appeared on the wall during King Belshazzar's feast, the queen mother advised her son to turn to Daniel for the interpretation of its meaning. Daniel announced God's judgment for Belshazzar's wicked acts, one of which was the serving of wine from the vessels of gold and of silver which Nebuchadnezzar's father had taken from the temple in Jerusalem.

Because the people recognized that Daniel lived "in the spirit of the holy gods," he later was clothed with purple and a chain of gold was placed about his neck. Furthermore, he was strengthened, encouraged, and promised the power of revelation. In him at this time was born a new hope for his oppressed people.

Amid all of his blessings, Daniel never forgot to thank God. In his hymn of thanksgiving (Dan. 2:20–23, NEB), he says in part:

> Blessed be God's name from age to age,
> for all wisdom and power are his.
> He changes seasons and times;
> he deposes kings and sets them up;
> he gives wisdom to the wise
> and all their store of knowledge to the men who know;
> he reveals deep mysteries;
> he knows what lies in darkness,
> and light has its dwelling with him.
> To thee, God of my fathers, I give thanks and praise,
> for thou hast given me wisdom and power . . .

Although the Book of Daniel comes between the books of the two prophets Ezekiel and Hosea, it is not included with the other prophecies because it is regarded as apocalyptic, which, like the Revelation of John, inspires people to endure suffering in the hope of a wondrous future, while prophecy rouses them to righteous living.

Chapter 7 of Daniel is one of the most illuminating of all. It predicts with positive faith the ultimate triumph of God and the coming of his son. One of the night visions reads in part:

> and behold, with the clouds of heaven
>   there came one like a son of man,
> and he came to the Ancient of Days
>   and was presented before him.
> And to him was given dominion
>   and glory and kingdom,
> that all peoples, nations, and languages
>   should serve him;
> his dominion is an everlasting dominion,
>   which shall not pass away,
> and his kingdom one
>   that shall not be destroyed.
>   (Dan. 7:13–14)

Jesus referred to this passage when the high priest asked him if he were "the Christ, the Son of the blessed," and he answered, "I am; and you will see the Son of man sitting at the right hand of Power, and coming with the clouds of heaven" (Mark 14:62).

Daniel's wisdom, righteousness, and unshakable faith qualify him for the hopeful revelations in the latter part of the book, which sets forth glorious expectations that transcend material beliefs.

DEMAS: THE "OFF-AND-ON" CHRISTIAN

(Col. 4:14; Philem. 24; II Tim. 4:10)

Demas was one of those "off-and-on" fellow Christians. Sometimes he was very eager for the gospel of Christ as introduced by Paul and other times he was "in love with this present world," as Paul said of him when Demas deserted him while he was a prisoner in Rome, to go to Thessalonica.

Of the four once with Paul—Demas, Crescens, Luke, and Titus —only Luke remained to serve him. Demas' hope in Christianity was like a weather barometer, moving up and down with uncertainty, but at least he was trying to be a Christian.

ENOCH: A WALK INTO ETERNITY

(Gen. 5:18, 19, 21–24; I Chron. 1:3; Luke 3:37; Heb. 11:5; Jude 14)

Enoch was a descendant of Adam and Eve's third son, Seth.

The passage most descriptive of Enoch reports that when he was three hundred and sixty-five years old he "walked with God; and he was not, for God took him" (Gen. 5:24). This passage seems to tell us that the soul of a godly man never sleeps, for he dwells in the breath of the Eternal, and that his life goes right on, unbroken by death.

The full-fledged hope of the New Testament Christians had its birth in the primitive hope expressed in the miraculous removal of Enoch from the world of the flesh to the world of the spirit:

"By faith Enoch was taken up so that he should not see death; and he was not found, because God had taken him. Now before he was taken he was attested as having pleased God. And without faith it is impossible to please him. For whoever would draw near to God must believe that he exists and that he rewards those who seek him" (Heb. 11:5–6).

In his *Greater Men and Women of the Bible*, James Hastings expresses it well when he says Enoch's "walk was on the high hills, so high that he simply stepped into the next world without troubling death to go through its long dark process . . . He seems to have been a seer, a man who went out under the midnight sky, and felt the infinite, touched the eternal, was bathed in the presence of God. Men looked at him, felt that there was a glory in him, a soul in him, a consciousness of the Divine in him that they did not possess, and he stood out a giant among his contemporaries" (Vol. 1, pp. 65–66).

Enoch lived in such close communion with God that he could not stand ungodliness in any form. These lines in the Apocrypha suggest the finality of evil, such as Enoch would detest:

the hope of the wicked is like
thistledown borne on the wind,
and like fine, tempest-driven foam;
Like smoke scattered by the wind,
and like the passing memory of the
nomad camping for a single day.
But the just live forever . . .
For he [God] shall shelter them with his
right hand,
and protect them with his arm.
(Wis. 5:14–16, NAB)

The facts regarding Enoch's life are so brief that we learn little about him except that he was a son of the obscure Jared and the father of Methuselah, well known because he lived to be nine hundred and sixty-nine years old (Gen. 5:27). Through Methuselah, Enoch became the grandfather of Lamech and the great-grandfather of Noah.

Enoch, this antediluvian patriarch, is regarded as the most spiritually oriented man of the primitive period before the great

flood. He seems to have been a very wise man too. It is no wonder
that his life shines like a star in the night of this period, about
which so little is known.

EPAPHRAS: A PREACHER OF COLOSSAE

(Col. 1:7, 4:12; Philem. 23)

Epaphras taught the good news of Christ in his native city of
Colossae and in nearby Laodicea and Hierapolis. Paul commends
Epaphras for his service to these three Christian communities,
which he himself supposedly never visited.

Colossae, the largest, was a textile center. Jewish and Greek
merchants traveling the highway made it buzz with racial preju-
dices and political and philosophical arguments. Because Colossae
has been called "a hotbed of fantastic theological theories," it is
easy for us to imagine that this ancient Phrygian city, now in
ruins, was a difficult place to spread the good news of Christ, even
for a faithful believer like Epaphras.

The loyal Epaphras also carried to the imprisoned Paul a report of heresy at Colossae and its neighboring towns.

Paul's finest description of Epaphras is recorded when he sends
greetings to the Colossians and refers to him as "one of yourselves,
a servant of Christ Jesus [who] greets you, always remembering
you earnestly in his prayers, that you may stand mature and fully
assured in all the will of God. For I bear him witness that he has
worked hard for you and for those in Laodicea and in Hierapolis"
(Col. 4:12–13).

EZRA: THE RESTORER OF TEMPLE WORSHIP

(Ezra; Nehemiah)

The head of one of the twenty-two priestly groups who came
back to Jerusalem with Nehemiah after exile in Babylon, Ezra was

a scribe skilled in the laws of Moses and a priest who made glorious the priestly side of religion.

He was commissioned by Artaxerxes, king of Persia, to lead his God-loving countrymen back from Babylon to Jerusalem. Ezra's primary objective was to restore the religious ideals of the temple at Jerusalem, the heart of the Jewish religion. Ezra had the confident hope that he could accomplish this mission, and he did. The year of the journey is not clear from the Book of Ezra, since it is not stated which of two kings of Persia bearing the same name, Artaxerxes I (465–425 B.C.) and Artaxerxes II (405–359 B.C.), is meant.

Ezra assembled the refugees on one of the canals of Babylonia, along the river Ahava, for the journey back to Jerusalem. In the caravan were priests, menservants, maidservants, and families, as well as horses, mules, camels, and asses. It is not known exactly how many people there were. The books of Ezra and Nehemiah differ, but it is generally thought there were more than five thousand.

The religious purpose of the journey became more evident as the sacred vessels for the embellishment of the temple services were assembled and packed. As preparations were made, again and again Ezra assured the people that the hand of the Lord was upon them and that they would be able to accomplish the miraculous. The perilous journey from Babylon to Jerusalem, largely on foot, required more than four months.

Without Ezra's leadership, his unbending firmness of will, unselfish patriotism, energy, initiative, and evangelistic spirit, the journey might have been a failure. But he went forward with one objective, to bring a renaissance to the holy city, Jerusalem.

When the returning exiles arrived in Jerusalem, Ezra summoned the congregation to the temple to rebuild the altar and to offer sacrifices. But first of all, he stood and thanked God, and then he read the Book of the Law, emphasizing not the penal side of the law as cited in Deuteronomy, but the goodness of God in giving the law to Israel.

Then the work on the temple was begun with vigor, but adversaries from Judah and Benjamin came forward to protest. They even hired counselors to frustrate Ezra's work, and for a time, the work was halted completely, but finally the temple was restored and the people celebrated the dedication of the temple with much joy. The Feast of the Tabernacle also was observed, during which Ezra gave his long penitential psalm (Neh. 9:6–38), which, in a sense, is a review of the whole religious history of his people and their long search for God.

Ezra initiated other reforms—the dissolution of mixed marriages, the observation of the Sabbath, the payment of a temple tax, and so on. But nothing was more meaningful than the restoration of the temple. These words of the Psalmist suggest the spirit of his undertaking.

> One thing have I asked of the Lord,
>   that will I seek after;
> that I may dwell in the house of the Lord
>   all the days of my life,
> to behold the beauty of the Lord,
>   and to inquire in his temple.
>   (Ps. 27:4)

FORTUNATUS: GLADNESS AT HIS PRESENCE

(I Cor. 16:17)

Fortunatus was one in whom Paul rejoiced at his coming to Ephesus from Corinth. Paul wrote to the Corinthians that the visit of Fortunatus, along with Stephanas and Achaicus, made up for the absence of his other Corinthian friends.

He said of them, "they refreshed my spirit as they did yours. You should recognize the worth of such men" (I Cor. 16:18). What a valuable credential for Fortunatus and his two other Corinthian friends, all worthy men, eager to aid in spreading the gospel of Christ.

GAMALIEL: AN ADVOCATE OF JUSTICE

(Acts 5:34, 22:3)

A Pharisee and a celebrated doctor of the law, Gamaliel, after the crucifixion of Jesus, pleaded for conformity to moral principle, not death for the apostles.

This was at the time of the Church's emergence immediately following Pentecost, when the apostles, miraculously released from prison, went forth to teach, preach, and heal in the name of "this just man" Jesus, who had been crucified. But when the high priest of Jerusalem and his jealous colleagues witnessed the success of the apostles, once more they demanded their arrest and ordered them to appear before the council in Jerusalem. There the high priest addressed them in these words,

> "We gave you formal warning," he said "not to preach in this name, and what have you done? You have filled Jerusalem with your teaching, and seem determined to fix the guilt of this man's death on us." In reply Peter and the apostles said, "Obedience to God comes before obedience to men; it was the God of our ancestors who raised up Jesus, but it was you who had him executed by hanging on a tree. By his own right hand God has now raised him up to be a leader and saviour, to give repentance and forgiveness of sins through him to Israel. We are witnesses to all this, we and the Holy Spirit. . . ." This so infuriated them that they wanted to put them to death.
>
> (Acts 5:28–33, JB)

Then Gamaliel, this just Pharisee who was president of the Sanhedrin, the full legal council of the Jews, stepped forth to speak, during great tumult, excitement, and anger, in defense of the apostles, who could have been hung on a cross as Jesus had been. Their ruthless enemies feared them now because their Christian converts were multiplying too fast.

Although there is no evidence that Gamaliel ever became a Christian, he was so tolerant and just that he saw that all, Jews, Gentiles, and Christians alike, were given fair trials. Having witnessed the power and purpose of God at work, Gamaliel desired to protect Pharisaic Judaism, in so many respects at one with Christianity on the resurrection of the dead.

There was silence in the court when the wise and distinguished Gamaliel spoke, for he was a man of great stature in the legal circles of Jerusalem, highly respected as the grandson of the famous Hillel, president of the Sanhedrin, for whom the School of Hillel was named.

Through his wise caution, Gamaliel was able to turn the tide in favor of the apostles when their enemies would have executed them on the spot. Diplomatically, Gamaliel asked the apostles to step aside while he addressed members of the Sanhedrin. And they listened.

"Men of Israel, be careful how you deal with these people. There was Theudas who became notorious not so long ago. He claimed to be someone important, and he even collected about four hundred followers; but when he was killed, all his followers scattered and that was the end of them. And then there was Judas the Galilean, at the time of the census, who attracted crowds of supporters; but he got killed too, and all his followers dispersed. What I suggest, therefore, is that you leave these men alone and let them go. If this enterprise, this movement of theirs, is of human origin it will break up of its own accord; but if it does in fact come from God you will not only be unable to destroy them, but you might find yourselves fighting against God."

(Acts 5:36–39, JB)

Gamaliel's wise advice was accepted. Orders were then given by the high priest to call the apostles in, flog them, warn them not to speak in the name of Jesus, and then release them. The apostles left the council rejoicing that they were counted worthy to suffer dishonor in the name of Jesus.

Every time after this when they went forth to preach and teach the Gospel in the temple and in private houses, they lovingly remembered Gamaliel, their defender.

After his conversion, Paul spoke of going as a youth from Tarsus to Jerusalem to study "at the feet of Gamaliel." In ancient times this was literally true, because a teacher of Gamaliel's prominence then sat on a raised bench in front of his pupils, where he commanded the same respect he later won in the courtroom.

GIDEON: THE MIGHTY DELIVERER

(Judg. 6, 7, 8; Heb. 11:32–34)

Liberated Israel from the oppression of the Midianites, Gideon is honored as one of the heroes of Heb. 11, "who through faith conquered kingdoms, enforced justice, received promises . . . won strength out of weakness, became mighty in war, put foreign armies to flight."

He is called one of the most remarkable military leaders in the Old Testament, one who went up against seemingly impossible odds and came out the conqueror.

While he was threshing wheat one day in the wine press of his father, Joash, a well-to-do farmer who lived in the border territory of Manasseh, Gideon was miraculously called to aid his people in a time of distress. The call came through an angel who appeared, addressing him as a mighty man of valor, and assured him that God was with him.

Since his father was a Baal worshiper, the first thing Gideon did was to tear down his father's altar to Baal, after which he erected an altar to God. Then he set about to deliver his people, weakened physically and spiritually by their constant oppression at the hands of Midianite marauders and pillagers, who at harvest time forcibly took their lands. Conflicts became so numerous that many Israelites were driven to caves, dens, and rocky strongholds for safety. When their future seemed hopeless, the young Gideon appeared to deliver them.

Then Gideon hopefully set forth to fight hordes of desert raiders, who swooped down like locusts and destroyed his people's sheep, oxen, and produce until they had no provisions; they seemed unable to fight against forces so powerful in size and equipment. Gideon had earlier appealed to God and asked, "How can I deliver Israel? . . . my clan is the weakest in Manasseh, and I am the least in my family" (Judg. 6:15).

With the spirit of the Lord upon him, Gideon grew strong in valor and sensed an ultimate, confident assurance of victory. Soon he was able to accomplish the miraculous.

He then set forth with thirty-two thousand defenders, but the Lord spoke to him again saying, "The people with you are too many . . . [say to them,] 'Whoever is fearful and trembling, let him return home' . . . Twenty-two thousand returned but ten thousand remained" (Judg. 7:2–3). This still was too many, for God wanted the victory to come through divine, not human strength.

As Gideon's remaining forces drank water beside a brook, God tested them and found a mere three hundred who proved worthy.

Gideon's access to God became the ground of his hope as he pressed on, with forces reduced from thirty-two thousand to three hundred.

He divided these into three equal bands. All were supplied with lighted torches and trumpets as they advanced upon the enemy from three sides. In the brilliant light from their torches and the thunderous noise from their trumpets, they appeared much more formidable than they were. The frightened enemy, plunged into panic, made a wild flight toward the Jordan Valley.

Gideon later sent messengers through the hill country for reinforcements. Soon victory was his. Later, the proud Ephraimites upbraided Gideon for not calling them into battle, but Gideon humbly asked them, "Is not the gleaning of the grapes of Ephraim better than the vintage of Abiezer?" (Judg. 8:2). Gideon's father was an Abiezerite, and his initial support came from this clan. By magnifying their accomplishments and depreciating his own, Gideon showed clearly that he was a master of diplomacy as well as of strategy.

Later, Gideon, this man of valor, was asked to become king of Israel, but he refused, saying that God alone was Israel's rightful ruler. He chose instead to return to his own family, village, and farm.

One of the finest tributes is paid to Gideon, the warrior, at the end of his Bible biography, "and the land had rest for forty years" (Judg. 8:28).

In honor of Gideon and his small band of men dedicated to the service of God, an organization founded in 1898 and called the Gideons has circulated Bibles all over the world. Millions of strangers in motels and hotels, some lonely and hopeless, have found the Gideon Bible in their rooms.

The Gideons, originally comprising a handful of traveling salesmen, now include business and professional men, doctors, lawyers, and teachers, who contribute generously to the organization's annual budget. Their Gideon Bibles help to keep alive the name of this early deliverer of Israel, but more than that, these Bibles help others to find victorious hope in God's word.

HEZEKIAH: JUDAH'S MOST GODLY KING

Hezekiah, referred to many times in II Kings, I and II Chronicles, Isaiah, Jeremiah, Hosea, Micah, and Ecclesiasticus in the Apocrypha, was Judah's most godly king.

During his rule, he held to the hope that he would be worthy of God's faithfulness. He is best remembered for the purging of the nation of idolatry, his support of Isaiah in civil and religious reforms, the restoration of true worship, his refusal to accept death during a serious illness, and his miraculous prayer of thanksgiving afterward.

Hezekiah's love for God was something of an enigma, for neither his father, Ahaz, nor his son Manasseh possessed it. He seems to have inherited his own lofty enthusiasm for the ancient faith from his mother Abi (Abijah). Apparently, she was descended from Zechariah, the favorite prophet of King Uzziah, a godly king also.

The fidelity and courage of King Hezekiah, the zeal of Isaiah, and the prayers of the righteous remnant brought about miracles in Israel during Hezekiah's reign.

Early in his reign, Hezekiah opened the doors of the temple, closed by his father, and then he set forth on a reformation of the religious principles laid down in Deuteronomy. He had the lamps in the temple lighted, the ceremonial vessels arranged before the altar, the long neglected Passover restored, and the choir trained. He assembled the priests and the Levites and called the people together in an assembly, during which they were inspired with new religious zeal. In all this Hezekiah paved the way for the religious reformation of King Josiah in the next century.

During Hezekiah's twenty-nine-year reign (715–687 B.C.), the powerful Assyrian oppressors also were routed. Water conduits or tunnels were cut under the walls of Jerusalem. They were fed by springs so that the city might be prepared to withstand a siege.

Israel also reached a literary height at this time, during which some of the Psalms and Proverbs were written, for there was a new spiritual vigor among the men of letters. Probably the Book of the Law, found in the temple during the reign of Josiah and sent to Huldah, who confirmed its authenticity, belonged to this creative period of Hezekiah. Temple devotees acclaimed Hezekiah's remarkable influence for good by giving his name to a guild of copyists (Prov. 25:1).

King Hezekiah was fortunate in the support he received from the prophet Isaiah, who was often in and out of his court and influential in his civil and religious decisions. Isaiah was at the palace with Hezekiah during the king's serious illness. When Hezekiah was almost at the point of death, Isaiah predicted he would die. More hopeful than the great prophet, the king turned his face to the wall and prayed that he might recover. As Isaiah made his way out of the royal chamber and reached the courtyard, he turned back to tell Hezekiah that God had heard his prayer and that he would recover and live fifteen years longer.

When the devout Hezekiah was well again, he arose in all of his strength to serve God, during which he wrote his famous Psalm of Praise (Isa. 38:9–20). He said in part:

> O Lord, I am oppressed; be thou my security! . . .
> All my sleep has fled
> > because of the bitterness of my soul. . . .
> > Oh, restore me to health and make me live! . . .
> those who go down to the pit cannot hope
> > for thy faithfulness.
> The living, the living, he thanks thee,
> > as I do this day;
> the father makes known to the children
> > thy faithfulness.
>
> The Lord will save me,
> > and we will sing to stringed instruments
> all the days of our life,
> > at the house of the Lord.
>
> (vs. 14–16, 18–20)

So exuberant was Hezekiah after some of his miraculous experiences, especially his recovery from a serious illness, that when the Assyrians sent an envoy to him with messages and presents, he committed a folly by gratifying his pride and showing his enemy the great extent of his possessions: silver and gold, precious stones, spices, shields, costly vessels, storehouses of grain, armory, wine and oil, and stalls for cattle. Isaiah later prophesied that the enemy would carry these kingly possessions into Babylonia but that this would not happen during Hezekiah's lifetime. Isaiah prophesied that Hezekiah and his people would enjoy peace and prosperity during the closing years of his reign.

Despite Hezekiah's pride and folly, he is remembered as a mild and just administrator, a man of integrity, intelligence, refinement, humility, and spiritual steadfastness. His very name is surrounded with a light he brought into his religious reform and a hope in God's power to heal. No wonder it is written of him: "He trusted in the Lord the God of Israel; so there was none like him among all the kings of Judah after him, nor among those who were before him" (II Kings 18:5).

John the Unknown: The Prophet-Exile on the Isle of Patmos

(I, II, III John; Revelation)

Often referred to as St. John the Divine, John is identified as the prophet exiled on Patmos, a thirteen-square-mile island in the Aegean. Here he wrote the Book of Revelation, which discloses revelations of the ultimate divine purpose.

This John, some scholars believe, wrote I John, often called "The Letter of Love," and II John, "The Letter of Love's Limitation." Some authorities also think that this John might also have written the fourth Gospel. The *Interpreter's Dictionary of the Bible* cites "a close resemblance of vocabulary, style, and thought between [I John and the fourth Gospel]. Both works employ a small vocabulary to express a small number of ideas which are constantly repeated in new forms" (Vol. 2, p. 950).

Traditionally, the author of Revelation has been identified with John the Apostle, son of Zebedee, but later scholars say Revelation was written in the latter part of the reign of the Emperor Domitian (A.D. 81–96). If so, it is not likely that he was the earlier John, the disciple of Christ's time.

This John identifies himself as a servant of Christ (Rev. 1:1) and as a brother in tribulation (v. 9). He mentions "the twelve apostles of the lamb" but does not connect himself with them.

From a ship passing by Patmos, a sparsely settled island in the Dodecanese, with its glistening white crags set in the beautiful Aegean, one gains a new understanding of the vision of John the mystic, in which he saw a new heaven and a new earth, "the holy city, new Jerusalem, coming down out of heaven from God, prepared as a bride adorned for her husband" (Rev. 21:2), "in heaven an open door" (4:1), a "sea of glass, like crystal" (4:6), etc. The book goes into many lofty flights of imagination like this. It is thought that the author received his visions while a prisoner on Patmos, where he no doubt, like other enemies of Rome, quarried the white stone while in exile.

The Monastery of St. John now owns most of the south half of Patmos, an excellent example of a geographical setting that is conducive to the meditation of a mystic.

Since I and II John, also III John, do not bear the author's name, he and the author of Revelation still remain a mystery.

Jonathan: Devoted Friend of David

(I Sam. 13, 14, 18, 19, 20, 23, 31; II Sam. 1:4–5, 12, 17, 22–23, 25–26, 4:4, 9:1, 3, 6–7, 21:7, 12–13, 21:14; I Chron. 8:33–34, 9:39–40, 10:2)

Jonathan, King Saul's crown prince son and David's boyhood friend, paved the way for David to become king of Israel instead of himself.

The love between Jonathan and David is the Bible's most beautiful example of friendship. It signifies a hope that is intricately woven into love at its best and is typical of God's love for man, a love that springs from God's creative power and moves toward a good that is harmonious with that power.

After his victory over the Philistine giant Goliath, the young David visited the court of King Saul and met his son Jonathan. There grew up between them "a love passing the love of women."

Their friendship was sealed by a covenant they made together (I Sam. 18:1–4), at which time Jonathan, to show his love and respect for David, gave him his princely armor, even his sword, his bow, and his girdle.

The armor filled David with new confidence, and he soon met with meteoric success in battle. Jonathan took pride in David's achievements as a warrior, but King Saul grew jealous of his prowess. The love of David and Jonathan, however, survived the difficult father-and-son relationship.

King Saul even sought to kill David, but Jonathan warned David of the impending danger to his life and told him to go and hide. While David was in hiding, Jonathan went to his father and spoke well of David. "And Saul hearkened to the voice of Jonathan." But jealousy again filled King Saul's heart, and while David played his lyre, Saul sought to pin him to the wall with a spear.

A second time Jonathan delivered David from oncoming danger. They met in a field again to discuss Saul's jealousy and mental disturbance and to reason together on how to deal with it. No doubt Jonathan also had a premonition of his own impending death in battle, for he said to David, "If I am still alive, show me the loyal love of the Lord, that I may not die; and do not cut off your loyalty from my house for ever" (I Sam. 20:14–15). David and Jonathan concluded their visit with another oath of their love and allegiance to each other.

Afterward Jonathan pleaded with his father for David's safety, but the disturbed Saul was more infuriated than ever. All Jonathan could do was warn David once more of his father's mental sickness.

In order to strengthen David's courage, Jonathan said to him, "'Fear not; the hand of Saul my father shall not find you. You shall be king over Israel, and I shall be next to you; Saul my father also knows this.' And the two of them made a covenant [the third time] before the Lord" (I Sam. 23:16–18).

When David fled again from Saul, he continued to be victorious in battle and Jonathan continued to sustain him with his steadfast friendship. Finally, however, the sad news reached David that Jonathan and his father and two brothers had been killed in battle at Mount Gilboa. This prompted David's moving elegy (II Sam. 1:17–27), in which he lamented,

> Jonathan lies slain upon thy high places.
> I am distressed for you, my brother Jonathan;
> very pleasant have you been to me;
> your love to me was wonderful,
> passing the love of women.
>
> (vs. 25–26)

At news of his father's death, Jonathan's five-year-old son, Mephibosheth, in a fall, was crippled in his feet when his nurse fled with him from the palace. The brotherly covenant David and Jonathan had entered into secured for this lame prince the lands of Saul, entrance to the royal court, where David was now king, and protection from the death that befell the other heirs of Saul.

This remarkable friendship was based upon great qualities in both Jonathan and David. David first of all had marvelous ability, diplomacy, and strength. The gentle, discerning Jonathan was so self-effacing that he was glad to pave the way for David to succeed his father as king. And David had such a steadfast love toward Jonathan that their friendship survived the tension created by the impetuous, unreasonable, and mentally sick King Saul, who, though torn from his son in life, was at last united with him in death.

JOSEPH OF ARIMATHEA: IN HIS OWN TOMB LAY THE BODY OF JESUS

(Matt. 27:57, 59; Mark 15:43; Luke 23:50; John 19:38)

A wealthy member of the Sanhedrin, the legal council that condemned Jesus, Joseph of Arimathea gave the garden tomb he had set aside for himself as a burial place for Christ.

Matthew describes Joseph as a rich man. Mark calls him a respected member of the Sanhedrin. Luke pictures him as "a good and righteous man." John tells that he was a disciple of Jesus.

When Joseph sat with the legal council that condemned Jesus, he either abstained or refused to vote with them for his execution.

Though apprehensive about a negative vote before this august group, Joseph afterward had the courage to go before Pontius Pilate, the Roman procurator, to petition to remove the body of Jesus from the Cross.

In providing for Jesus his own new, roughly hewn sepulchre near Calvary, Joseph of Arimathea assumed the responsibility of a relative. He showed even greater love and kindness when he wrapped Jesus' crucified body in linens and assisted Nicodemus in sweetening the linens with spices.

As his final thoughtful act, Joseph rolled a stone against the door of the tomb so as to protect Jesus' body from vandals. Mark reports that the witnesses to this final loving care of Jesus were Mary the mother of Jesus (Mark 15:47) and Mary Magdalene, the only person also there three days later when Jesus arose from the tomb.

This garden tomb provided by Joseph, it is thought, was on the present site of the Church of the Holy Sepulchre.

JOSEPH OF GALILEE: THE HUSBAND OF MARY, THE MOTHER OF JESUS

(Matt. 1:16–20, 24, 2:13, 19; Luke 1:27, 2:4, 16, 33, 43, 3:23, 4:22; John 1:45, 6:42)

Joseph of Galilee trusted in God's messengers each time they appeared to him.

First an angel said, "Joseph, son of David, do not fear to take Mary your wife, for that which is conceived of her is of the Holy Spirit; she will bear a son, and you shall call his name Jesus" (Matt. 1:20–21). And Joseph did as the angel of the Lord commanded. He took his wife, but "he knew her not until she had borne a son" (v. 25).

A second time, after Jesus was born, "an angel of the Lord appeared to Joseph in a dream and said, 'Rise, take the child and his mother, and flee to Egypt, and remain there till I tell you; for Herod is about to search for the child, to destroy him'" (Matt. 2:13). Again Joseph heeded the angel's warning, and he departed for Egypt.

A third time an angel appeared in a dream to tell Joseph to return to Israel "for those who sought the child's life are dead" (Matt. 2:20).

The final mention of Joseph is when he attended the Passover feast at Jerusalem with his wife and twelve-year-old child (Luke 2:41–51). After being missing for three days, Jesus was found sitting among the teachers in the temple. Now Jesus spoke of God as his true Father. At first neither his mother nor his father understood the full impact of his words. Later, however, Jesus went back with his parents to Nazareth.

From the age twelve he remained in Nazareth until he was a young man. Joseph now disappears from the record.

Joseph is honorably mentioned wherever his name appears, and he is ever the attentive husband and father. He was with Mary on the arduous trek from Nazareth to Bethlehem when the decree had gone out from Caesar Augustus that a census of the Roman world had to be taken. Mary rode the ninety miles by donkey, and it is easy to imagine that Joseph walked beside her most of the way.

He next took her and the child Jesus to the temple at Jerusalem, when it was time, according to Jewish custom, for Mary's purification rites. Mary and Joseph were together all the way to the altar when they placed their son in the arms of Simeon, who saw that the light of God was on the child's face. Joseph remained with his wife, Mary, and the child Jesus in Egypt until the death of Herod, and then Joseph carefully watched over his family as they journeyed back to Nazareth.

Joseph trained Jesus in his own carpenter's trade, teaching him how to make tables, benches and stools, probably a new chest for the scrolls of the Law, and yokes for the farmers' oxen.

Every mention of Joseph indicates that he was a worthy son of the line of David, a God-fearing man, willing to take second place beside his wife, Mary, through whom her son, Jesus, was spiritually conceived, according to the record of Luke 1:27, which calls her "a virgin betrothed to a man whose name was Joseph."

Much confusion has arisen through the centuries among several branches of the Christian faith regarding the birth of Jesus, and many questions still remain unanswered.

One great branch of the Christian faith believes that Joseph
was many years older than Mary and had been married before, and that his children by this former marriage are the
brothers and sisters mentioned in Mark 6:3 . . . Other com-
mentators conjecture that Mary and Joseph, after the birth
of Jesus, had several children, born the normal way. Still
others suggest that the "brothers" and "sisters" could have
been Jesus' cousins by his mother's sister (John 19:25)."

All of the Women of the Bible, p. 161

JOSIAH: DISCOVERER OF THE LOST BOOK OF THE LAW

(I Kings 13:2; II Kings 21, 22, 23; I Chron. 3:14–15; II Chron. 33,
34, 35, 36; Jer. 1, 3, 22, 25, 26, 35, 36, 37, 45, 46; Zeph. 1:1; Matt.
1:10–11)

Josiah was a godly king of Judah, who "in lawless times made
godliness prevail" (Ecclesiasticus 49:3, NEB). In his appraisal of
famous men, the writer declares that all the kings of Judah were
wicked, except David, Hezekiah, and Josiah (49:4).

Josiah is best remembered for his restoration of the temple at
Jerusalem and his renewal of the covenant of God given to Moses
and documented in the lost Book of the Law. This was found
while repairs were under way in the temple.

Josiah was "eight years old when he began to reign, and he
reigned thirty-one years in Jerusalem" (II Chron. 34:1). He became king after his father Amon was murdered by his servants in
the palace. Both Amon and his father, Manasseh, are described
as wicked kings, but Josiah's mother, Jedidah (II Kings 22:1), is
thought to have been a godly woman.

When Josiah was sixteen years old "he began to seek the God
of David" (II Chron. 34:3), and he set out to conduct his own
life and that of his court according to God's laws. When he was
twenty-six he took energetic steps to repair the temple. While
this was under way, Hilkiah the priest found the lost Book of the
Law there. He handed it over to the scribe Shaphan, who in turn
read it to Josiah, who was so deeply impressed that he humbled
himself before God and determined to inaugurate his great reform according to the laws in the book.

However, before Josiah took this step he had the foresight to send the book by five of his messengers to the prophetess Huldah, who verified its authenticity. Josiah then had it read publicly before the elders, prophets, priests, and populace, and so the book, which comprised a large part of the commandments, testimonies, and statutes in Deuteronomy, became the constitution of the Jewish faith.

Josiah set about with religious zeal to put the book into effect. He ordered that all vessels made for idol worship be destroyed, that idolatrous priests be deposed, that the houses of the male cult prostitutes be broken down, that the chariots of the sun be burned, and that the mediums, wizards, the teraphim, the idols, and all other abominations against God be wiped out.

Then Josiah instituted a Passover on a scale unheard of since the time of Samuel and other judges. This and other religious festivals were all according to the documented material in the lost Book of the Law.

Because of Josiah's fight against evils which had so long prevailed, the religious remnant found new hope in this young king who "turned to the Lord with all his heart and all his soul and with all his might" (II Kings 23:25). Other texts on Josiah in II Kings 22 and 23 and II Chron. 34 and 35 provide an inspiring commentary on his reforms, and Jeremiah and Zephaniah begin their prophecies by saying that the word of the Lord first came to them in the days of Josiah.

He met an untimely death when he went into battle at age thirty-nine against Neco king of Egypt at Carchemish on the Euphrates. He was so badly wounded at Megiddo that he died soon afterward. His death was greatly mourned. Even Jeremiah and all the singing men and women uttered a lament for Josiah.

"In his untimely death the fervid hopes of the pious received a set-back which was long lamented as one of the cardinal disasters of Israel. It was a sore calamity, but also a stern education. Israel must learn not only the enthusiasm but also the prudence and wisdom of its new-found faith," says John Franklin Genung in *The International Standard Bible Encyclopaedia* (Vol. III, pp. 1753.)

Although Josiah's fervid hopes were torn asunder in the reigns

of his wicked sons, Jehoiakim and Zedekiah, and although Jerusalem and its temple fell during the latter's reign, at least in
Josiah's reign we see God's transcendence and obedience to God's
laws and statutes as the power of Israel's future.

JULIUS THE CENTURION: PAUL'S KIND ROMAN FRIEND

(Acts 27:1, 3)

Julius was the man who probably saved Paul from death when
Roman soldiers threatened to kill him after their ship was
grounded off Malta. Julius was a centurion of the Augustan Cohort stationed at Caesarea in Syria and a member of the Julian
family, of which Julius Caesar was the most distinguished.

Paul had just appeared before the Roman governor, Festus,
and the puppet king of Chalcis, Agrippa, at Caesarea, where he
was accused of being a disturber of the peace (Acts 24:1–9). He
needed a friend like Julius, in whose custody he was placed for
the trip from Caesarea to Rome. Because the journey was made in
a merchant ship, not a military vessel, some of Paul's companions,
including Aristarchus, were able to accompany him. This courtesy
came through Julius' faith in Paul. Although Paul was a prisoner,
Julius allowed him to go ashore at Sidon, where he visited friends,
who also showed him many kindnesses.

As the ship neared Malta on the voyage to Italy, "striking a
shoal, they ran the vessel aground; the bow stuck and remained
immovable, and the stern was broken by the surf. The soldiers'
plan was to kill the prisoners [including Paul], lest they should
swim away and escape; but the centurion [Julius], wishing to save
Paul, kept them from carrying out their purpose" (Acts 27:41–43).

In every crisis, whether a close call from death or a violent
storm at sea, Paul was renewed by his faith and hope in God, so
that he pressed forward, despite the crisis. The Roman Julius, who
was the channel for Paul's triumph over tragedy this time, is me-
morialized as a trusting, kind man. Were it not for this quality,
the name of Julius no doubt would have been lost in the pages
of time.

Koheleth: Author of Book on Unrealized Hopes

Koheleth (Qoheleth) is the author of Ecclesiastes, the twenty-first book in the Bible. "Koheleth," signifying one who preaches in an assembly, is the Hebrew title. "Ecclesiastes," which has the same meaning, comes from the Septuagint, the Greek translation of the Old Testament used by the early Church. Little is known of Koheleth himself. Probably he was a public figure well known for his wisdom.

The Book of Ecclesiastes has been connected with the wisdom literature for centuries. It was once thought to have been written by Solomon, but scholars are now certain he did not write it, though some of its examples (Ecc. 2:4–11) quoted earlier in the story of Solomon well apply to him.

Regardless of who the author was, the book is regarded as Solomon's confidential autobiography. He used his own experiences and those of other public figures in Israel's history. The book was written during the postexilic period, probably 430–400 B.C., but it is thought other editorial hands touched it later.

Koheleth probably was a man of wealth, who could entertain, travel, and indulge himself in other ways. His theme throughout is "Vanity of vanities! All is vanity!" This is stated at the beginning and repeated at the conclusion. The book is filled with the hopelessness of vain pursuits, such as fame, wealth, and honor, but also with hopefulness for the reconciliation that comes amid all the trials and perplexities in life, if we remember our whole duty is to keep God's commandments.

"Man's days," Koheleth says, "are painful." In death, human aspirations vanish like the wind.

The author, a realist, seems to be goading us to accept reality. He reminds us that too many selfish ambitions and human desires can be frustrating. For that reason we must learn to invest our lives in acts of charity and in dedication to God. He also tells us that we must learn to make the best of each day's challenges, remembering that history and nature move in an ever-revolving circle.

He also says that we must learn to be satisfied with relative good, willing to compromise, and able to seek enjoyment in the midst of aimless disorder, since all things are vanity anyway.

Koheleth also teaches that we must willingly accept what God has for us, that without hardships, sorrow, and disappointments there is no progress anyway. The most profound and most quoted discourse in the book is that there is a time for every thing:

a time to be born, and a time to die;
a time to plant, and a time to pluck up what is planted;
a time to kill, and a time to heal;
a time to break down, and a time to build up;
a time to weep, and a time to laugh;
a time to mourn, and a time to dance;
a time to cast away stones, and a time to gather stones together;
a time to embrace, and a time to refrain from embracing;
a time to seek, and a time to lose;
a time to keep, and a time to cast away;
a time to rend, and a time to sew;
a time to keep silence, and a time to speak;
a time to love, and a time to hate;
a time for war, and a time for peace.

(Ecc. 3:2-8)

This appears in the second discourse on the frustrating experiences of life (Ecc. 3:1-5:20), following the first discourse (1:1-2:26) on the vanity of human wisdom. The third discourse, on the vanity of honor and riches (6:1-8:17) reminds us that our lives pass like a shadow in the sunlight.

In the author's counsel on how to be prudent in a world filled with sin, he makes the point that "a good name is better than precious ointment" (Ecc. 7:1), that wisdom is of more value than wealth, that we must learn to respect authority and to accept injustices we can do nothing about.

Finally, in the fourth discourse (Ecc. 9:1-12:8), Koheleth stresses that we must leave our destiny to God, knowing he has a plan for our lives if we seek to live according to the best in us and if we do not fret too much when we can not find the answers to all the puzzling questions of life.

Although there are contradictory thoughts in the book, it holds interest to the end because it is a story of our human pilgrimage, and most of our own experiences are common to other lives described here. We learn, too, that life, with all its disappointments and uncertainties, has purpose and meaning.

Lazarus: The Center of a Hope

(John 11:1–2, 5, 11, 14, 43, 12:1–2, 9–10, 17)

Lazarus rose from the grave in the presence of a great crowd of witnesses when Jesus spoke to him, "Lazarus come out" (John 11:43). Some were hostile, but others looking on, including Lazarus' sisters, Martha and Mary, believed in the resurrection.

Soon after this, Christ was on his way to the Cross. The great miracle of raising Lazarus did two things at the time. It made Christ's enemies more jealous of him, but made his followers stronger believers.

Four days before the miracle, while Jesus was on a mission in a nearby village, Lazarus had died of a short illness. When Jesus arrived at his tomb he "wept" (John 11:35), for he loved Lazarus, as he did Lazarus' sisters, at whose home in Bethany he had visited often.

When Lazarus was first stricken, Mary and Martha sent word to Jesus, saying, "'Lord, he whom you love is ill.' But when Jesus heard it he said, 'This illness is not unto death; it is for the glory of God, so that the Son of God may be glorified by means of it'" (John 11:3–4).

In his one-volume *Commentary on the Holy Bible,* J. R. Dummelow says of this physical miracle "that it was definitely worked to produce faith in Christ; that more than any other miracle it was performed under test conditions" (pp. 792–93).

The triumphal climax comes in Christ's declaration to Martha: "I am the resurrection and the life; he who believes in me, though he die, yet shall he live, and whoever lives and believes in me shall never die" (John 11:25–26).

We can assume that Lazarus was a man of hope before the miracle took place. If not, there is no doubt of his confident faith after that. The only time he is mentioned before his death is in an incident that occurred six days before the Passover, as he sat at the table where Martha served and where "Mary took a pound of costly ointment of pure nard and anointed the feet of Jesus and wiped his feet with her hair, and the house was filled with the fragrance of the ointment" (John 12:3).

We can confidently assume that Lazarus later was aware that the miracle surrounding his life brought a crowd of witnesses to Jerusalem, when Jesus made his triumphal entry there on Palm Sunday.

Today's disbelievers discount so wondrous a miracle. But what of it? God is the one "who gives life to the dead and calls into existence the things that do not exist" (Rom. 3:17). Christ demonstrated this to the fullest when he raised Lazarus from the grave. This miracle raises the voice of hope to say there is a way out. Hopelessness would say, "There is absolutely no exit."

In the miracle of Lazarus is humanization at its best: two grieving sisters; Christ filled with love for a friend, even to the point of weeping; and disciples at the graveside, soon to look beyond the grave for their hope and to see the wonder of God in all his mystery.

The story of Lazarus is a continuation of the biblical record of the way hope was won, of its struggle and its triumph.

Luke: The Joyful Historian

(Luke; Acts; Col. 4:14; II Tim. 4:11; Philem. 23)

In about A.D. 70 Luke wrote the third Gospel, which bears his name. An indefinable light surrounds his narrative, from the Annunciation and the song of Mary, to the appearance of the risen Lord at Emmaus.

Gladness is ever present, from the angels' song, "Glory to God in the highest and on earth peace among men with whom he is pleased" (Luke 2:14) to Christ's ascension. Here we see the disciples jubilantly returning to Jerusalem and going to the temple to bless God for his goodness. All of these biblical tableaus regenerate hope in Christ the Redeemer.

Luke also includes some of the most uplifting hymns in Christianity, Mary's "Magnificat," Zechariah's "Benedictus," the angels' "Gloria in Excelsis," and Simeon's "Nunc Dimittis," all inspiring parts of Handel's *Messiah*. In all of these, God communicates his will and purpose to man.

A modest, sympathetic, and tender man, Luke accords to women a more prominent and radiant place than any writer in the Bible. He deals with all women, even the sinful woman and the woman stooped in body for eighteen years, compassionately and lovingly. In the foreground is Mary, the morally perfect mother of Christ, whose very presence sheds an indefinable light over Luke's entire Gospel.

According to tradition, Luke is also the author of Acts, supposedly written soon after his Gospel. A radiance surrounds many parts of Acts, too, especially at Pentecost when the people are blessed with the gift of the Holy Spirit and afterward when this same brotherhood of believers in the risen Christ partake of food "with glad and generous hearts." Finally, Luke writes of Paul, who stands on trial "for hope in the promise made by God to our fathers" (Acts 26:7).

In addition to being an author, Luke was a physician. His style and choice of words, particularly in his Gospel, suggest a physician's thoughts and speech. Paul honors Luke by calling him "the beloved physician" (Col. 4:14).

Luke and "the man of Macedonia" (Acts 16:9) seem to be identical. If so, Luke said to Paul, "Come over to Macedonia and help us" (16:10). Together they opened to Christianity the door to what was later to be known as Europe. The two met at Troas, in Asia Minor, and afterward evangelized together in Jerusalem and Rome.

Paul speaks of Luke tenderly when he says, "Luke alone is with me" (II Tim. 4:11). Another time Paul mentions him as one of his fellow workers, along with Mark, Aristarchus, and Demas (Philem. 24).

En route to Rome for the last time, when Paul was a prisoner in the custody of Julius, the Roman centurion, he and Luke were in a dangerous storm in the Adriatic, during which their ship was wrecked near Malta, where they found safety. Several months later they journeyed on to Rome.

Whatever their relationship, it seems that Luke was with Paul until the end when Paul died a martyr's death, probably in Rome. If so, Luke, the beloved physician and companion, was there administering to Paul with his compassion, knowledge and love.

MARK, JOHN: THE ENLIGHTENED AUTHOR OF FIRST GOSPEL

(Mark; Acts 12:12, 25, 15:37, 39; Col. 4:10; II Tim. 4:11; Philem. 24; I Peter 5:12)

A relative of Barnabas, the companion of Paul, John Mark is author of the Gospel of Mark, the first gospel written, the basis of Matthew and Luke and a support for the Gospel of John.

Mark, as he is usually called, seems to have been with Peter on some of his apostolic missions when Christ was present. Mark depicts Christ as the Lord who was rich and became poor, as the suffering servant of God who gave his ransom for many, and as the exalted one who will appear again.

Mark receives a special greeting when Peter refers to him as "my son Mark." Tradition has associated Mark with Peter as the latter's interpreter. Mark is honored again when Paul calls him one of his "fellow workers for the kingdom of God" (Col. 4:11), one who has been "a great comfort to me." Another time Paul says "get Mark and bring him with you; for he is very useful in serving me" (II Tim. 4:11). Again Mark is called a fellow worker of Paul's in Phil. 24. In all of these references we have a picture of Mark, a disciple of both Peter and Paul, who diligently served and comforted each of them.

The young Mark was with Barnabas and Paul on Paul's first missionary journey, but for some unknown reason, probably homesickness or a physical disability, he left the party and went back to Jerusalem. There his mother Mary was one of the influential women in the church. It is thought that her home could have been the meeting place for believers during Pentecost.

Mark's Gospel, the shortest of the four, is written in a graphic, vigorous style and seemingly from an eye-witness point of view. For example, when Mark describes the hungry villagers fed by the compassionate Christ, he recounts that "he commanded them all to sit down by companies upon the green grass" (Mark 6:39).

Earlier, Mark writes of the apostles going in a boat "to a lonely place by themselves" (6:32). Later, Mark says that after Jesus walked on the sea, he got into a boat with the apostles "and the wind ceased" (6:51). These probably first-hand touches add special interest to Mark's Gospel.

Mark is regarded as the founder of the first Jewish-Greek church at Alexandria, where it is thought that he died and was buried. Many churches in Christendom have been named "St. Mark's" after Mark the Gospel writer.

MELCHIZEDEK: THE "KING OF RIGHTEOUSNESS"

(Gen. 14:18; Ps. 110:4; Heb. 6:20, 7:1, 10, 11, 15, 17)

Melchizedek symbolizes the ideal king-priest of whose order Christ was called a member.

Melchizedek's name first appears in quite a remarkable way in the story of Abraham (Gen. 14:18). While Abraham (or Abram, as he was called then) dwelt in tents under the oaks of Mamre, he had word that the king of Elam and three confederate kings, all warriors and plunderers, had taken Sodom and led away its inhabitants as captives. Among these were Lot, Abraham's nephew, and his family. When Abraham had word of this, he went forth with his three hundred and eighteen trained servants, pursued the conquerors, and brought Lot and his family back safely.

The king of Sodom rode forth to express his gratitude to Abraham, his deliverer. A more notable person, Melchizedek, king of Salem, suddenly appeared on the scene to bless Abraham and refresh him with bread and wine, during which he declared, "Blessed be Abram by God Most High, maker of heaven and earth." Abraham, in turn, gave Melchizedek a tenth of everything he had.

Melchizedek then emerged from obscurity. He is described as a king "without father or mother or genealogy, and has neither beginning of days nor end of life, but resembling the Son of God he continues a priest for ever . . . not according to a legal requirement concerning bodily descent but by the power of an indestructible life" (Heb. 7:3, 16).

Melchizedek's home city of Salem is identified with Jerusalem —Uru-salim (City of Peace), as it is called in the Tell el-Amarna tablets of 1400 B.C., in the Zagros Mountains. The king of Elam ruled over an area in the southwestern part of what is now Iran. The Elamites were an ancient people, thought to be a part of the pre-Sumerian population of Babylonia.

Hope for a rulership such as Melchizedek's is proclaimed in Ps. 110:4, which praises the ideal king after the Melchizedek order. The name suggests righteousness, royalty, and a priesthood higher than the order of Aaron, the first head of the Hebrew priesthood. Everywhere Melchizedek is mentioned, the priestly work rather than the priestly person is emphasized.

Though Christ bore a likeness to Melchizedek, Christ's priesthood took in so much more—a spiritual not a temporal covenant, a heavenly not an earthly tabernacle, a sacrifice not symbolical but real. So there emerges in Christ the superior priesthood of Melchizedek, one filled with hope universal in scope, a divine Sonship with the ability to suffer, to sympathize, and to save; one under an eternal covenant and eternal redemption. All of these come into their fullness in Heb. 7, which presents an outline of the new covenant under Christ, the true king of righteousness.

NATHAN: DAVID'S MORAL AND SPIRITUAL INSPIRER

(II Sam. 7:2, 3, 4, 17, 12:1, 5, 7, 13, 15, 25; I Kings 1:8, 10, 11, 22–24, 32, 34, 45; I Chron. 2:36, 17:1, 2, 3, 15, 29:29; II Chron. 9:29, 29:25)

Nathan, a prophet and a chaplain in the court of King David, lifted Israel morally and spiritually.

When King David committed adultery with Bathsheba, the wife of Uriah, who was serving in David's army, Nathan, using a parable of a rich man who took away the one ewe lamb of a poor man, courageously confronted David with his adultery and with his later murder of Uriah. Nathan recited the parable (II Sam. 12:1–6) to David and boldly told him, "You are the man." Admitting his guilt, David penitently answered, "I have sinned against the Lord."

When the child of the adulterous union died, Nathan had been so effective in calling David to what was morally right that the repentant David "went into the house of the Lord and worshipped."

This so-called "penitent's Psalm" (Psalm 51), one of the great biblical passages on confession and cleansing from sin, rings out in all its fullness in David's prayer and vow:

> Create in me a clean heart, O God,
>   and put a new and right spirit within me.
> Cast me not away from thy presence,
>   and take not thy holy Spirit from me.
> Restore to me the joy of thy salvation,
>   and uphold me with a willing spirit.
>
> Then I will teach transgressors thy ways,
>   and sinners will return to thee.
> Deliver me from bloodguiltiness, O God,
>   thou God of my salvation,
>   and my tongue will sing aloud of thy deliverance.
>
> (vs. 10–14)

This moment of prayer and confession was one of the most dramatic and meaningful hours in David's life. In his willingness to admit guilt and to repent before God, he was at his best.

By helping to give the king and all Israel a look toward God, Nathan, the most God-inspired man in the kingdom, succeeded in arousing all Israel's trust in doing what was right.

Nathan as court chaplain also counseled David concerning the building of the first temple. David desired a new temple, but Nathan saw that the time was not right, and so the temple was not built until the reign of Solomon.

Nathan ministered to Solomon from his birth. When the child

was born to David and Bathsheba (after she had become his wife), Nathan called Solomon "Jedidiah," meaning "because of the Lord" (II Sam. 12:25).

Nathan, who was politically active in encouraging godly actions in the king's family, also aided Bathsheba when Solomon was appointed to succeed David as king.

Nathan's good life lived on through his children—two sons—Azariah, who was over Solomon's officers, and Zabad, the king's friend.

Nathan and his successors over the centuries have hopefully raised the moral tone of the world.

Nehemiah: The Restorer of the Laws and the Walls

(Ezra, Nehemiah)

Nehemiah served as governor of Judah from 445 to 433 B.C., with a special commission to rebuild Jerusalem. One of his first accomplishments was to restore belief in the importance of obeying the laws set up by Moses.

The Book of Nehemiah relates that one of the first steps that the people took after returning with Ezra and Nehemiah from the exile in Babylon was to gather "into the square before the Water Gate . . . from early morning until midday, in the presence of the men and the women and those who could understand; and the ears of all the people were attentive to the book of law" (Neh. 8:1, 3).

Because of the scarcity of water, the people in Bible times liked to relax where there were streams or wells or springs of water. To them, watering places were for refreshment and light. In the time of Moses a gate—the Water Gate mentioned above—at the eastern side of the tabernacle provided the entrance to the sanctuary enclosure. It may be presumed that it was also where legal cases, referred to the jurisdiction of the sanctuary (the only trial court then), were heard. So the Water Gate, then as now, in the twentieth-century Senate hearing, signified a place where laws had been broken, and also where justice finally was meted out.

While living at the court of Artaxerxes, king of Persia, in Susa, Nehemiah learned that survivors in Jerusalem, who had escaped exile, were in "great trouble and shame" (Neh. 1:3). More than a century earlier the city had fallen. Its walls were still broken down, its burned gates in shambles, and now its people suffered harsher afflictions.

Nehemiah, who introduces himself as "a cupbearer of the king," was a man of great wealth. His memoirs in the Book of Nehemiah, regarded as the finest autobiography in the Old Testament, furnish a continuous narrative of his work in Jerusalem and of his own thoughts regarding himself and his time. His well-written narrative is fresh and rich in color. He comes through as one who loses himself in the service of God and his people, as a leader decisive, fearless, democratic, reliable, persistent, humble, and full of national pride. Nehemiah had his faults, such as narrow nationalism, harsh discipline, and bitterness toward non-Jews, but his good qualities outweighed these.

Nehemiah entered Jerusalem at a time of heartbreaking discouragement, but he brought hope as he began to tackle impossible situations. He went about his mammoth task with sadness and joy, sadness because "the place of his fathers' sepulchres" was in ruins, joy because the "good hand of God" was upon him as he sought to restore and revitalize his homeland. Now, finally, Nehemiah's once despairing people were renewed in expectancy for a new Jerusalem moving confidently into a future with hope.

"Come let us rebuild the walls of Jerusalem, that we may no longer suffer disgrace" (Neh. 2:17), Nehemiah said to his people. And they promptly answered, " 'Let us rise and build,' so they strengthened their hands for the good work" (2:18). In fifty-two days the walls were restored.

There were setbacks, though. Three men, "Sanballat the Horonite and Tobiah the servant, the Ammonite, and Geshem the Arab" (Neh. 2:19) derided and despised Nehemiah as he directed the work.

Sanballat scoffingly asked, "What are these feeble Jews doing?" (Neh. 4:2). Tobiah criticized the construction, saying, "If a fox goes up on it he will break down their stone walls" (v. 3). But Nehemiah went forward in a triumphant spirit: "So we built the wall . . . For the people had a mind to work" (v. 6), it is recorded. As the wall began to close in, Sanballat, Tobiah, Geshem, and others were so angry that they threatened to fight those inside the wall.

Nehemiah endured other adversities. The Jews complained because the costs were too high. Sanballat and Tobiah continued to taunt the workers as they went about the restoration. But Nehemiah persevered.

He not only furthered the economic well-being of his people, but he settled families in villages outside Jerusalem. He recorded the genealogy of the remnant returning from Babylon and added these names to those who had returned earlier. He had a listing made of the priests and Levites who came back, and appointed collectors and gatekeepers. He also fought the greed of the wealthy Jews and championed the poor.

After restoring and governing for twelve years, Nehemiah returned to Susa. In his absence the people of Jerusalem broke the covenant.

He returned to Jerusalem a second time, only to find, on the Sabbath, men treading wine presses, bringing in sheaves and leading asses with foodstuff, and peddlers from Tyre selling fish and other wares. Nehemiah closed the gates on the Sabbath, but the merchants opened booths outside the gates; he put a stop to these violations when he placed Levites over the gates as wardens.

His final prayer, closing his memoirs, is "Remember me, O my God, for good" (Neh. 13:31). His prayer was answered. He is venerated as one of the most dedicated leaders of the postexilic period.

Nicodemus: The New Birth in Its Fullness

(John 3:1, 4, 9, 7:50, 19:39)

An orthodox rabbi and a legalistic conservative of the Sanhedrin, Nicodemus sought from Jesus an answer to the question,

"What is the new birth?" As a matter of caution, he timidly went to Jesus by night, probably to John's house in Jerusalem, for his discourse with Jesus.

Nicodemus approached Jesus, saying, "Rabbi, we know that you are a teacher come from God. Tell us how can a man be born again?" And Jesus explained to Nicodemus that he must be born anew, that the nature we inherit from our parents is material, but that the new nature which comes with the new birth is spiritual. The inner life, Jesus told Nicodemus, is as difficult to trace in words as the source of the wind.

This new birth, Jesus further explained to Nicodemus, must reveal itself in a new heart and a new nature. The evidence for this new birth must establish itself in many ways: in humble trust in God; in personal faith in Jesus; in love that manifests itself in deeds of mercy to others. In such acts of faith one becomes a new creation, a new being, as it were.

Jesus knew that the rabbis frequently alluded to a proselyte baptism as a "regeneration," a new birth, and that this rabbi, Nicodemus, would understand what involved a new birth of the spirit.

But Nicodemus, an orthodox and pious believer in his own faith, a ruler and a Pharisee, probably could not undergo such a radical change in his thinking so hastily. He seems to be out of the discourse as Jesus continues his teaching on eternal life.

Nicodemus is not mentioned again until a later controversy arose over whether Jesus was the Messiah. During the last day of the Feast of the Tabernacle in Galilee, Jesus cried out, "If anyone thirst, let him come to me and drink. He who believes in me, as the scripture has said, 'Out of his heart shall flow rivers of living water'" (John 7:37–38).

The skeptical doubted this. During the questioning, Nicodemus, showing moral and compassionate concern for Jesus, intervened to ask, "Does our law judge a man without first giving him a hearing and learning what he does?" (John 7:51). The unbelievers then asked Nicodemus, "Are you from Galilee too? Search and you will see that no prophet is to rise from Galilee" (v. 52).

After the Crucifixion, Nicodemus proved his love for Jesus when he went to Joseph of Arimathea with a mixture of myrrh and aloes,

more than half a hundredweight, to wrap with the burial linens
provided by Joseph.

Faithful to the end, Nicodemus, like Joseph of Arimathea, adds
beauty to the story of the entombment. In their last act of love
for Jesus, these two shed an indefinable light around Jesus before
his resurrection three days later. Nicodemus was now prepared
to understand the Resurrection, truly a new birth, discussed in
depth with him by Jesus when they had their first discourse together.

Noah: A New Hope in a Rainbow

(Gen. 5:29, 30, 32, 6:8–10, 13, 22, 7:1, 5–7, 9, 11, 13, 15, 23, 8:1,
6, 11, 13, 15, 18, 20, 9:1, 8, 17–20, 24, 28–29, 10:1, 32; I Chron. 1:4;
Isa. 54:9; Ezek. 14:14, 20; Matt. 24:37–38; Luke 3:36, 17:26–27;
Heb. 11:7; I Pet. 3:20; II Pet. 2:5)

Son of Lamech and father of Shem, Ham, and Japheth, Noah
was the first to see an arc of prismatic color appearing in the
heavens and signifying that the great flood was over.

This rainbow became a lasting token of God's covenant with
Noah (Gen. 9:8–17), which embraced the orderliness and regu-
larity of the seasons, the promise that Noah's seed would replenish
the earth, the emergence of a system of law and government,
and the promise of food in abundance.

Because Noah had the courage and foresight to follow God's
command to build an ark in which to ride out the great flood, the
Book of Hebrews lists him among the fathers of faith. "Noah,
being warned by God concerning events as yet unseen, took heed
and constructed an ark for the saving of his household; by this he
condemned the world and became an heir of the righteousness
which comes by faith" (Heb. 11:7).

Patiently and diligently, Noah entered upon his tremendous
task with hope in God's promise. The people scoffed at Noah for
being so presumptuous as to think that the earth would be destroyed by a flood. But when God saw that the earth was corrupt

and filled with violence, he commanded Noah, "a righteous man," to prepare for the deluge.

His task of building the gopherwood ark, probably four hundred and fifty feet long, seventy-five feet wide, and three stories high, consumed much time and enormous labor. Afterward, Noah had to gather the animals, probably some seven thousand—a pair of every kind of beast, creeping thing, and bird. He prepared special quarters for them and for his family, for he did not know how long they would have to ride out the storm or how far they would have to voyage. When the deluge started, Noah entered the ark with his animals and his family—his wife, his sons, Shem, Ham, and Japheth, and their wives. "The waters prevailed and increased greatly upon the earth; and the ark floated on the face of the waters" (Gen. 7:18).

The whole earth, according to the Bible tradition, was flooded. The ark floated on the waters until it came to rest on the highest visible mountain, said to be Ararat, in eastern Turkey, near the borders of modern Soviet Union and Iran.

In order to determine whether the waters had subsided, Noah opened a window of the ark and sent forth a raven, but this flew back and forth, for there was no dry land to light upon. Next Noah sent a dove, but the dove, finding no place either, also returned to the ark. Noah waited another seven days and then sent forth the dove again, and when she came back this time, in her mouth was a freshly plucked olive leaf. Now he knew that the waters had subsided. After waiting another seven days, he sent forth the dove once more, but she did not return this time.

Finally, Noah removed the covering from the ark. On discovering that the earth was dry, he and his wife and his sons and their wives followed God's command to leave the ark and to take with them birds and animals and every creeping thing, in order that they might breed abundantly on the earth.

The first thing Noah did after he was settled on land again was to build an altar to the Lord and, according to the primitive custom of the time, to offer one of every clean animal and bird as burnt offerings upon the altar. After that, God established the Noahic covenant mentioned earlier, with the rainbow as its symbol.

A rainbow of hope, piercing the heavens with light and irides-
cent colors, just like the one that Noah first saw before he left the
ark, has become a lasting symbol that the storm has subsided and
tranquillity reigns again. Like the stars, the rainbow never ceases
to appear when hope is most needed. Like the stars, too, it represents the order and constancy of the universe and assures us of
God's infinite goodness.

The author of Ecclesiasticus in the Apocrypha (42:11–12), writing many centuries later on the wonders of Creation, declared,

> Look at the rainbow and praise its Maker;
> it shines with a supreme beauty,
> rounding the sky with its gleaming arc,
> a bow bent by the hands of the Most High.

ONESIMUS: THE SLAVE WITH A NEW MASTER—CHRIST

(Col. 4:9; Philem.)

Onesimus was a slave who ran away from his master, Philemon.
Although Onesimus probably had stolen from Philemon (Philem.
10), under Paul's tutelage he became "a faithful and beloved
brother" in Christ.

He, along with Tychicus, "a fellow minister and faithful servant in the Lord" (Col. 4:7), later bore Paul's letter addressed to
Philemon his master, to his master's wife, Apphia, to Archippus, a
fellow minister in the Gospel, and to the church in their house,
either at Colossae or Laodicea.

In the letter Paul begged Philemon to forgive Onesimus. Paul
believed that "he who was called in the Lord as a slave is a freed-
man of the Lord. Likewise he who was free when called is a slave
of Christ" (I Cor. 7:22).

Paul, who had great hope for Onesimus' release from slavery,
told Philemon in the letter that his losses, if any, caused by
Onesimus should be charged to his (Paul's) account. In sending
Onesimus back, Paul wrote that he was sending his "very heart,"
for he had come to think of Onesimus as a beloved son. Actually,
Paul needed the faithful and helpful Onesimus, but his first

thought was not for himself but for Onesimus, and he desired that he be received back by Philemon not through compulsion but in Christian love and faith.

According to the law of the time, Onesimus could have been severely punished by his master, but tradition has it that Onesimus was forgiven and taken back into the household of Philemon, not as a slave but as a Christian brother.

ONESIPHORUS: PAUL'S STEADFAST FRIEND

(II Tim. 1:16, 4:19)

Onesiphorus befriended Paul when others had deserted him. Many did not even know where Paul was, but Onesiphorus, a disciple in Ephesus, searched until he found Paul imprisoned in chains in Rome.

Afterward, writing to the household of Onesiphorus, Paul commends him as one "not ashamed of my chains" (1:16). This letter suggests that Onesiphorus was dead and that Paul was writing a letter of condolence to his family.

Paul, soon to die a martyr's death, asked God to grant mercy to the household of this humble, devout, and faithful friend, Onesiphorus.

PAUL'S MANY FRIENDS: CHURCH FELLOWSHIP AT ITS BEST

These friends, more than twenty of them, whom Paul greets in the last chapter of Romans (16), were all no doubt hopeful believers in the good news about Christ. Paul, a very personal as well as a triumphant leader, lovingly calls each by name.

Whether they were members of the Roman Church is still a question. One scholar says "the most natural address is Ephesus." Another says "the letter could have been sent to Rome or Ephesus, for dissemination in Europe."

The vital point is that Paul expressed a warm feeling for each one and had something kind to say about each. Brief though his comments are, they give the reader an excellent understanding of the warm fellowship that existed in the New Testament Churches established by Paul.

Among the more than twenty listed appear six women—Priscilla, Mary, Tryphaena, Tryphosa, Persis, Julia, and Olympas—but the men far outnumber the women. These are:

Aquila and his wife Priscilla, who are addressed as "fellow workers in Christ Jesus, who risked their necks for my life."

Epaenetus, "my beloved," who was the first convert in Asia for Christ.

Andronicus and Junias, "my kinsmen and my fellow prisoners," both "men of note among the apostles."

Ampliatus, "my beloved in the Lord."

Urbanus, "our fellow worker in Christ."

Stachys, "my beloved."

Apelles, one "who is approved in Christ."

Aristobulus and his family.

Herodion, "my kinsman."

Narcissus (there is question about whether a man or woman) and his family.

Rufus, "eminent in the Lord."

Asyncritus, Phlegon, Hermes, Patrobas, Hermas, and other "brethren with them."

Philologus and Nereus and "all the saints who are with them."

"Greet one another with a holy kiss," says Paul, as he concludes the greetings.

Then he begs all of these "to take note of those who create dissensions and difficulties, in opposition to the doctrine which you have been taught; avoid them. For such persons do not serve our Lord Christ" (Rom. 16:17–18).

Paul concludes his letter also with greetings from those with him—Timothy, his fellow worker; Lucius, Jason, and Sosipater, his kinsmen; Tertius, the secretary who wrote the letter; Gaius, who was host to Paul at the time it was written; Erastus, the city treasurer; and Quartus, a brother in the faith, all probably in Corinth from where it is thought the letter was written.

PHILEMON: A CHURCHMAN IN HIS OWN HOUSE

(Philemon)

Philemon was Paul's "beloved brother" in Christ, who, with his wife Apphia, had a church in his house, either at Colossae or Laodicea, both in the same Phrygian area. Philemon was the owner of a runaway slave, Onesimus, whom Paul had converted, probably in Rome.

Paul, who had great faith in the power of the gospel to destroy slavery, appealed to Philemon to free his slave. This would sweep away one of the strongest barriers in human relationships at this time.

Paul's letter to Philemon, in one chapter of only twenty-five verses, was written from a prison in Rome. The two probably enjoyed Christian fellowship together at Ephesus, where it is thought that Paul had converted Philemon.

When Paul wrote this brief letter, he probably had no idea that it would be preserved. However, it was preserved, to become one of the canonized books of the Bible. After many centuries this eighteenth book in the New Testament still has tremendous appeal. The basic reason for this is the diplomatic, warmhearted manner in which Paul approaches a very controversial matter, that of a runaway slave.

Paul requests Philemon to restore Onesimus to his household again, not as a slave but as a free individual. He begins the letter with an expression of his great love for Philemon, adding, "I hear of your love and of the faith which you have expressed toward the Lord Jesus" (Philem. 5).

The twentieth century theologian John Knox (who is a Philemon expert), has called this one of the most convincing letters ever written, because Paul makes the request so diplomatically.

The high point of the letter is Paul's request that the slave's freedom be a gift of the spirit, not granted as an act compelled by outward authority. And since Paul introduces himself as a prisoner for Jesus Christ, the letter is all the more effective, especially when

Paul offers to pay Philemon for what Onesimus owes him.

There remains this question about the slave Onesimus, whose name in the Greek means "useful." Did Paul want Onesimus to be freed for evangelizing or for further service in Philemon's household? Whatever the answer, this is a minor point. Paul's plea, that Christians, whether slaves or free men, are all in the same fellowship of Christ, is of primary significance.

In stressing this, Paul sows the seed for a more spiritual type of revolution, the transformation of many other troubling human relationships. And he gives immortality to Philemon, who would have been lost in the centuries of time were it not for this small but great book which bears his name—and which speaks a message of hope for transforming other human relationships, such as those between nations today.

PHILIP: THE EVANGELIST "FULL OF THE SPIRIT AND WISDOM"

(Acts 6:5, 8:5–6, 12–13, 26, 29–31, 34–40, 21:8)

Philip the Evangelist was one of the first seven chosen as deacons of the early Church in Jerusalem. The others were Stephen and five little known men: Prochorus, Nicanor, Timon, Parmenas, and Nicolaus.

Philip the Evangelist, who is not to be confused with Philip the Apostle, had many later accomplishments to his credit. After the martyrdom of Stephen, he fled from Jerusalem to Samaria. Here he proclaimed the Christ, and many were healed and also baptized by him. The report of Philip's work in Samaria concludes, "So there was much joy in that city" (Acts 8:8) because of his visit.

Among Philip's most notable converts in Samaria was Simon, the magician, who claimed he could perform all kinds of miracles. When he found himself eclipsed by Philip, he joined his company and was baptized, but he thought he could obtain the gift of God with money, as well as buy influence and popularity for himself. Philip's aim was to attract others to the Savior, but Simon's was to attract others to himself.

Simon, this sorcerer who put the work of the holy Diety on a level with the deceptive achievements of men, passes from the record, while Philip moves on to greater spiritual achievements.

On his way from Jerusalem to Gaza, Philip was directed to an Ethiopian statesman, a eunuch and treasurer for Candace, queen of the Ethiopians. This eunuch was a seeker of God, who had traveled over a thousand miles by chariot to worship in Jerusalem. Philip, who came upon him as he was returning to Ethiopia, holding in his hand the Book of Isaiah, asked " 'Do you understand what you are reading?' And he said 'How can I, unless some one guides me?' And he invited Philip to come up and sit with him" (Acts 8:30–31).

Philip sat down and explained to the eunuch the meaning of Isaiah 53, which he was reading. Then Philip told him the good news about Christ, whose coming Isaiah prophesied. The eunuch asked Philip to baptize him, and they both went into the water together. The eunuch went back to Ethiopia, no doubt carrying the same good news of the gospel with him.

After this experience Philip traveled along the seaboard, preaching from city to city, until he reached his home in Caesarea. Here Philip was host to Paul (Acts 21:8–9). Assisting Philip in his hospitality were his four unmarried daughters "who prophesied." They, like their father, were "illumined expounders of God's word."

SETH: ADAM AND EVE'S SON OF HOPE

(Gen. 4:25–26, 5:3–8; I Chron. 1:1; Luke 3:38)

Seth was thought to be the third son of Adam and Eve, who filled a need for hope in their lives at a time of tragedy.

When Seth was born, his disheartened mother, comforted by his birth, said of him, "God has appointed for me another child instead of Abel, for Cain slew him" (Gen. 4:25). Seth was the father of Enosh, in whose time men first "began to call upon the name of the Lord" (v. 26).

Seth is mentioned in Luke's genealogy of Christ's mother Mary.

This went back to "the son of Enosh, the son of Seth, the son of Adam, the son of God" (Luke 3:38).

SILAS: PETER AND PAUL'S FAITHFUL HELPER

(Acts 15:22, 27, 32, 34, 40, 16:19, 25, 29, 17:4, 10, 14, 15, 18:5; II Cor. 1:19; I Thess. 1:1; II Thess. 1:1)

Silas (also called Silvanus) is thought to have been the scribe of the first letter of Peter, often called "the epistle of grace and hope." Some authorities think Silas was the bearer of this letter to provinces in northern Asia Minor. He also played a significant role as Paul's associate on his second missionary journey through Asia Minor and Macedonia.

Paul's letters to the Thessalonians, written from Corinth, contain salutations from Paul, Timothy, and Silas. Because of the "we" used by Paul in these letters, scholars also conjecture that Silas and Timothy assisted in assembling them. If Silas, thought to be a Jew with Roman citizenship, co-operated in compiling these epistles, he was a scholar, a devout believer in the risen Christ, and willing to suffer in spreading the Gospel.

Silas is first introduced as a responsible member of the mother Church in Jerusalem. He was one of those sent by that Church with Paul and Barnabas to Antioch. Silas and his companion Judas Barsabbas carried a special communication to the Antioch Church. This explained the Jerusalem Church's stand on Church problems. Silas, along with Judas Barsabbas, is described as a prophet, who "exhorted the brethren with many words and strengthened them" (Acts 15:32). He had a great understanding of the demands on new Christians, designated as "a royal priesthood, a holy nation, God's own people . . . called out of darkness into his marvelous light" (I Pet. 2:9).

Silas is never mentioned except in the company of someone else, but his part as an aide was always significant. In facing the first antagonism in Europe to the Gospel, he was with Paul. When Silas and Paul were imprisoned at Philippi, the magistrates tore the apostles' clothes off and beat them unmercifully. Then their feet were put in stocks.

That night, despite their discomfort, Silas and Paul prayed and sang together. About midnight, as other prisoners listened to them, there was an earthquake and the doors of the prison were miraculously opened. When the jailer awoke and saw the prison door ajar, he was about to kill himself for letting his prisoners escape.

Silas was beside Paul when Paul called out to the jailer in a loud voice, "Do not harm yourself, for we are all here." Calling for lights, the jailer fearfully rushed in and fell down before Silas and Paul. He asked them what he must do to be saved, and they told him, "Believe in the Lord Jesus" (Acts 16:31). After this the jailer brought Silas and Paul into the house, washed their bleeding wounds, and then the jailer and all his family were baptized.

When the magistrates finally released Paul and Silas, they continued to Thessalonica and Beroea. At the latter place they went into the Jewish synagogue together, and the people received them eagerly. Silas did not go with Paul to Athens, but he was reunited with him and Timothy at Corinth, where he remained after Paul left.

"Silas," used in Acts, is thought to be his original Semitic (Aramaic?) name. "Silvanus," used in the letters, is thought to be an adopted Roman form.

SIMEON: THE HOPEFUL PROPHET OF CHRIST'S TIME

(Luke 2:25, 34)

A just and devout man in Jerusalem, Simeon saw in the child Jesus the long expected Messiah who would redeem Israel.

Now hopeful about the future, Simeon was ready to depart the world in peace. His words in the "Nunc Dimittis," a part of the Christian liturgy, echo Isa. 49:6, in which it is prophesied that God shall send one who will be "a light to the nations."

Simeon was looking for this new spiritual leader, for it had been revealed to him that he should not see death until he had seen Christ.

When Mary and Joseph came to the temple in Jerusalem to

present their child to the Lord there, Simeon declared he saw God's salvation in this child. Taking Jesus in his arms and thanking God, Simeon was filled with new hope, which he expressed in the now famous Song of Simeon (Luke 2:29–35).

Mary and Joseph marveled at what Simeon prophesied about their child. After blessing them too, Simeon told Mary that "this child is set for the fall and rising of many in Israel . . . (and a sword will pierce through your own soul also), that thoughts out of many hearts may be revealed" (Luke 2:34–35). Simeon's prophetic words are better understood now than then.

SIMON OF CYRENE: THE BEARER OF CHRIST'S CROSS

(Matt. 27:32; Mark 15:21; Luke 23:26)

By chance, Simon was nearby when Jesus, on his way from the hall of judgment in Jerusalem to the place of execution, gave way beneath the weight of his cross. Simon, a native of Cyrene in North Africa but now a resident of Jerusalem, took up Christ's cross and carried it for him.

The brief verses about him by the three Gospel writers merely relate that he chanced to be walking at Christ's side on the way to Calvary.

Like many others, Simon was not waiting to bear another's cross, especially one as heavy as Christ's. But when the need arose, he aided this weary man on his way to the Crucifixion. And Simon's acceptance of Christ's cross stands out as the one kindly act done for the living Jesus that day.

Simon had two sons, Rufus and Alexander, who doubtless became cross-bearing Christians too. Paul sends greeting to Rufus (Rom. 16:13), who must have been the same Rufus as that in Mark 15:21.

Stephanas: Paul's Worthy Convert

(I Cor. 1:16, 16:15, 17)

Stephanas' conversion in Achaia was one of the first fruits of Paul's ministry in this province. Its capital was Corinth, and Stephanas and his household were baptized there together.

He is mentioned with Fortunatus and Achaicus, and the three made up a delegation from the Corinthian Church to consult with Paul at Ephesus. Their coming refreshed Paul's spirit. It is thought they brought a letter from the Corinthian Church to Paul and took back with them the letter known as I Corinthians.

Stephanas and his family, because of their early baptism and their dedication to the service of the pioneering Church, represent hope in the new Christian faith at its best.

Stephen: The First Martyr for Christ

(Acts 6:5, 8–9, 7:2, 59, 8:2, 11:19, 22:20)

Stephen was one of the first seven deacons chosen by the twelve apostles to minister to the spiritual and temporal needs of the poor in the Jerusalem Church. The demands arose when the native Jews, who were also Christians, criticized the Hellenists (Greek-speaking Jews) for neglecting the widows among them in the daily distribution of food.

Stephen and the other six little known deacons, Philip, Prochorus, Nicanor, Timon, Parmenas, and Nicolaus of Antioch, were assigned these new duties in order to leave the apostles more time for their spiritual ministry.

Some of the tasks of the seven deacons were menial, such as waiting on tables, but they also taught and preached in the synagogues. Stephen, the most conspicuous of the deacons, went about his work in a spirit of humility and "did great wonders and signs among the people" (Acts 6:8). So excellent was his example in the solution of problems in the Christian community that some of those who belonged to the "Synagogue of Freedmen," made up of the Jews from Cyrene, Alexandria, Cilicia, and Asia, became jealous of Stephen, a man both wise and good.

They "secretly instigated" a charge that Stephen had spoken blasphemies against Moses and God. The elders and scribes were so incited against Stephen that they brought in false witnesses who said, "This man never ceases to speak words against this holy place and the law" (Acts 6:13). They expressed fear that Stephen, this devout believer in Jesus of Nazareth, would change the age-old customs of Moses and destroy their religious heritage.

When the high priest asked Stephen, "Is this so?" Stephen went into a long discourse (Acts 7:2–53) on the glory of God in the history of the Jewish people, from the time of the patriarchs on through Moses, Solomon, and the prophets. Stephen made four stirring points. First, he asserted, God gave his greatest revelations of truth not in Palestine but outside—to Abraham in Mesopotamia, not in Canaan; to Joseph in Egypt, not in Judea; to Moses on Mount Sinai, not in the Promised Land. The second point stressed by Stephen was that Israel always rebelled, not only against God but against his prophets. His third point was that the "Just One," the prophet whose coming Moses had predicted, was betrayed and killed. Finally, Stephen told them that the Law was holy but they had not kept it.

Stephen concluded with this vigorous accusation of his accusers: "You stiff-necked people, uncircumcised in heart and ears, you always resist the Holy Spirit. As your fathers did, so do you. Which of the prophets did not your fathers persecute? And they killed those who announced beforehand the coming of the Righteous One, whom you have betrayed and murdered, you who received the law as delivered by angels and did not keep it" (Acts 7:51–53).

From this moment on, Stephen's suffering almost paralleled that of Jesus after his accusation by the Sanhedrin. Men ground their teeth with anger against Stephen and finally closed up their ears when he courageously declared, "Behold, I see the heavens opened, and the Son of man standing at the right hand of God" (Acts 7:56), a statement similar to that in Mark when Jesus was asked,

"Are You the Christ?" And his answer was, "I am; and you will see the Son of man sitting at the right hand of Power, and coming with the clouds of heaven" (Mark 14:62).

Then Stephen's accusers cast him out of the city and stoned him as he prayed, "Lord Jesus, receive my spirit." His final words were "Lord, do not hold this sin against them." And after he spoke these words, he died. Saul, a young man at whose feet the witnesses had piled their cloaks after they stoned Stephen, "was consenting to his death" (Acts 8:1).

But a new hope came into the hearts of Christian believers, and the differences between Judaism and Christianity began to appear. Evidence of this was in the converted Paul, who no longer bore any of the traits of Saul, his earlier self.

Symeon Niger: The Antioch Priest and Prophet

(Acts 13:1)

Symeon Niger is listed next after Barnabas as a prophet and priest in the Antioch Church. Next come Lucius of Cyrene, Manaen, a member of the court of Herod, the tetrarch, and Saul (Paul).

While these priests were worshiping and fasting, they heard the Holy Spirit say, "Set apart for me Barnabas and Saul for the work to which I have called them."

What better credentials could Symeon and his companions have, first to be identified as prophets and teachers who believed in the good news about Christ, next as to be those who blessed Barnabas and Paul and sent them forth on their memorable missionary journey from Syrian Antioch?

Tertius: Paul's Faithful Secretary

(Rom. 16:22)

Tertius was the man to whom Paul dictated his letter to the Romans. Sometimes Paul wrote a small part of certain letters with his own hand, but most often he dictated in order to save time and trouble.

Tertius is remembered for having interposed his own greeting between Paul's salutations. In this he said, "I Tertius, the writer of this letter, greet you in the Lord." Then Paul himself inserts the name of Gaius, host to Paul and to the whole Church at Corinth, as well as those of Erastus, the city treasurer of Corinth, who was with Paul when he sent the letter to the Romans, and Quartus, a fellow Christian.

THEOPHILUS: HIS NAME A LIGHT OF HOPE

(Luke 1:3; Acts 1:1)

Theophilus was a nobleman to whom the books of Luke and Acts are dedicated. Who he was remains obscure. Some scholars ask, "Was he only the symbol of the ideal Christian?" The majority maintain that he was a real person, identified by Luke as "noble" or "most excellent."

He may have been a Gentile official, a true but anonymous friend to Christians. Whatever the answer, the name Theophilus, appearing at the beginning of two great books, sets him apart from others.

In the first book he is called "most excellent Theophilus" by Luke, who says, "it seemed good to me . . . to write an orderly account for you . . . that you may know the truth concerning the things of which you have been informed" (Luke 1:3–4).

In the Acts preface, also written by Luke, he again addresses Theophilus on church matters that only a man of hope in the Risen Christ could fully comprehend.

Timothy: Paul's Adopted Son and Helper

(Acts 16:1, 17:14–15, 18:5, 19:22, 20:4; Rom. 16:21; I Cor. 4:17, 16:10; II Cor. 1:1, 19; Phil. 1:1, 2:19; Col. 1:1; I Thess. 1:1, 3:2, 3:6; II Thess. 1:1; I Tim.; II Tim.; Philem. 1; Heb. 13:23)

The faithful son, whom Paul circumcised and took on his travels, Timothy was with Paul longer than any other helper. Paul regarded him as his adopted son, of whom he was the spiritual father.

Timothy, who spent his early years at Lystra and Derbe, probably was born at one of these places. His faithful mother, Eunice, was a Jewess and his father was a Greek, about whom little else is known. His mother and his grandmother Lois trained him well from childhood in the sacred writings (II Tim. 3:15).

Timothy was about fifteen years old when Paul converted him, probably at Lystra on his first missionary journey. Paul had lost a brother in the faith, Barnabas, but he had found a son in Timothy.

Leaving his widowed mother, Timothy set forth with Paul to Macedonia and Asia as "God's servant in the gospel of Christ" (I Thess. 3:2). Earlier he helped to organize the offering for the Church at Jerusalem.

When Paul did not have the close companionship of others, Timothy accompanied him. Timothy also went as Paul's emissary on the most confidential missions, to Philippi, Athens, Thessalonica, and Beroea, and he had charge of the most important congregations.

When Paul sent Timothy to the Philippians, he wrote them, "I have no one like him, who will be genuinely anxious for your welfare. They all look after their own interests, not those of Jesus Christ. But Timothy's worth you know, how as a son with a father he has served me in the gospel" (Phil. 2:20–22).

Here we come to know a Timothy trained by Paul himself, a Timothy in whom he had explicit confidence, a Timothy willing to suffer for the gospel, one who fully understood the power of Christ and who brought life and immortality through the gospel.

The godly training that Timothy received through Paul comes out in every statement Paul writes to him, such as this, "O Timothy, guard what has been entrusted to you. Avoid the godless chatter and contradiction of what is falsely called knowledge, for by professing it some have missed the mark as regards the faith" (I Tim. 6:20–21).

The teaching that Timothy received from this, his spiritual father, illuminates the true meaning of sound doctrine, such as Church order, the character of a Christian minister, the duties and requirements of deacons, elders, and bishops, the evils of false doctrines and false teachers, and the wise use of wealth. These exhortations appear in I and II Timothy, which with the letter to Titus, are referred to as "The Pastoral Epistles."

Paul's love for Timothy comes out best in this letter to him, purportedly written from prison in Rome shortly before Paul's death:

> . . . I remember you in my prayers—as indeed I do constantly, night and day. Recalling your tears when we parted, I yearn to see you again. That would make my happiness complete. I find myself thinking of your sincere faith—faith which first belonged to your grandmother Lois and to your mother Eunice, and which (I am confident) you also have.
>
> For this reason, I remind you to stir into flame the gift of God bestowed when my hands were laid on you. The Spirit God has given us is no cowardly spirit, but rather one that makes us strong, loving, and wise. Therefore, never be ashamed of your testimony to our Lord, nor of me, a prisoner for his sake; but with the strength which comes from God bear your share of the hardship which the gospel entails.
>
> (II Tim. 1:3–10, NAB)

Timothy is alleged to have served Paul as a secretary or editorial assistant for the letters to the Philippians and Colossians and to Philemon, however there is some confusion about this.

Timothy's importance is not to be underestimated. He is mentioned in twelve books of the New Testament, two of which, I and II Timothy, bear his name.

The final reference in Heb. 13:23 alludes to Timothy as having been released, probably from prison. If so, he, like Paul, suffered to the end of his life for the Gospel of Christ.

Titus: "My True Child in a Common Faith"

(II Cor. 2:13, 7:6, 13, 14, 8:6, 16, 23, 12:18; Gal. 2:1, 3; II Tim.
4:10; Tit. 1:4)

Titus was one of those to whom Paul addressed one of his letters and of whom Paul said, "God, who comforts the downcast,
comforted us by the coming of Titus" (II Cor. 7:6).

Titus was left by Paul in Crete, a mid-Mediterranean island,
"to amend," as he said, "what was defective." A man of unim-
peachable character, who never took advantage of others and was
earnest in the care of others, Titus was ideally equipped to lead
others. His task in Crete was not easy, for the Cretans were described then as an untruthful, vicious, and lazy people.

Titus was directed to train the Cretans in the Christian way of
life, to try to make them see that "to the pure all things are pure,
but to the corrupt and unbelieving nothing is pure; their very
minds and consciences are corrupted" (Tit. 1:15). Later Paul encouraged Titus when he wrote him in Crete, "we are disciplined
to renounce godless ways and worldly desires, and to live a life of
temperance, honesty, and godliness" (Tit. 2:11, NEB). Titus set
these ideals as his goals as he served among the Cretans.

Andrew of Crete, the seventh-century archbishop, wrote that
Titus laid the foundation of the Church in Crete and was the
pillar of the truth there and the strong supporter of the faith.

Titus, a Gentile Greek, is thought to have carried Paul's first
letter to the Corinthians and probably was one of three who took
the second letter. To this disorganized Church Titus was first sent
by Paul to bring peace. He succeeded so well in his mission there
that Paul later praised him for his zeal and sympathy, for his grief
at the sight of evil, and for his rejoicing over good. He also lauded
Titus for collecting from the Church at Corinth a generous sum
for the needy Christians in Judea.

After serving with Paul in Rome and Nicopolis, Titus is last
mentioned as assisting the Church in Dalmatia. Wherever he
went, he was "a true child in a common faith" (Tit. 1:4), who,

like Paul, though weary and afflicted at every turn, brought new light to disbelievers.

TROPHIMUS AND TYCHICUS: PAUL'S MISSIONARY COMPANIONS

(Acts 20:4, 21:29; II Tim. 4:20) (Acts 20:4; Eph. 6:21; Col. 4:7; II Tim. 4:12; Tit. 3:12)

Trophimus and Tychicus were both Gentiles and Asians, who assisted Paul in his last missionary activities in Macedonia, where he went after spending three months in Greece preceding the Ephesus riot.

Trophimus, according to II Tim. 4:20, was finally left ill at Miletus. Earlier he had gone with Paul to Jerusalem bearing gifts to the Church. When he entered the inner court of the temple with Paul through a barrier forbidding Gentiles, both were unjustly accused of being Gentiles and arrested. Injuries received in the temple could have caused the later illness of Trophimus.

Tychicus, according to Eph. 6:21, was bearer of Paul's letter to the Ephesians. Paul calls him "the beloved brother and faithful minister in the Lord." He tells the Ephesians that he has sent Tychicus to them, in order "that he may encourage your hearts" (v. 22). Tychicus played a similar role as bearer of Paul's letter to the Colossians. Paul sends him to Colossae, as he says, to comfort the Christians there. Tychicus, it seems, was supposed to assist Titus in Crete, but he went to the Ephesians instead.

Wherever Trophimus and Tychicus were, they seemed to have been one in their role, that of comforting others.

TWO UNNAMED CRIPPLES WALK AGAIN: HEALINGS BY PETER AND PAUL

An unnamed cripple who begged alms at the gate of the temple was healed by Peter (Acts 3:1–10). Another was healed by Paul at Lystra (Acts 14:8–10).

The first man, sensing new strength in his feet and ankles, leaped and walked and praised God, and all of the people were filled with wonder and amazement.

The second man had been a cripple from birth. "He listened to Paul, speaking; and Paul, looking intently at him and seeing that he had faith to be made well, said in a loud voice, 'Stand upright on your feet.' And he sprang up and walked" (Acts 14:9). The people lifted up their voices, saying, "The gods have come down to us in the likeness of men!" (v. 11).

This was the beginning of other healings by Paul. When he stopped in Malta he healed the father of Publius (Acts 28:7–10), who had fever and dysentery. After this, other sick people on the island came to Paul, were cured and filled with new hope.

UNNAMED ONES HEALED BY CHRIST: HOPE IN TIME OF DISEASE

The miracles centering around various unnamed people are intimately interwoven into the life of Jesus. He, who lived in a realm of hope, miraculously restored to wholeness many who had been hopeless about their numerous and varied diseases, including blindness, leprosy, and paralysis. Jesus' healing of them, both when he was in their presence and when he was far away, is evidence of his understanding of prayer and faith and of his unique relationship with God. These nameless men, twenty-five in all, who were healed are:

Two blind men who could see again (Matt. 9:27–33).
Two other blind men healed near Jericho (Matt. 20:29–34; Mark 10:46–52; Luke 18:35–43).
The blind man healed near Bethsaida (Mark 8:22–26).
The man born blind whose sight is restored (John 9:1–34).
The dumb demoniac who could speak again (Matt. 9:32–34).
The deaf mute healed (Mark 7:31–37).
The man whose withered hand was restored to usefulness (Matt. 12:9–14; Mark 3:1–6; Luke 6:6–11).
The man with dropsy made whole again (Luke 14:2–6).

The ten lepers cleansed of their disease (Luke 17:11–19).
The son of an official, at the point of death, raised by Jesus (John 4:46–54).
The man ill for thirty-eight years who took up his pallet and walked (John 5:5–16).
The paralyzed man healed (Matt. 9:1–8; Mark 2:1–12; Luke 5:17–26).
The man with the unclean spirit renewed (Mark 1:23–28; Luke 4:31–37).
The centurion's servant healed of paralysis (Matt. 18:5–13; Luke 7:1–10).

These and other healings, not cited individually, incomprehensible events to many in Jesus' time, had value as evidence of the power of the Christian faith. They also characterized Jesus' high moral purpose in making divine good available to all those in need, regardless of their needs or their stations in life.

Those healed reacted in a variety of ways. Many felt a new personal confidence. Some ignored what Christ had taught them. Several boasted of Christ's miraculous power, even when he had charged them to tell no one. Others, including nine of the ten lepers, failed to express thanks. Others healed on the Sabbath heard Christ criticized by the Pharisees because he should have chosen another day for healing. Those restored said nothing, little realizing that these criticisms were a prelude to his persecution and crucifixion.

Amid all of these human reactions, the good and the bad, Christ's miracles continue to inspire sincere believers in his power to bring God's law from the mysterious to the real. They also help believers to remember that God's goodness never fails the faithful, no matter how hopeless their condition.

ZERUBBABEL: THE TEMPLE REBUILDER AND ANCESTOR
OF CHRIST

(I Chron. 3:19; Ezra 2:2, 3:2, 8, 4:2–3, 5:2; Neh. 7:7, 12:1, 12:47;
Hag. 1:1, 12, 14, 2:2, 4, 21, 23; Zech. 4:6–7, 9:10; Ecclesiasticus
49:11)

An ancestor of Christ (Matt. 1:12), Zerubbabel led the first
band of exiles back from Babylonia. In Jerusalem he took an active part as governor of Judah under the Persian King Darius I.

It took a man of fervent hope like Zerubbabel, a grandson of
the exiled king of Judah, Jehoiachin (I Chron. 3:17–19), to inspire the exiles and to help them to look forward and not backward in a time of such uncertainty. His faith in the God of Israel
guided and encouraged them as they trudged to the land of their
fathers.

The journey was long and arduous. It could have been a time
of despair and hopelessness for the returning exiles. Although
they were going to the beloved home of their ancestors, many of
them represented a new generation born in Babylon. A few others, almost too old to travel, had been deported to Babylon by
King Nebuchadnezzar after the fall of Jerusalem in 586 B.C. Such
a change was not easy at best, especially now that Judah was a
smaller province and Jerusalem had been devastated by war.

When they arrived, the people were beset with spiritual difficulties too. But Zerubbabel courageously led them forward in the
restoration of the altar of God and in rebuilding the temple. The
work was halted for a while by Samaritan interference and other
hostility, but finally it was completed in the second year of the
reign of Darius. So important was Zerubbabel in creating this new
national and religious center that it is sometimes called "Zerubbabel's temple."

Both Ezra and Nehemiah mention Zerubbabel prominently as
a rebuilder of the temple and a leader of God's people, and the
prophets, too, praise him. Haggai likens him to "a signet ring" on
God's hand. Zechariah, in one of his visions, refers to him as "the

Branch," meaning David's worthy descendant. Ecclesiasticus, in the Apocrypha, asks, "How can we tell the greatness of Zerubbabel?" (49:11, NEB). He it was who raised to the Lord a holy temple, destined for eternal glory.

Zerubbabel's immortal place in Hebrew history lives on, as an ancestor of Christ, as testified in the Matthew genealogy of Christ.

Epilogue

The Old Testament heroes of faith and hope are acclaimed by Ecclesiasticus as men who revealed God's majesty in each succeeding age. He describes them as men who held sway over kingdoms and made themselves a name by their exploits, as sage counselors who spoke out with prophetic power, as men who, by their counsels and their knowledge of the nation's law, . . . gave instruction. Furthermore, he describes them as men who won fame in their own generation and were the pride of their times. Their immortality is certain, for

> Their line will endure for all time,
> and their fame will never be blotted out . . .
> Nations will recount their wisdom,
> and God's people will sing their praises.
> (Ecclesiasticus 44:13, 15, NEB)

The inspiring Old Testament heroes recorded in this book are a living testament to man's fidelity, a fidelity that produced a Christ, who fulfilled all the hopes expressed by those who came before them and who went even beyond their hopes.

Christ towers majestically above all others as the one who discharged his mission as a true servant of God, even unto death, and finally as the only one who by his resurrection from the dead enriched our lives with a living hope, an inheritance which is "imperishable, undefiled, and unfading" (I Pet. 1:3).

At the birth of the new Church, Peter speaks eloquently in his Pentecostal Sermon when he declares,

> Men of Israel, listen to me: I speak of Jesus of Nazareth, a man singled out by God and made known to you through miracles, portents, and signs, which God worked among you through him, as you well know. When he had been given up to you, by the deliberate will and plan of God, you used heathen men to crucify and kill him. But God raised him to life again, setting him free from the pangs of death, because it could not be that death should keep him in its grip.
>
> (Acts 2:22–24, NEB)

This Jesus of Nazareth, this true Son of God, is therefore "the hope set before us . . . an anchor for our lives, an anchor safe and sure. It enters through the veil" (Heb. 6:18–19) where Jesus is.

The whole future of the Christian life resides in him, the light of the world, and our lasting hope.

Bibliography

RECENT BOOKS ON HOPE

ALVES, RUBEM AZEVEDO. *Theology of Human Hope*, Corpus Books, Washington, D.C., 1969.

BRAATEN, CARL E. *The Future of God: The Revolutionary Dynamics of Hope*, Harper & Row, New York, 1969.

CAPPS, WALTER H. *The Future of Hope*, Fortress Press, paperback, Philadelphia, 1970.

——. *Time Invades the Cathedral*, Fortress Press, paperback, Philadelphia, 1970.

FACKRE, GABRIEL J. *The Rainbow Sign*, Eerdmans, paperback, Grand Rapids, Mich., 1969.

FROMM, ERICH. *The Revolution of Hope*, Bantam, paperback, New York, 1968; Harper & Row, hardback, New York, 1968.

HÄRING, BERNARD. *Hope Is the Remedy*, Doubleday, Garden City, N.Y., 1972.

LYNCH, WILLIAM F. *Images of Hope*, Metro-Omega Books, paperback, New American Library, New York, 1965.

MARTY, MARTIN E., and DEAN G. PEERMAN, eds. *New Theology No. 5*, Macmillan, Toronto, New York, London, 1969.

MENNINGER, KARL. "The Academic Lecture on Hope," *American Journal of Psychiatry*, April–May, 1959.

MOLTMANN, JURGEN. *Theology of Hope*, tr. by James W. Leitch, Harper & Row, New York, 1965.

MURRAY, RALPH L. *The Biblical Shape of Hope*, Broadman Press, paperback, Nashville, Tenn., 1971.

O'COLLINS, GERALD. *Man and His Hopes*, Herder & Herder, New York, 1969.

SHERMAN, FRANKLIN E., ed. *Christian Hope and the Future of Humanity*, Augsburg, paperback, Minneapolis, 1970.

WOODYARD, DAVID. *Beyond Cynicism: The Practice of Hope*, Westminster Press, Philadelphia, 1952.

ZIMMERLI, WALTHER. *Man and His Hope in the Old Testment*, Alex R. Allenson, Naperville, Ill., 1971.

BIBLE VERSIONS USED IN TEXT
(With abbreviations)

The Authorized King James Version (KJV), Harper, New York.

The Jerusalem Bible (JB), Alexander Jones, gen. ed., Doubleday, Garden City, N.Y., 1966.

The New American Bible (NAB), tr. by the Catholic Biblical Association of America, Catholic Press, Chicago, 1971.

The New English Bible, with Apocrypha (NEB), Oxford University Press/Cambridge University Press, London, 1970.

The Revised Standard Version, Harper Study Bible (RSV), Harold Lindsell, ed. Harper & Row, New York, 1964.

The New Testament in Modern English, tr. by J. B. Phillips, Macmillan, New York, 1959.

GENERAL REFERENCE BOOKS

AVI-YONAH, MICHAEL, and EMIL G. KRAELING. *Our Living Bible*, McGraw-Hill, New York, 1962.

BARCLAY, WILLIAM. *The Mind of Jesus*, Harper & Row, New York, 1961.

BLUMRICH, J. F. *The Space Ships of Ezekiel*, paperback, Bantam, New York, 1974.

BORNKAMM, GUNTHER. *Paul*, tr. by D. M. G. Stalker, Harper & Row, New York, 1971.

BUTTRICK, GEORGE ARTHUR, ed. *The Interpreter's Dictionary of the Bible*, Abingdon Press, Nashville, Tenn., 1962.

BRUCE, A. B. *The Training of the Twelve*, Harper & Brothers, New York and London, 1871; rev. ed., Kregel, Grand Rapids, Mich., 1971.

CALKINS, RAYMOND. *The Modern Message of the Minor Prophets*, Harper, New York, 1947.

CHASE, MARY ELLEN. Preface to *The Book of Job*, Heritage Press, New York, 1946.

DEEN, EDITH. *All of the Women of the Bible*, Harper, 1955.

DUMMELOW, J. R. *Commentary on the Holy Bible* (1909), Macmillan, New York, 1955.

FOSDICK, HARRY EMERSON. *The Hope of the World*, Country Life Press, Garden City, N.Y. 1953.

HAMILTON, EDITH. *Spokesmen for God: The Great Teachers of the Old Testament*, Norton, New York, 1963.

HASTINGS, JAMES. *Greater Men and Women of the Bible*, 6 vols., Scribner's, New York, 1914.

JAMES, FLEMING. *Personalities of the Old Testament*, Scribner's, New York, 1939.

KRAELING, EMIL G. *I Have Kept the Faith: The Life of the Apostle Paul*, Rand McNally, Chicago, 1965.

———. *The Disciples*, Rand McNally, Chicago, 1966.

LAYMON, CHARLES M., ed. *The Interpreter's One-Volume Commentary on the Bible*, Abingdon Press, Nashville, 1971.

MILLER, MADELEINE S., and J. LANE MILLER. *Harper's Bible Dictionary*, Harper, New York, 1956.

MOULD, ELMER K. *Essentials of Bible History*, Ronald Press, New York, 1966.

ORR, JAMES, gen. ed. *The International Standard Bible Encyclopedia*, 5 vols., Eerdmans, Grand Rapids, Mich., 1949.

PATERSON, JOHN. *The Goodly Fellowship of the Prophets*, Scribner's, 1948.

PHILLIPS, J. B., trans. *Letters to Young Churches*, Macmillan, New York, 1951.

———. *God Our Contemporary*, Macmillan, paperback, New York, 1960.

POLLOCK, JOHN. *The Apostle: A Life of Paul*, Doubleday, Garden City, N.Y., 1969.

TILLICH, PAUL. *The New Being*, Scribner's, New York, 1955.

VELIKOVSKY, IMMANUEL. *Worlds in Collision*, Doubleday, Garden City, N.Y., 1952.

Index

Chronology of the Bible Wheel of Time

In the Beginning—
Gen. 1–11, before 4000 B.C.
Seth (Adam and Eve's godly son)

The Patriarchs: A Time of Promise
Gen. 12–50, about 1800–1650 B.C.
Abraham, Isaac, Jacob, Joseph

The Exodus, Civil and Religious Law, Return to Canaan
Ex., Num., Lev., Deut., Josh.
1500–1250 B.C. (?)
Moses and Joshua

A New Hope: A Rulership Under God
Judg., I and II Sam., I Kings 1–11, I Chron., II Chron. 1–9
1200–931 B.C.
Samuel, David, Solomon

Two Kingdoms: Judah and Israel
I Kings 12–22, II Kings 1–17, II Chron. 10–28, Amos., Hos., Isa., Mic.
931–721 B.C.
Elijah, Elisha: Beginning of Prophecy

Period of Despair and Rebirth
721–333 B.C.
Jerusalem falls, 586 B.C.
Exiles taken into Babylon
Ezra, Nehemiah return to restore Jerusalem
Major and minor prophets expect a Messiah

The Hellenistic Period
333–63 B.C.
Nameless biblical writers recall the glorious past

Wheel of Time Begins to Turn to Christ and His Church
The New Testament, 4 B.C. – A.D. 125
Birth of John the Baptist
Birth of Jesus Christ
Disciples begin their mission
Christ crucified
Paul and his helpers begin their work
Pentecost, new churches established
Period of martyrdom